Ultimate Android Design Patterns

Master Android Design Patterns with Real-World Projects for Scalable, Secure, and High-Performance Apps

Lorenzo Vainigli

www.orangeava.com

First Published: May 2025

Published By: Orange Education Pvt Ltd, AVA®

Address: 9, Daryaganj, Delhi, 110002, India

275 New North Road Islington Suite 1314 London,
N1 7AA, United Kingdom

ISBN (PBK): 978-93-48107-40-4
ISBN (E-BOOK): 978-93-48107-45-9

Scan the QR code to explore our entire catalogue

www.orangeava.com

Dedicated To

Those who Persevere in Pursuing their Ideals and Inspire Others Through Small yet Meaningful Actions, Igniting a Positive Change in the World

About the Author

Lorenzo Vainigli is an Italian Android engineer, born in 1994, with a deep passion for computer science and mobile technologies. His curiosity has led him to explore various fields, including artificial intelligence, open-source software, and the latest trends in Android development.

After obtaining a diploma in accounting from the Istituto Bandini in Siena, where he was introduced to the basics of programming. He continued his studies at the University of Bologna. There, he earned a bachelor's degree in Computer Science in 2017, presenting a thesis on an Android application for managing personal financial flows. Later, in 2021, he obtained a master's degree in Computer Science with a thesis on the use of deep convolutional neural networks for diagnosing COVID-19 through voice recordings.

He began his career in Android development a few weeks after obtaining his master's degree in 2021, working on software solutions for monitoring and testing mobile network infrastructures. After two and a half years, in 2023, he transitioned to the field of automotive infotainment systems, focusing on the integration of Android-based solutions into next-generation vehicles.

Beyond his professional activities, he is a strong advocate of open-source software and actively contributes to the Android development community. He has created several Android applications, including Nice Places, a virtual travel guide launched in 2018, and Food Expiration Dates, a free and open-source application designed to help users track food expiration dates and reduce waste. His projects have gained global reach, with downloads spanning over 120 countries.

Lorenzo believes in the power of knowledge sharing and is dedicated to writing about Android development, best practices, and emerging technologies. Through his blog and contributions on platforms including LinkedIn, Medium, and GitHub, he shares insights on Jetpack Compose, Kotlin, and modern Android architectures, helping developers navigate the complexities of mobile development.

Beyond Android development, Lorenzo explores Japanese culture and astronomy, drawing parallels to software discipline and innovation. He is dedicated to building efficient applications and fostering a collaborative developer ecosystem.

About the Technical Reviewer

Aish Kodali is a senior iOS developer with expertise in UIKit and Swift.

She is enthusiastic and curious about how technology can improve human lives. She is a great admirer of Steve Jobs, who inspired her belief that one can "put a dent in the universe." These inspirations and dreams have driven her to develop impactful apps and understand the importance of user-friendly technology.

Aish Kodali is also a career ambassador for the chooseMaths campaign by the Australian Mathematical Sciences Institute, which encourages young girls to pursue mathematics and careers in STEM fields. As a career ambassador, Aish Kodali educates younger generations on how mathematics is a crucial building block for app algorithms.

Aish Kodali has received two state-level awards at GovHack, Australia's largest hackathon: the Government as a Platform award and the Social Hack award. In this hackathon, Aish's team developed an app that allows users to report vandalized or problematic public properties directly to the council.

Acknowledgements

I would like to express my deepest gratitude to the entire team at Orange AVA for inviting me on this incredible journey. Achieving this milestone is truly a dream come true, and it feels like reaching a whole new level. Publishing a book is something I consider incredibly significant, and their unwavering support and step-by-step guidance throughout the entire process have been invaluable. They believed in me even when I doubted myself, and for that, I am profoundly grateful.

To the fantastic people in my life who continually contribute to my growth, both professionally and personally, I am equally grateful. Reaching this point makes me feel incredibly fortunate, and I hope to give back all the luck I have received to those who have believed in me and done something meaningful for me.

I would also like to extend my gratitude to all the developers who generously share learning resources online for free. Through their willingness to share knowledge, I have been able to learn so much and continue to deepen my understanding every day.

And to all the developers who have contributed to my open-source projects, thank you for your invaluable support.

Preface

Android app development is a constantly evolving field, shaped by new challenges and the need to write scalable, maintainable, and testable code. In this landscape, design patterns are essential tools for tackling recurring problems with well-established solutions, helping to avoid fragile and hard-to-reuse code.

This book was created as a practical and structured guide to the key design patterns used in Android development, covering everything from fundamental concepts to real-world applications. Through a step-by-step journey, we will explore creational, structural, and architectural patterns, analyzing their impact on code quality and developer experience.

Beyond the theory, this book stands out for its hands-on approach, featuring three real-world projects: an e-commerce app, a social media app, and an instant-messaging app. Each project is an opportunity to see design patterns in action, applying concepts such as MVVM, Dependency Injection, Repository, and many more.

Whether you are an Android developer just starting out or an experienced professional looking to deepen your knowledge, this book will guide you in effectively integrating design patterns into your code, helping you build robust, modular, and maintainable applications.

This book is divided into 15 chapters, covering in detail the main design patterns used in Android development. Starting with the fundamentals and the importance of patterns, we will explore their applications in creational, structural, behavioral, and architectural contexts, leading up to their combination for building modular and scalable systems. The book concludes with three practical projects – an e-commerce app, a social network, and a chat system – to see design patterns applied in real-world scenarios. The details of each chapter are outlined as follows:

Chapter 1 will introduce the concept of design patterns, explaining their origins and why they are fundamental in software development. We will explore historical examples and their application in modern software architectures, with a focus on Android.

Chapter 2 will deepen into the importance of design patterns in Android development, highlighting key challenges such as fragmentation, memory management, and UI complexity. Practical examples will demonstrate how patterns enhance maintainability, modularity, and testability in Android applications.

Chapter 3 will explore creational design patterns, covering Singleton, Factory, Builder, and Dependency Injection. We will examine the advantages of each pattern, their implementations in Android, and when they are recommended to improve code scalability.

Chapter 4 will cover structural design patterns, demonstrating how to organize classes to ensure a more efficient and maintainable structure. We will explore Adapter, Facade, Proxy, and Decorator, with practical examples of their application in Android to reduce component coupling and promote code reuse.

Chapter 5 will delve into behavioral design patterns, focusing on Observer, Command, and Strategy. These patterns help manage events and interactions between app components efficiently, improving state management and object communication.

Chapter 6 will explore the most commonly used architectural design patterns in Android development, such as MVC, MVP, MVVM, and MVI. We will analyze the evolution of Android architectures and why MVVM and MVI are now the most widely adopted solutions for separating business logic from the UI.

Chapter 7 will focus on patterns for managing concurrency, networking, and security. We will explore Thread Pool and Producer-Consumer for thread management, Repository and Caching for networking, and Encryption and Authentication to ensure data security in Android apps.

Chapter 8 will explain how to combine different design patterns to build modular and scalable architectures. We will analyze real-world cases of integrating patterns to create more flexible and reusable systems.

Chapter 9 will discuss performance optimization in Android applications, demonstrating how the proper use of design patterns can improve memory management, reduce CPU load, and ensure a smooth user experience. We will introduce profiling tools and best practices for writing more efficient code.

Chapter 10 will explore the importance of testing in Android applications and how design patterns can help write reliable tests. We will introduce tools such as JUnit, Espresso, and Mockito, with examples of unit, integration, and UI tests applied to real app components.

Chapter 11 will focus on refactoring existing code using design patterns. We will showcase scenarios where patterns such as Factory, Builder, or Strategy can be introduced to improve code quality and maintainability without drastically changing the existing architecture.

Chapter 12 will guide the reader through the development of an e-commerce app, applying the studied design patterns. From design to implementation, we will demonstrate best practices for structuring code in a modular and scalable way, enhancing both the user experience and data management.

Chapter 13 will demonstrate how to develop a social media app, implementing design patterns for feed management, user profiles, and notifications. A modular approach will be adopted to separate functionalities, improving code reusability and integration between components.

Chapter 14 will guide the development of a chat app based on Model-View-Intent (MVI), showing how to manage application state and simulate real-time message reception without a backend. Patterns will be applied for conversation management, data persistence, and UI reactivity.

Chapter 15 will discuss the future evolution of Android development, driven by Jetpack Compose, Kotlin Multiplatform, and AI-assisted development. MVI and reactive state management are becoming the new standard, enhancing scalability and modularity, while integration with IoT and wearable devices will lead to new interaction models and increasingly adaptive architectures.

Get a Free eBook

We hope you are enjoying your recently purchased book! Your feedback is incredibly valuable to us, and to all other readers looking for great books.

If you found this book helpful or enjoyable, we would truly appreciate it, if you could take a moment to leave a short review with a 5 star rating on Amazon. It helps us grow, and lets other readers discover our books.

As a thank you, we would love to send you a free digital copy of this book, and a **30%** discount code on your next cart value on our official websites:

www.orangeava.com

www.orangeava.in (For Indian Subcontinent)

☑ **Here's how:**

Leave a review for the book on Amazon.

Take a screenshot of your review, and send an email to **info@orangeava.com** (it can be just the confirmation screen).

Once, we receive your screenshot, we will send you the digital file, within 24 hours.

Thank you so much for your support – it means a lot to us!

Downloading the code bundles and colored images

Please follow the links or scan the QR codes to download the
Code Bundles and Images of the book:

https://github.com/ava-orange-education/Ultimate-Android-Design-Patterns

The code bundles and images of the book are also hosted on
https://rebrand.ly/1aw4gaj

In case there's an update to the code, it will be updated on the existing GitHub repository.

Errata

We take immense pride in our work at **Orange Education Pvt Ltd,** and follow best practices to ensure the accuracy of our content to provide an indulging reading experience to our subscribers. Our readers are our mirrors, and we use their inputs to reflect and improve upon human errors, if any, that may have occurred during the publishing processes involved. To let us maintain the quality and help us reach out to any readers who might be having difficulties due to any unforeseen errors, please write to us at :

errata@orangeava.com

Your support, suggestions, and feedback are highly appreciated.

DID YOU KNOW

Did you know that Orange Education Pvt Ltd offers eBook versions of every book published, with PDF and ePub files available? You can upgrade to the eBook version at **www.orangeava.com** and as a print book customer, you are entitled to a discount on the eBook copy. Get in touch with us at: **info@orangeava.com** for more details.

At **www.orangeava.com**, you can also read a collection of free technical articles, sign up for a range of free newsletters, and receive exclusive discounts and offers on Print Books and eBooks.

PIRACY

If you come across any illegal copies of our works in any form on the internet, we would be grateful if you would provide us with the location address or website name. Please contact us at **info@orangeava.com** with a link to the material.

ARE YOU INTERESTED IN AUTHORING WITH US?

If there is a topic that you have expertise in, and you are interested in either writing or contributing to a book, please write to us at **business@orangeava.com**. We are on a journey to help developers and tech professionals to gain insights on the present technological advancements and innovations happening across the globe and build a community that believes Knowledge is best acquired by sharing and learning with others. Please reach out to us to learn what our audience demands and how you can be part of this educational reform. We also welcome ideas from tech experts and help them build learning and development content for their domains.

REVIEWS

Please leave a review. Once you have read and used this book, why not leave a review on the site that you purchased it from? Potential readers can then see and use your unbiased opinion to make purchase decisions. We at Orange Education would love to know what you think about our products, and our authors can learn from your feedback. Thank you!

For more information about Orange Education, please visit **www.orangeava.com**.

Table of Contents

CHAPTER 1
Overview of Design Patterns

Introduction

This chapter introduces the concept of design patterns that are essential tools to solve common problems in software development. We will explore the definition of design patterns, and their origins and evolution. We will then examine *SOLID* principles because they represent fundamental concepts in understanding design patterns. Finally, we will explore the different types of design patterns.

Knowledge of the basis of design patterns will equip the readers with an understanding of how these structured solutions can make the software development process easier and improve code quality in Android applications.

Structure

In this chapter, the following topics will be covered:

- Definition of Design Patterns
- History and Evolution of Design Patterns
- SOLID Principles
- Types of Design Patterns
  - Creational Patterns
  - Structural Patterns
  - Architectural Patterns
  - Concurrency, Network, and Security Patterns

Understanding Design Patterns

Design patterns are not just solutions, they are the building blocks of any software. Design patterns provide a wireframe for any seamless software. They provide a reusable method to solve specific problems, making code more flexible and easier to maintain. These patterns are not finished projects that can be translated directly into code, instead, they are schemes that can be reused in many different situations. Adoption of design patterns by developers can ensure that their code is modular, understandable, and easy to maintain.

Design patterns can be very helpful in dealing with big projects where more developers work together. They provide common guidelines for developers to communicate and develop the project. This way of communication can lead to a more efficient collaboration and a more coherent code. Furthermore, design patterns can help developers to avoid issues and common counterproductive solutions (that is, *anti-patterns*).

History and Evolution of Design Patterns

The concept of design pattern has its roots in the work of architect Christopher Alexander, who introduced the idea of pattern in the context of urban and architectural design. In his book A *Pattern Language: Towns, Buildings, Construction* (1977), he described a *pattern* as a reusable solution for a recurrent problem in a particular context.

Figure 1.1: *Cover of the book "A Pattern Language" by Christopher Alexander*

"Each pattern describes a problem which occurs over and over again in our environment, and then describes the core of the solution to that problem, in such a way that you can use this solution a million times over, without ever doing it the same way twice" – Christopher Alexander, A *Pattern Language: Towns, Buildings, Construction* (1977).

Alexander's work has been successively adapted to software engineering by a group of programmers known as the "Gang of Four" (Erich Gamma, Richard Helm, Ralph Johnson, and John Vlissides). Their fundamental book, *Design Patterns: Elements of Reusable Object-Oriented Software*, published in 1994 (the year in which the author of this book was born), set the basis to the use of design patterns in software development. This book authored by the "Gang of Four" divided design patterns in three main categories: creational patterns, structural patterns, and behavioral patterns.

Creational patterns are related to the mechanisms of creation of objects, structural patterns deal with the composition of classes and objects, and behavioral patterns define the ways in which objects should interact and their responsibilities.

Over the years, the use of design patterns evolved to adapt to new programming paradigms and technologies. The rise of object-oriented programming in the 90s favored the application of design patterns. With the evolution of software design and development methods, the design patterns also have undergone changes.

In the context of Android development, design patterns become mandatory due to the platform complexity and the need for efficient resource management. The Android ecosystem's rapid growth saw the adoption of tailored patterns for mobile app development, ensuring applications perform well and continue to be maintainable, no matter the challenges created by different device configurations and resource constraints.

The evolution of design patterns also includes the development of new patterns and improvement of the existing ones. As developers face new challenges and technologies evolve, new patterns emerge to address these problems. For example, the pattern **Model-View-ViewModel (MVVM)** has become popular in app development for its ability to separate concerns and make it easy to test and maintain apps.

Adhering to established patterns, developers can write more predictable and maintainable code that is easier to understand and can be modified for others. Design patterns are very important for code maintenance, for both large and small projects, and can help developers to debug code when there are any issues in the app.

SOLID Principles

SOLID principles are a set of guidelines written to design object-oriented software proposed by Robert C. Martin (also known as "Uncle Bob"). These principles aim to make software more comprehensible, flexible, and maintainable. SOLID is an acronym for the following:

- **S**: Single Responsibility Principle (SRP)
- **O**: Open/Closed Principle (OCP)
- **L**: Liskov Substitution Principle (LSP)

- **I**: Interface Segregation Principle (ISP)
- **D**: Dependency Inversion Principle (DIP)

Single Responsibility Principle

The Single Responsibility Principle (SRP) states that a class should have only one reason to change, and that means that it should have only one responsibility. This principle aims to achieve the separation of concerns, making the code easier to understand and maintain.

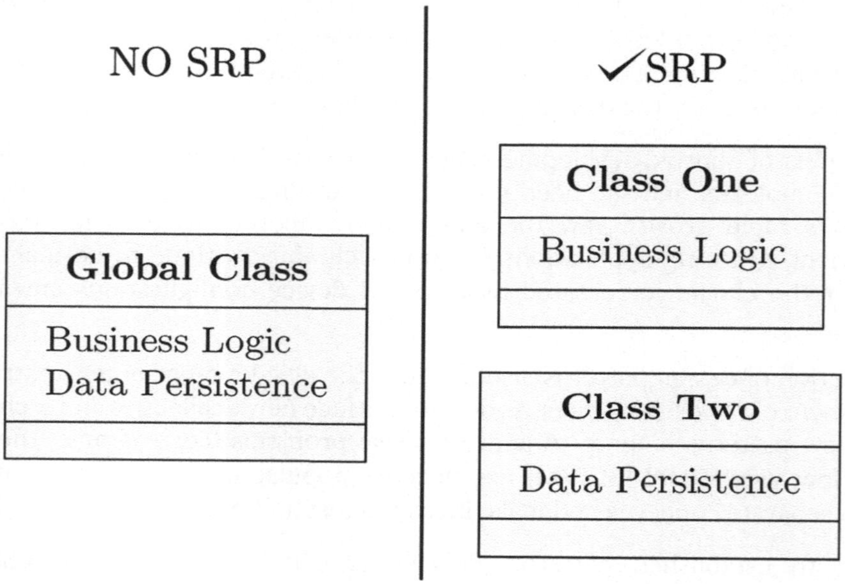

***Figure 1.2**: A design that does not satisfy the SRP principle (left) and the same design refactored to follow the SRP principle (right)*

Example: A class that manages both business logic and data persistence violates SRP. In this case, following SRP, we should have one class to handle the business logic, and another class to handle data persistence.

Open/Closed Principle

The Open/Closed Principle (OCP) states that the software should be open to extension but closed to modification. This means that the behavior of a class can be extended without modifying the existing code. This principle favors the use of interfaces and abstract classes to allow extension of the behavior of a class through inheritance and polymorphism.

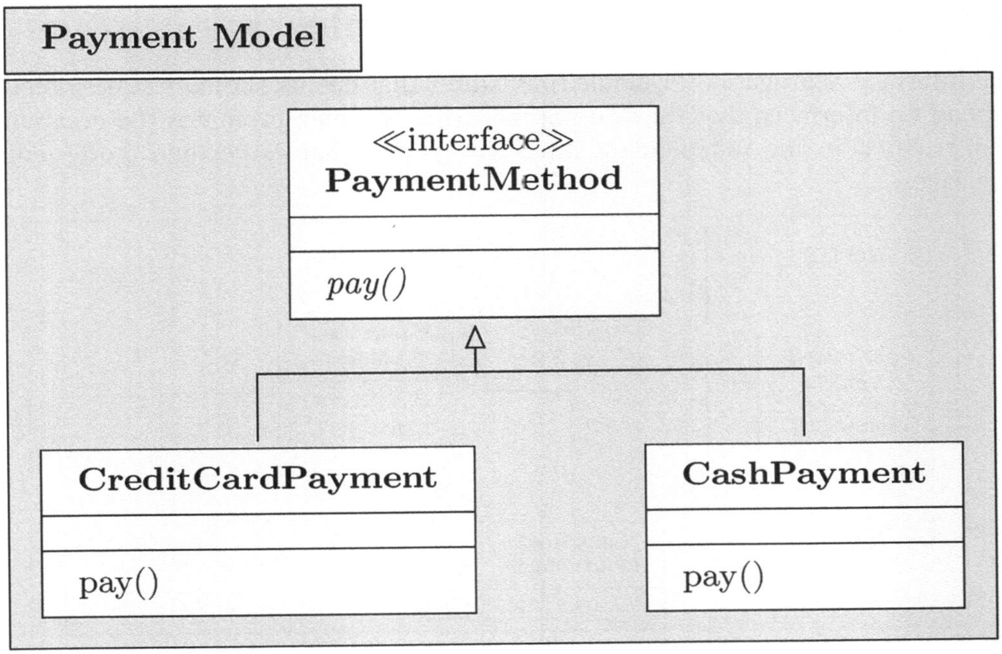

***Figure 1.3**: A design that follows the OCP principle*

Example: A payment model can be designed to support new payment methods without modifying the existent code, implementing a common interface for all payment methods.

Liskov Substitution Principle

The Liskov Substitution Principle (LSP) states that the derived class should be replaceable with their base classes without altering the soul behavior of the class. In other words, derived classes should extend base classes without changing their expected behavior.

`val cat = Feline()`
`val tiger = Feline()`
 	
`// Here cat and tiger have type Feline`
`cat.hunt()`
`tiger.hunt()`
	should be equal to	`val cat = Cat()`
		`val tiger = Tiger()`
		
		`// Here cat has type Cat and tiger has type Tiger`
		`cat.hunt()`
		`tiger.hunt()`

Example: If a base class **`Feline`** has a method **`hunt()`**, all of its subclasses (such as **`Cat`** or **`Tiger`**) should be able to use the method **`hunt()`** without modifying the internal code of the method.

Interface Segregation Principle

The Interface Segregation Principle (ISP) states that clients should not be forced to depend on interfaces that they do not use. This principle promotes the creation of smaller, specific and independent interfaces, rather than larger and more generic interfaces.

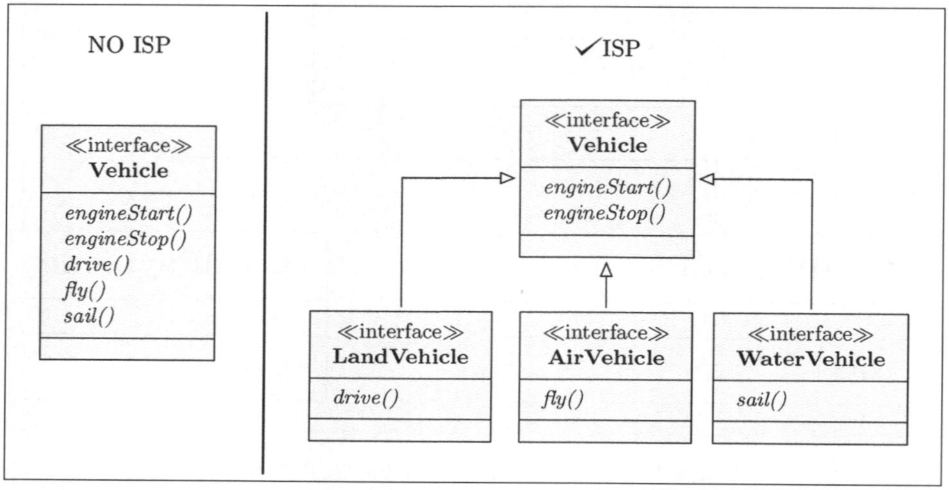

***Figure 1.4**: A design that does not satisfy the ISP principle (left) and the same design refactored to follow the ISP principle (right)*

Example: Rather than having a single interface **`Vehicle`** with methods such as **`start`**, **`stop`**, **`fly`** and **`sail`**, it would be better to have separate interfaces like **`LandVehicle`**, **`AirVehicle`**, **`WaterVehicle`** for specific functionalities.

Dependency Inversion Principle

The Dependency Inversion Principle (DIP) states that high-level components should not directly depend on low-level components. Instead, both should rely on abstractions (such as interfaces). Additionally, these abstractions (rules) should not depend on specific implementations (details), instead, the implementations should depend on abstractions.

In other words, the system should be designed so that the details follow the rules, rather than the rules being shaped by the details.

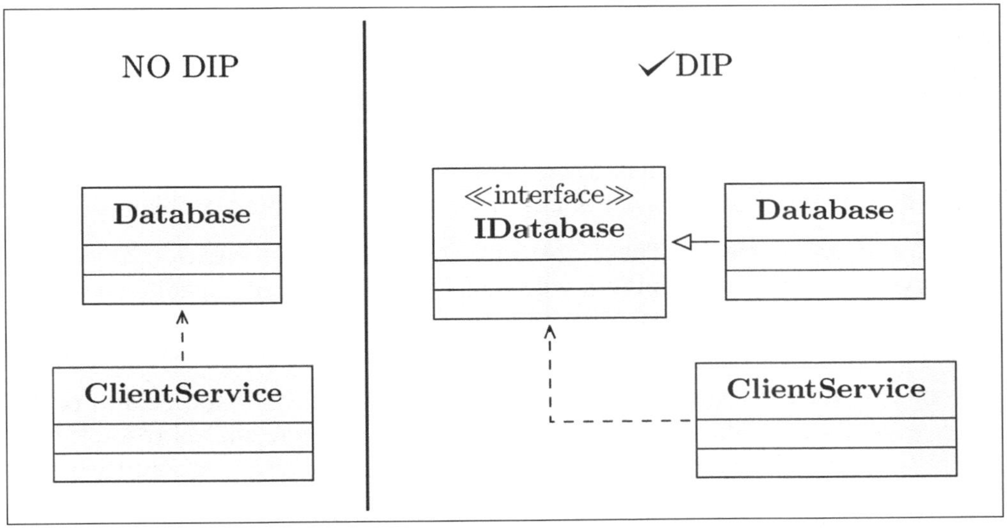

Figure 1.5: *A design that does not satisfy the DIP principle (left) and the same design refactored to follow the DIP principle (right)*

Example: Instead of a class **`ClientService`** that depends directly on a concrete class **`Database`**, **`ClientService`** should depend on an interface **`IDatabase`**, and the concrete class **`Database`** should implement the interface **`IDatabase`**. This way of design allows us to easily replace the database without modifying **`ClientService`**.

Influence of SOLID Principles on Design Patterns

SOLID principles deeply influence design patterns, as both aim to create a software that is easy to extend and maintain. Most design patterns implicitly follow these principles:

- **Single Responsibility Principle (SRP):** Patterns such as Singleton and Factory help to separate responsibilities in different classes.
- **Open/Closed Principle (OCP):** Patterns such as Decorator and Strategy let us extend the behavior of the classes without modifying them.
- **Liskov Substitution Principle (LSP):** Patterns such as Adapter ensure that derived classes can replace base classes without problems.
- **Interface Segregation Principle (ISP):** Patterns such as Facade promote the use of specific and tailored interfaces.
- **Dependency Inversion Principle (DIP):** Patterns such as Dependency Injection apply this principle, making it easy to manage the dependency between classes.

Types of Design Patterns

The design patterns presented in this book are divided into four main categories: creational, structural, behavioral, architectural, and specialized patterns (concurrency, network, and security patterns). Each category is related to a specific aspect of software design and provides a set of patterns for solving related problems.

- **Creational Patterns:** These patterns deal with object creation mechanisms, trying to create objects in a way that is suitable for the specific situation in which they will be used. They help to make a system independent of how its objects are created, composed, and represented. Creational patterns include:
    - **Singleton:** It guarantees that a class has only one instance and provides a global entry point to it. This is useful to manage shared resources such as a database or an object which can be accessed throughout the project.
    - **Factory:** It defines an interface to create an object, but it lets the subclasses decide which class to instantiate. This promotes loose coupling, delegating the instantiation process to the subclasses.
    - **Builder:** It separates the creation of an object from its representation, letting the same construction process create different representations. This is useful in building objects with many configuration options.
- **Structural Patterns:** These patterns concern object composition and typically identify simple methods to create relations between different objects. They help to guarantee that if a part of a system changes, the whole system structure does not have to change. Structural patterns include:
    - **Adapter:** It allows incompatible interfaces to communicate together. It acts as a bridge between the two interfaces, converting the first interface in a way that the second one can communicate with it. Conceptually, the adapter pattern acts like a translator between two people that speak different languages.
    - **Decorator:** Adds responsibilities to objects in a dynamic and transparent way, providing a flexible alternative to sub-classification in order to extend the functionalities. This pattern is useful to adhere to the principle of unique responsibility.
    - **Facade:** Provides a simplified interface to a complex subsystem, making the subsystem easier to use. It helps to hide the complexity of the system and provides an interface that the client can use easily.
- **Behavioral Patterns:** These patterns concentrate on the communication between objects, defining how objects interact and how their responsibilities are distributed among them. They help to reduce the complexity of the flow of information inside a system. Behavioral patterns include:

- **Observer:** Defines a one-to-many dependency between objects. When an object (the observable) changes state, the objects that are watching it (the observers) get notified and get updated automatically. This pattern is widely used to implement distributed event management systems.
- **Strategy:** Defines a family of algorithms, encapsulates them and makes them interchangeable. This pattern lets the algorithm change, regardless of the clients who use it.
- **Command:** It encapsulates a request as an object, letting the clients to be parameterized with queues, requests, and operations. This pattern also supports cancelable operations, making it suitable to implement transactional systems.

- **Architectural Patterns:** These patterns deal with the high-level structure of an application and define the overall layout and the interaction between all of its components. They are crucial to keeping the separation of concerns, improving the scalability, and making the app easy to maintain. Common architectural patterns are:
  - **Model-View-Controller (MVC):** Separates an application in three main components: Model (the data), View (the user interface), and Controller (the business logic). This separation helps to manage complex applications, promoting clean code and improving testability.
  - **Model-View-Presenter (MVP):** Similar to MVC, but Presenter assumes a more prominent role, because it is responsible not only for the business logic, but also for the update of the View. In this pattern, the View is more passive–it only visualizes the information and forwards user actions to the Presenter.
  - **Model-View-ViewModel (MVVM):** This has been designed to make it easy to separate the development of the user interface (the View) and the development of the business logic (the Model). The ViewModel acts as an intermediary between the View and the Model, handling user input and system responses.
  - **Model-View-Intent (MVI):** This is the newest among the architectural patterns. It focuses on a unidirectional data flow, making it easy to reason about state changes and handling complex user interaction. This pattern is useful when we deal with reactive programming.
- **Specialized Patterns:** These other types of patterns, which are covered in this book, provide tailored solutions to the domains of concurrency, network, and security.
  - **Concurrency Patterns:** These patterns help to handle the execution of multiple threads or processes in order to optimize performance and resource usage.

        - **Thread Pool:** It manages a pool of threads, assigning new tasks to existing threads rather than creating new threads, thus improving performances.
        - **Executor:** Provides a high level abstraction for handling threads, abstracting task execution.
    - **Network Patterns:** These patterns make the network communication of an application simple and maintainable.
        - **Repository:** Encapsulates the data logic or the business logic, providing a clean API to access data and decoupling the application from the data source.
    - **Security Patterns:** These patterns guarantee that applications manage data in a secure way, protecting them from common threats.
        - **Encryption:** Protects data by converting them into an unreadable format for those who do not have a decryption key. It protects sensitive information.
        - **Secure Storage:** Guarantees that sensitive data are stored in a secure way, preventing unauthorized access and data violation.

By understanding these categories and what pattern belongs to each, developers can better identify the pattern to be applied to a specific problem, leading to a more robust and readable code.

Conclusion

In this chapter, we explored the concept of design patterns, starting with their origins and moving to their evolution over time. We saw how design patterns represent standardized solutions to recurrent problems in software design and how they can help to write more efficient, maintainable, and scalable code. Furthermore, we explored SOLID principles that provide the basis to a lot of best practices in software design, thus influencing design patterns.

Design patterns not only help to solve common problems, but they also promote better comprehension and collaboration among developers, making the code cleaner and more readable. Understanding and applying design patterns is fundamental to everybody wanting to develop complex applications, especially in the context of Android development, where robust and flexible solutions are mandatory to face challenges about resource usage and different device configurations.

As you continue to read this book, you will explore every design pattern more deeply, not only learning how to implement each of these, but also how to adapt to the requirements of your application. The knowledge about design patterns will provide to you essential skills to address challenges in software design in a structured and professional way, improving the quality of your code.

In the next chapter, we will analyze the importance of design patterns in designing and developing high-quality Android apps.

Points to Remember

- **Design patterns**: Design patterns are standardized solutions to common problems in software design. They make it easier to write flexible, modular, and maintainable code.
- **Origins of design patterns**: The concept of design patterns originated from the work of architect Christopher Alexander and was adapted to software design by the "Gang of Four".
- **Main categories**: Design patterns are divided into five main categories:
  - **Creational patterns**: These patterns deal with object creation (Singleton, Factory, Builder).
  - **Structural patterns**: These patterns deal with object composition (Adapter, Decorator, Facade).
  - **Behavioral patterns**: These patterns deal with object interaction (Observer, Strategy, Command).
  - **Architectural patterns**: These patterns deal with the overall architecture of an application (MVC, MVP, MVVM, MVI).
  - **Specialized patterns:** (Concurrency patterns, Network patterns, and Security patterns).
- **SOLID principles**: SOLID principles are a set of guidelines created to improve software maintainability and flexibility. The five principles are:
  - **Single Responsibility Principle (SRP)**
  - **Open/Closed Principle (OCP)**
  - **Liskov Substitution Principle (LSP)**
  - **Interface Segregation Principle (ISP)**
  - **Dependency Inversion Principle (DIP)**

These points summarize the key concepts explored in this chapter and they offer a comprehensive base to understand the importance of using design patterns in software development.

Multiple Choice Questions

1. Which SOLID principles says that a class should have only one reason to change?
   a. Open/Closed Principle (OCP)
   b. Single Responsibility Principle (SRP)
   c. Dependency Inversion Principle (DIP)
   d. Interface Segregation Principle (ISP)
2. Which design pattern is used to ensure that a class has only one global instance?
   a. Factory
   b. Builder
   c. Singleton
   d. Adapter
3. Which of the following is a behavioral design pattern?
   a. Adapter
   b. Observer
   c. Facade
   d. Singleton
4. Which of the following design patterns promotes code reuse separating object creation from its representation?
   a. Builder
   b. Factory
   c. Strategy
   d. Adapter
5. The Model-View-ViewModel (MVVM) pattern is mainly used for:
   a. Manage object creation
   b. Separate the business logic from user interface
   c. Handle communication between objects
   d. Provide a simple interface to a complex subsystem

Answers

1. b
2. c
3. b
4. a
5. b

Questions

1. How does the Open/Closed principle help you design flexible and extensible software?
2. Describe the use of the Singleton pattern to manage the connection to a database.
3. What are the main differences between MVP and MVVM patterns?
4. How can the Strategy pattern improve the flexibility of an application?
5. Explain how the Observer pattern can handle automatic updates in the UI of an Android app.

References

1. **Alexander, Christopher. A Pattern Language**: *Towns, Buildings, Construction*, 1977.
2. ***Gamma, Erich, Richard Helm, Ralph Johnson, and John Vlissides.* Design Patterns**: *Elements of Reusable Object-Oriented Software*, 1994.

CHAPTER 2
Design Patterns in Android Development

Introduction

This chapter explores the common challenges in Android development, showing how to address these challenges using design patterns.

We will start examining the challenges that an Android developer must face. After that, we will discover the benefits of using design patterns and also explore how to find the appropriate design pattern to use. Further, scenarios in which it is better to avoid design patterns, as well as practical examples of real-world usage of design patterns are presented.

Structure

In this chapter, we will cover the following topics:

- Challenges in Android Development
  - Platform Complexity
  - Limited Resources
  - Variety of Devices and Android Versions
  - User Experience and App Reactiveness
  - Code Maintainability in Large Projects
- Benefits of Using Design Patterns
- Real-World Examples of Design Patterns Improving Android Apps
  - Singleton Pattern to Handle Network Connections
  - Observer Pattern to Update User Interface
  - Repository Pattern to Manage Multi-Source Data
  - MVC/MVVM to Organize Code in Modules

Challenges in Android Development

The development of Android apps involves different challenges due to the complexity of the platform and the characteristics of the Android ecosystem. Understanding these challenges is fundamental to appreciate the role of design patterns in improving the development process and ensuring robust and maintainable apps.

Platform Complexity

Android is a complex and extensive platform, with a multitude of components and API. Developers must navigate through numerous libraries, frameworks, and tools to create applications that provide the best experience to the users. This complexity can lead to writing code that is hard to maintain and to errors that may compromise the app functionality.

Design patterns help to manage this complexity by providing standard solutions to common problems, reducing the probability of errors, simplifying code management, and offering a structured foundation for the project.

Limited Resources

Unlike laptop or personal computers, mobile devices have limited resources, both in memory and computational power. Thus, Android developers must optimize their applications in order to guarantee that they execute smoothly even on less powerful devices. A bad management of resources can lead to crashes, slowdowns, and a poor user experience.

Design patterns help to optimize resource usage, ensuring better performance. For example, the Singleton pattern helps to manage shared resources, while Builder makes object creation more efficient.

Variety of Devices and Android Versions

One of the major challenges in Android development is fragmentation. Since device vendors choose to pick Android and customize it, rather than write from scratch their own operating system, there are hundreds of device models that run Android. These differences can be screen size, Android OS version, and hardware capacity. This fragmentation makes it harder to ensure that an app performs well on every device.

Design patterns can help to handle fragmentation, for example, using Factory we can create objects that adapt dynamically to device configuration, or Adapter to ensure compatibility with different APIs.

User Experience and App Reactiveness

Users expect that Android apps run fast and smoothly. Every delay on the user interface after a user interaction can lead to a bad user experience, and the user may decide to uninstall the app. The management of background tasks, such as data loading or the execution of complex tasks, must be performed in a way that the user interface can stay smooth and reactive.

Patterns such as Observer and Command can be used to handle interaction between user and background tasks, ensuring that the user interface reflects the current status of the app without losing performance.

Code Maintainability in Large Projects

The more an Android project grows in dimensions and complexity, the harder it becomes to keep the code maintainable. The tight coupling between components, code repetition, and the lack of a clear separation of responsibilities can lead to writing code that is hard to understand, to modify, and to scale.

Design patterns such as MVC, MVP, or MVVM help to structure the code in an organized way, clearly separating responsibilities and making it easy to maintain and scale the project.

Benefits of Using Design Patterns

Design patterns offer numerous benefits that contribute to software quality development. These benefits are particularly important in complex and large scale Android apps, where maintainability, scalability, and code reuse are critical.

- **Better maintainability:** Design patterns provide a clear structure and guidelines for writing code, making the code base easy to comprehend and modify. Following stable patterns, developers can avoid spaghetti code that results in apps that are better organized and maintainable. This is important when there is a project that involves more developers, because it ensures consistency and makes collaboration easier.
- **Greater scalability:** One of the main advantages of design patterns is their power to create scalable solutions. Using patterns that promote loose coupling and high cohesion, developers can design apps that can grow and evolve without forcing them to significantly rewrite the code.

  For example, Factory pattern allows to add new types of products without modifying the existing code, thus supporting scalability.
- **Easier reuse of code:** Design patterns encourage the reuse of proven solutions in multiple parts of a software or even in different projects. This not only

speeds up the development process, but also improves code quality, taking advantage of solutions that have been tested and refined over time.

Patterns such as Singleton and Observer can be used in different contexts, guaranteeing that common problems are solved in an efficient way.

- **Greater flexibility:** Design patterns help to build flexible software that can adapt itself to requirement changes. Defining clear roles and responsibilities for different components and patterns allows developers to make changes to a part of an app, without impacting the others.

  For example, Strategy permits to dynamically change algorithms at runtime, providing flexibility on how some tasks are executed.

- **Better communication:** The use of design patterns defines a common language between developers. This shared language makes it easy to discuss design concepts and solutions, letting team members better understand the work of their colleagues.

  When a developer speaks about Adapter or Proxy, the others immediately understand the scope and the purpose, creating more efficient communication and collaboration.

- **Promotion of best practices:** Design patterns embody best practices that have been identified and refined through years of software development. Following these patterns, developers can avoid common mistakes and anti-pattern, leading to a more robust and reliable code.

  Patterns such as MVVM (Model-View-ViewModel) promote separation of concerns, making the software architecture clean and modular.

- **Better testability:** A lot of design patterns intrinsically support better testability, promoting loose coupling and clear interfaces.

  For example, Dependency Injection makes it easy to mock dependencies in unit tests, promoting more complete and reliable tests. This leads to better quality software, reducing bugs and regressions.

How to Choose the Right Design Pattern

The adoption of a pattern should always be justified by a clear advantage. If a pattern adds complexity without providing real benefits, it may be better to avoid it.

Using design patterns helps write more organized, scalable, and maintainable code, but selecting the right pattern for each scenario is not always straightforward. To make an informed decision, it is essential to evaluate several factors, including project complexity, the need for modularity, testability, and performance.

Analyze Project Requirements

The choice of a design pattern depends on the specific needs of the application. Some patterns are better suited for improving modularity, others for reducing class coupling or ensuring a predictable data flow.

Purpose	Recommended pattern	Motivation
Separate business logic from UI	MVVM/MVI	Improves modularity and UI testability.
Ensure a single shared instance	Singleton	Prevents instance duplication for global services (for example, database, network).
Create objects flexibly	Factory	Hides creation logic, making the code more modular.
Configure complex objects with many properties	Builder	Simplifies object creation with optional parameters.
Avoid rigid dependencies between classes	Dependency Injection	Improves modularity and facilitates testing by easily replacing dependencies.

***Table 2.1**: Typical use cases of some design patterns*

Example: If you are developing an app that uses a centralized network client with Retrofit, the Singleton pattern is useful to ensure a single shared instance, reducing memory consumption. However, if you want to avoid a direct dependency between the HTTP client and the code that uses it, you can combine Factory with Dependency Injection for greater flexibility.

Increased Complexity versus Long-Term Benefits

Some patterns improve modularity and scalability, but they can make the code harder to read and maintain, especially for new developers.

Examples:

- Decorator is useful for adding functionalities without modifying the original code, but it introduces more classes, making the code harder to navigate.
- Proxy enhances access control and caching but can increase complexity, especially when implemented with multiple abstraction layers.

- MVVM/MVI effectively separate logic from the UI but require more boilerplate code compared to a direct implementation.

Aware Choice: If the project is small and does not require expandability, it is better to avoid overly complex architectures.

Performance versus Flexibility

Some patterns improve code extensibility, but they may negatively impact app performance.

- Dependency Injection (Hilt/Dagger) reduces coupling and improves testability but can slow down app startup due to automatic code generation.
- Singleton reduces memory consumption by maintaining a single instance, but if misused, it can introduce memory leaks and threading issues.
- Factory improves dependency management but may add overhead compared to direct object creation.

Aware Choice: If the app needs to start quickly (for example, a GPS navigation app), excessive use of Dependency Injection can cause issues.

Testability versus Simplicity

If the goal is to write easily testable code, some patterns are more suitable than others:

- MVVM/MVI allow testing the ViewModel separately from the UI.
- Dependency Injection makes it easier to replace dependencies with mocks during testing.
- Singleton can make testing more difficult due to its shared global state.

Aware Choice: If the project does not require high test coverage, adopting patterns like Dependency Injection may not be necessary.

The choice of a design pattern depends on the project context and the objectives to be achieved. There is no perfect pattern for every situation, but with a careful evaluation of benefits and trade-offs, it is possible to structure an Android application to be scalable, maintainable, and high-performing.

When to Avoid Design Patterns

Although design patterns are powerful tools for writing more organized and scalable code, they are not always the best choice. A pattern should be applied only when there is a real need, otherwise, it may unnecessarily complicate the code without providing tangible benefits.

Let us see some scenarios in which it is better to avoid the use of design patterns.

When a Pattern Adds Unnecessary Overhead

Some patterns, such as Factory or Builder, are introduced to make object creation more flexible, but they are not always necessary. If an object can be initialized directly with a constructor without additional logic, using a Factory Pattern may be excessive.

Example: If an app only handles two types of notifications (text-based and with an image), using a Factory might be unnecessary. A simple instance created with a constructor would be more efficient.

When a Pattern Overcomplicates Simple Code

Some patterns require more complex implementation, which can lead to increased boilerplate without providing real benefits. For example, MVVM and MVI are great for separating UI and business logic, but if a screen is very simple and lacks complex logic, it may be more practical to update the UI directly within the composable interface without introducing a ViewModel.

Example: A Splash Screen that displays a logo for a few seconds before navigating to the main screen does not need a ViewModel. Instead of using MVVM, a simple `LaunchedEffect` in Jetpack Compose provides a more direct and readable solution.

When Dependency Injection is Too Complex for Small Projects

Using Dependency Injection (DI), such as Hilt or Dagger, is very beneficial for large-scale projects, but in a simple app, it might add unnecessary complexity. In many cases, manual dependency injection is sufficient, avoiding the overhead of configuring a DI framework.

Example: If an app has only two repositories and a ViewModel, introducing Hilt is unnecessary. Passing dependencies directly as constructor parameters is a simpler and more efficient approach.

The use of design patterns should always be evaluated based on the context. If a pattern introduces more problems than it solves, it is better to avoid it and adopt a more straightforward solution. Simplicity, readability, and maintainability should always be the top priorities in Android app development.

Real-World Examples of Design Patterns Improving Android Apps

To fully comprehend the importance and the effectiveness of design patterns in Android development, it is useful to view some practical examples of their use in real scenarios. These examples show how design patterns can solve common problems, improve code quality, and optimize performance in Android applications.

Singleton Pattern to Handle Network Connections

Singleton pattern is widely used in Android development to ensure that there will be only one instance of a class inside the application lifecycle. A common example is the management of network connections. For a lot of applications (that is, social network apps or streaming services apps), it is mandatory to maintain a persistent network connection to a remote server to execute API calls or synchronize data.

Using a Singleton to handle network connection, we ensure that all network requests use the same connection instance, reducing resource consumption and preventing unnecessary multiple connections.

Observer Pattern to Update User Interface

Observer pattern is particularly useful to implement automatic update of user interface when data changes. In Android, this pattern is implemented using LiveData (or recently Flow and StateFlow) and ViewModel, which are components provided by Android Jetpack. LiveData allows users to observe data and update the user interface when data changes through a built-in mechanism of notification. ViewModel, which holds the business logic, sends notifications to observers through LiveData, ensuring that the user interface is always up-to-date with the state of the app.

Repository Pattern to Manage Multi-Source Data

Repository pattern is used to abstract and centralize access to data, providing a single source of truth that retrieves data from different sources, such as local databases, remote API or caching files. For example, an Android application that synchronizes data from a remote server but also uses a local cache to make data available offline. The Repository pattern can manage the logic to determine the source to be used depending on network availability. This not only simplifies the code, but makes the app more flexible and easier to maintain.

MVC/MVVM to Organize Code in Modules

Architectural patterns such as Model-View-Controller (MVC) and Model-View-ViewModel (MVVM) are fundamental to organize code in separate modules, dividing business logic from presentation logic. In Android, MVVM is popular, thanks to its capacity to make testability and maintainability easier. For example, in an application that uses MVVM, the Model manages data, the ViewModel contains the business logic and interacts with data, and the View focuses only on presenting data to the user. This approach allows developers to modify or extend each module without impacting the others, improving app modularity and flexibility.

These real-world examples prove how the correct use of design patterns in Android development leads to solving common problems, optimizing performances and making code more organized and maintainable. By applying these patterns strategically, developers can create more robust, scalable, and quality apps.

Conclusion

In this chapter, we explored the main challenges in Android development and how to use design patterns to create effective solutions for these problems.

Design patterns not only improve maintainability, scalability, and app performance, but also provide a structured approach to face the complexity of the Android platform. Through practical examples, we saw how patterns such as Singleton, Observer, and Repository could optimize the code and make it easy to develop high quality Android apps. The adoption of these patterns represents an essential step for every Android developer who aims to build robust and scalable apps.

In the next chapter, we will take an in-depth look at the different categories of design patterns.

Points to Remember

- **Design patterns help solve common problems** in Android development by providing structured solutions that enhance code organization, scalability, and maintainability.
- Challenges in Android development **include device fragmentation, memory management, and UI complexity**, and the use of design patterns can help mitigate these issues.
- Adopting the right patterns **reduces code duplication, improves reusability, and promotes separation of concerns** between different components of the app.

- **Using patterns simplifies testing and debugging**, making it easier to isolate individual parts of the code and reduce the risk of errors caused by tight coupling between components.
- Patterns such as **MVVM and MVI improve state management and code organization,** separating business logic from the UI and making testing easier.
- **Singleton and Dependency Injection** are essential for dependency management, but their use must be balanced to avoid global state issues or excessive complexity.
- **The trade-offs of design patterns should always be considered**, as a pattern may add complexity without real benefits if applied in an inappropriate context.
- **Using a design pattern is not always necessary**, and in some cases, simpler solutions (such as direct object creation or manual dependency injection) can be more efficient and readable.
- **Choosing the right pattern depends on project requirements.** An app with many interactions between components may benefit from a structural pattern, while an app with complex business logic may take advantage of a creational pattern.
- **Strategic use of design pattern** leads to more scalable, testable, and maintainable code in the long run, improving the overall quality of Android applications.

Multiple Choice Questions

1. Which of these is a common challenge in Android development?
    a. Resource management on mobile devices
    b. Desktop application development
    c. Unlimited access to hardware resources
    d. Legacy systems maintenance
2. Which design pattern is commonly used to guarantee that there is only one class during an application lifecycle?
    a. Factory
    b. Singleton
    c. Observer
    d. Adapter

3. How can the Observer pattern be useful in Android development?
    a. To handle complex object creation
    b. To automatically update user interface when data change
    c. To centralize access to data that come from different sources
    d. To separate business logic from presentation logic
4. Which design pattern is used to centralize the access to data that come from different sources, such as local databases or remote APIs?
    a. Singleton
    b. Observer
    c. Factory
    d. Repository
5. Which of these is a benefit of using design patterns in Android development?
    a. Increase of code complexity
    b. Reduction of app performances
    c. Improve code maintainability and scalability
    d. Limit the functionalities of an app

Answers

1. a
2. b
3. b
4. d
5. c

Questions

1. What are the main challenges in Android development and how can design patterns help overcome them?
2. Explain how the Singleton pattern can be used to manage network connections in an Android application.
3. How does the Repository pattern help centralize data access in an Android application?
4. Why should you use patterns such as MVC and MVVM?
5. What specific benefits do design patterns offer in developing complex Android applications?

CHAPTER 3
Creational Patterns

Introduction

In this chapter, we will dive into creational patterns, which are fundamental to improving the creation of objects in complex Android applications. These patterns help to solve common problems related to the instantiation of classes, improving decoupling, modularity, and testability of the app.

We will explore four key design patterns: **Singleton**, **Factory**, **Builder,** and **Dependency Injection**. Singleton is ideal for situations in which a class should have only one global instance, such as shared resource management. Factory makes it easy to create objects, centralizing the logic and allowing to create different variants without exposing the concrete implementation. Builder is useful when we work with complex objects that have a lot of parameters to configure, improving code readability and maintainability. Lastly, Dependency Injection is a powerful tool to improve decoupling between components, simplifying tests, and integrating new modules or dependencies.

Through practical examples and use cases, the reader will acquire a clear comprehension of how and when to apply these patterns, improving the quality and the flexibility of the code in his Android apps.

Structure

In this chapter, we will cover the following topics:

- Singleton Pattern
  - Use Cases
  - Structure
  - Implementing Singleton in Android
  - Advantages and Disadvantages
  - Final Thoughts
- Factory Pattern
  - Use Cases

Singleton Pattern

Singleton pattern is a creational design pattern that ensures that a class has only one instance at runtime, and it provides a single access point to that instance. In other words, the Singleton pattern ensures that there is only one representation of a class inside the whole application, preventing the creation of additional instances that can lead to inconsistencies and inefficiencies.

Figure 3.1: *The Android mascot as a public authority figure*

Use Cases

In the context of Android development, the Singleton pattern is particularly useful for managing shared resources that must have only one instance throughout the application lifecycle. For example, it is common to use Singleton to handle a database connection, a network client, a user preference controller, or a memory cache. These behaviors must be accessed from different components of the application, but they must not be recreated every time a component requests access to them, because this can lead to inefficient resource usage and concurrency problems.

A practical example could be the management of a network connection to a remote server for executing API calls. Instead of creating a new instance of the HTTP client every time a network call is requested, we can use Singleton to keep a single instance of the client, reducing overhead of continuous creation and disruption of an object and thus improving app performance.

The Singleton pattern, that we just saw to be very powerful, should be used carefully. If not handled correctly, it can introduce issues in unit tests (due to its strong coupling) and also can cause app crashes.

This introduction sets the basis to understand the importance of the Singleton pattern and its application in Android development, preparing the readers to delve deeper into its implementation, the advantages, the disadvantages, and the practical examples in the next sections.

Structure

The UML diagram of the Singleton pattern is very simple: it consists of a class that contains a static method which is responsible for the management of its unique instance. The following figure shows the UML diagram of a Singleton class;

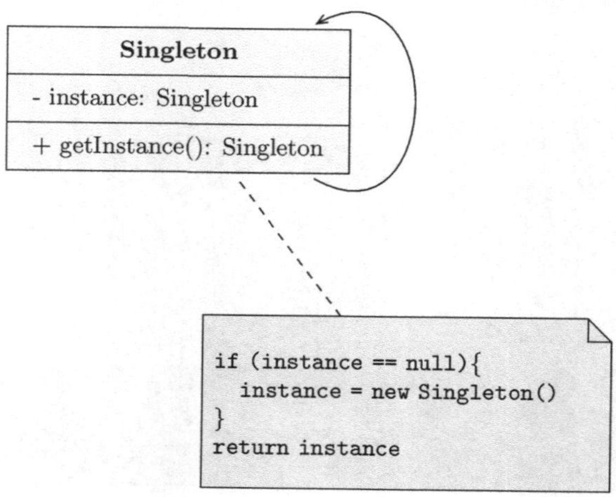

***Figure 3.2**: UML diagram of the Singleton pattern*

In the UML diagram, we can see:

- **`Singleton`**: A class that has global access, which is the subject of the Singleton pattern.
- **`instance`**: A static private field of Singleton class that holds the single instance of the class.
- **`getInstance()`**: A public method that returns the unique instance of the class. At the beginning, instance is null, but when the method **`getInstance()`** is called for the first time, a new instance of the class is created and assigned to instance.

  ```
  fun getInstance(): Singleton {
    if (instance == null){
      instance = new Singleton()
    }
    return instance
  }
  ```

  In this way, the next time **`getInstance()`** is called, the previously created instance is returned to the caller, without recreating it.

The structure of the Singleton pattern is designed to provide a class that has only one instance and that instance is easily accessible from everywhere in the app. This configuration is useful when it is necessary to monitor shared resources, having an object that holds a UI state, or centralizing crucial components of the application, such as data providers. Anyway, it is important to use this pattern carefully to avoid coupling problems and issues in unit tests.

Implementing Singleton in Android

To implement a Singleton object, Kotlin offers a very easy and clean way–just declare an object instead of a class:

```
object Singleton {
    // This is a singleton
}
fun main(){
    val instance1 = Singleton
    val instance2 = Singleton
    // Here instance1 and instance2 point to the same object
}
```

Anyway, for learning purposes, it is useful to see how Singleton can be implemented using a class and the classic **`getInstance()`** method, which is responsible to create one, and only one instance of the class:

```
class Singleton {
    companion object {
        private var instance: Singleton? = null
        fun getInstance(): Singleton {
            if (instance == null){
                instance = Singleton()
            }
          return instance!!
        }
    }
}

fun main(){
    val instance1 = Singleton.getInstance()
    val instance2 = Singleton.getInstance()
    // Here instance1 and instance2 point to the same object
}
```

Let us now look at a practical implementation of the Singleton pattern in the next section.

Database Connection Using Singleton

In this implementation, we can see an implementation using the **`object`** keyword, which is one of the features Kotlin introduced compared to Java. This is very helpful because it allows us to skip the declaration of the variable **`instance`** implementation of the method **`getInstance()`**. This behavior is already implemented under the hood when we use **`object`** instead of **`class`**.

The Singleton implemented here, which is called **`NetworkClient`**, has a method **`sendNetworkRequest()`** that simulates sending a network request and returns an **`Int`**.

```
// Implementation of Singleton
object NetworkClient {

    var requestCount: Int = 0

    fun sendNetworkRequest(): Int {
        // Perform network request
        requestCount++
        return 0
    }

}
```

- **`object NetworkClient`**: Automatically creates a Singleton of type **`NetworkClient`**. This instance is shared and accessible globally.
- **`sendNetworkRequest()`**: A method that simulates sending a network request.

In this case, it always returns **0**, but in a real application, it could return an HTTP response code or another code that identifies the result of the network call.

Now, let us test the implementation.

```
@Test
fun singletonTest() {
    // Get the first instance and update a property
    val instance1 = NetworkClient
    instance1.requestCount++

    // Get another instance and check if it reflects the update
    val instance2 = NetworkClient
    assert(instance2.requestCount == 1)

    // Modify again and check consistency
    instance2.requestCount += 2
    assert(instance1.requestCount == 3)
}
```

This test verifies the behavior of the Singleton pattern, ensuring **NetworkClient** is really a singleton, that is, even if the class is instantiated more than once, all the variables should point to the same, single instance.

The test first retrieves an instance and assigns it to **instance1**, then increments the **requestCount** property. A second instance, assigned to **instance2**, is then retrieved, and its **requestCount** is checked to ensure it reflects the previous modification. Since both **instance1** and **instance2** share the same state, the test confirms that **NetworkClient** is a singleton. If any modification in one instance is reflected in the other, it proves that only one instance exists and is shared across the application.

Advantages and Disadvantages

The Singleton pattern offers multiple benefits, mostly when we deal with efficient shared resource management. However, it also presents some disadvantages that should be considered carefully. Let us explore the main advantages and disadvantages of using the Singleton pattern.

Advantages:

- **Shared resource management**: This pattern is optimal to manage shared resources, such as database connection or user preferences, ensuring a single access point inside the whole app.
- **Global access:** This pattern provides a centralized access to the instance of the class, making it easy to manage shared resources.

- **Lifecycle aware:** The singleton instance is created the first time it is accessed and remains available until the end of the app execution.
- **Minimize creation overhead:** Since only one instance of Singleton can be created, the overhead of object creation is minimized. No multiple and useless instances will be created.
- **Easy to implement:** We saw how easy it is to create Singleton in Kotlin, and this means that it is a fast and bug free solution to adopt.

Disadvantages:

- **Testability challenges:** This pattern introduces a strong coupling, making it hard to mock the class in unit tests.
- **Concurrency problems:** In a multithreaded environment, this pattern can cause issues if it is not implemented correctly. When multiple threads access a shared resource, concurrency-safe mechanisms should be provided to avoid race conditions.
- **Coupling and global dependencies:** It can lead to global dependencies that are hard to manage and modify, reducing code flexibility, especially in large projects.
- **Fault tolerance:** What if the single instance of Singleton crashes? Is it acceptable to simply recreate it from scratch? Or should some mechanism of state saving and recovery be provided? These questions are not trivial, especially if we have to implement background tasks that run continuously.

The Singleton pattern is very useful to manage shared resources, but it should be used carefully to avoid testability, concurrency, and coupling problems.

Final Thoughts

The Singleton pattern is a powerful and widely used tool in Android development, especially when it is necessary to have the existence of a single instance of a class inside the entire application. Its implementation is relatively simple and it offers a way to manage shared resources, such as network or database connections, minimizing overheads and improving the performance of the app.

However, it is important to use it carefully. Even if it offers numerous advantages, it can introduce significant issues, such as difficulties in tests and race conditions in multithreaded environments. To mitigate these issues, it is recommended to use Singleton with other patterns, such as Dependency Injection, that can improve code flexibility and maintainability.

Ultimately, the Singleton pattern is a valid solution for specific scenarios, but it should be applied with awareness, taking into consideration its limits and other suitable alternatives available. If used in the right way, it can contribute to creating efficient and well-structured Android apps.

Factory Pattern

The Factory pattern, also called Factory Method, is a creational design pattern that provides an interface to create objects in a superclass, but it leaves to the subclasses the type of the object that will be created. In other words, Factory pattern allows the delegation of the object creation logic to specific "factories", allowing to centralize and control the creation of complex objects without exposing the details of the creation process.

Figure 3.3: *The Android mascot as a factory worker*

Use Cases

In Android development, Factory pattern is particularly useful when the application needs to create objects that share a common interface but require different implementations, based on the context. This pattern is optimal to handle situations in which the type of the object to be created is not known at compile time, but it will be decided at runtime.

A practical example could be the creation of custom components for user interface. Suppose we wish to have an app that needs to create different buttons depending on the theme chosen by the user (for example, rounded buttons for the modern theme and square buttons for the classic theme). Using the Factory pattern, we are able to centralize the logic of the creation of these buttons in a factory class, and the class will return the correct implementation based on the selected theme.

Another example could be the creation of objects to manage different data storage strategies. If the application must support data storage both on the local device and on the cloud, a factory could be used to instantiate the desired class following the current configuration at runtime.

The Factory pattern improves the modularity of the code and makes it easy to add new types of objects in the future, simply creating new factory subclasses without having to modify the existing code.

Structure

We will now explore the UML diagram of the Factory pattern. The diagram shows the structure of the pattern that centralizes the logic of object creation, separating the instantiation process from the client code. The pattern is used to create different types of objects, all of them implementing the same interface.

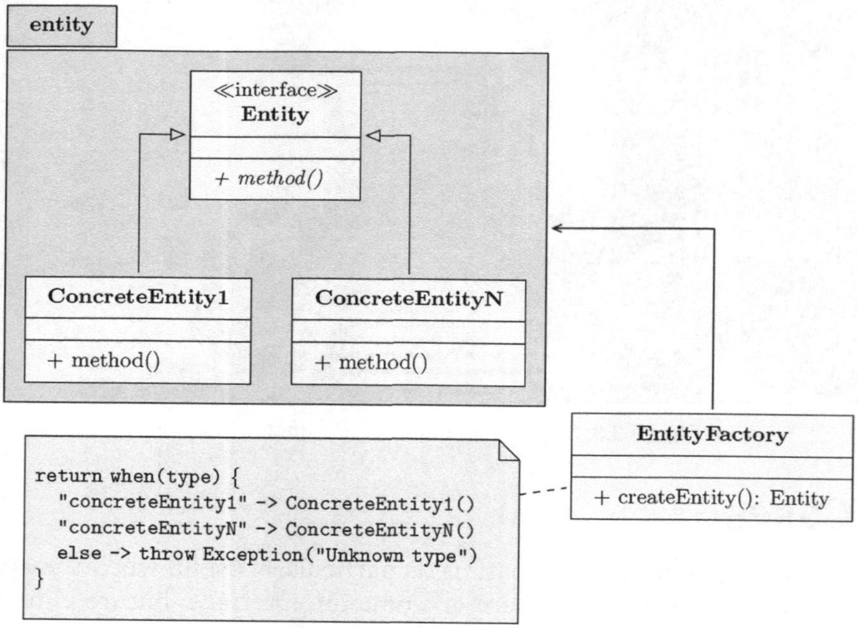

Figure 3.4: *UML diagram of the Factory pattern*

- **`Entity`**: This interface defines the common contract that all the concrete classes must implement. This ensures that all the concrete variants have the same behavior.
- **`ConcreteEntity1`**, **`ConcreteEntityN`**: These classes are the different implementations of **`Entity`**. Every subclass implements the method (or the methods) defined by the interface, and every subclass can implement its own logic to construct the object that it represents.

For the sake of simplicity we have created only two classes, but the names ending in 1 and N should suggest that there can be a custom number of subclasses.

- **`EntityFactory`**: This is the core of the pattern, the class that contains the method **`createEntity()`** that acts like a factory and is used to create the concrete instances of **`Entity`**. The factory decides what concrete object to create depending on the parameter received in input (for example, the string **`type`**). The green box at the bottom of *Figure* 3.4 shows the object creation mechanism. Based on the requested type, the factory creates an instance of the appropriate concrete class. If the requested type does not match with the types available, an exception is thrown.

The Factory pattern offers flexibility, allowing us to add new types of objects without modifying the existing code, simply creating new concrete classes, and extending the factory.

Implementing Factory in Android

The succeeding code implements the Factory pattern in Kotlin, following the structure shown in the UML diagram in the previous section. The factory centralizes the object creation logic returning instances of the different classes depending on an input parameter.

```
interface Entity {
    fun method()
}

class ConcreteEntity1: Entity {
    override fun method() {
        // Logic of ConcreteEntity1
    }
}

class ConcreteEntityN: Entity {
    override fun method() {
        // Logic of ConcreteEntityN
    }
}

class EntityFactory {
    companion object {
        fun createEntity(type: String): Entity {
            return when(type) {
                "concreteEntity1" -> ConcreteEntity1()
                "concreteEntityN" -> ConcreteEntityN()
```

```
                    else -> throw IllegalArgumentException("Unknown
type")
                }
            }
        }
}

fun main(){
    val entityType = "concreteEntity1"
    val entity = EntityFactory.createEntity(entityType)
    // Here entity has type ConcreteEntity1
    entity.method()
    // Here a method of ConcreteEntity1 has been called
}
```

This code has been written following a clear mapping between the conceptual elements of the UML diagram and its practical implementation. The interface **`Entity`** of the diagram is directly represented by the interface **`Entity`** in the code, that defines the common contract for concrete classes. The concrete classes **`ConcreteEntity1`** and **`ConcreteEntityN`** are the specific implementations of this interface, as we can see in the diagram. The **`EntityFactory`** deals with the object creation using the construct when that implements the logic shown in the green box of the diagram. In case an unknown type is requested, the code of the implementation throws an **`IllegalArgumentException`**, which is a specific type of the **`Exception`** suggested in the diagram.

Now let us test the code to see its correctness:

Test 1:

```
@Test
fun createConcreteEntityTest() {
    val entity1 = EntityFactory.createEntity("concreteEntity1")
    assert(entity1 is ConcreteEntity1)
    val entity2 = EntityFactory.createEntity("concreteEntityN")
    assert(entity2 is ConcreteEntityN)
}
```

This test checks if the instances created by the Factory correspond to the ones specified in the input parameter.

This code verifies that when the string **`"concreteEntity1"`** is passed to the factory, an instance of **`ConcreteEntity1`** is created, and the same verification is performed with **`"concreteEntityN"`** related to **`ConcreteEntityN`**.

The factory should create exactly the requested instances given by the input parameter; this is why this test is important. In other words, it ensures that the logic that selected the object type to instantiate is correctly implemented.

Test 2:

```
@Test(expected = IllegalArgumentException::class)
fun createUnknownEntityTest() {
    EntityFactory.createEntity("unknownEntity")
}
```

Before analyzing this test, it is important to notice something new with respect to the other tests we have seen so far. Instead of relying on the assert function to determine if the test passes or not, this time we are not expecting a boolean result, instead, we want the code of the test to throw an exception. When an **`IllegalArgumentException`** is expected, we need to specify it with the annotation **`@Test(expected = IllegalArgumentException::class)`**.

This second test verifies that the factory "fails correctly", and that means that when it receives an object type that it does not know, an exception of type **`IllegalArgumentException`** is thrown. This is very important because we do not want the factory to instantiate unwanted or invalid object types.

This implementation of the Factory pattern centralizes the creation of objects, making the code more flexible and scalable. It is possible to add new concrete classes without having to modify the existing code of the factory; adding new types with their instantiation logic is enough. Tests ensure that the factory works correctly, creating the appropriate instances and handling errors correctly.

Advantages and Disadvantages

The Factory pattern is a versatile solution to create objects that centralizes the creation logic, providing code flexibility and maintainability. However, as every pattern, it has pros and cons that should be considered carefully.

Advantages:

- **Centralization of the creation logic**: This pattern shifts the object's creation logic to a single point, simplifying the client code and reducing its duplication. This approach makes code maintainability easier, mostly in complex applications.
- **Extensibility**: It is easy to extend a system adding a new type of object without modifying a lot of code–we just have to create a new concrete class and add it to the factory logic. This makes the application flexible and scalable.
- **Removal of strong coupling**: This pattern lets us create objects without knowing their detailed implementation. The client interacts only with the factory, reducing the class coupling, thus improving code modularity.
- **Better choices at runtime**: The Factory pattern is particularly useful when we do not know the type of object to be created until runtime. The logic of

Factory allows dynamically creating an object based on specific conditions or parameters.

Disadvantages:

- **Growth of code complexity**: Even if this pattern reduces the complexity in the client code, it introduces a bit of complexity in the overall system. Adding a factory implies introducing an additional layer of abstraction that could complicate the code structure, especially in small and simple projects.
- **Factory's maintainability**: As the number of objects increases, the factory could become hard to maintain, in particular if the creation logic becomes complex or there are a lot of conditions to handle. Here it is important to find a balance between modularity and simplicity.
- **Reduced testability**: Even if this pattern enhances the decoupling, it could make some parts of the code hard to test. If the factory becomes too complex, it might be necessary to write specific tests, or rewrite the existing ones, to cover all the possible conditions, increasing the testing workload.
- **Risk of excessive use**: As with many design patterns, the risk of using Factory in a context in which it is not needed is real. In some cases, a simple class constructor might be sufficient, with the use of Factory would only add complexity without a real benefit.

The Factory pattern is particularly useful when we want to make the object's creation more flexible and improve the scalability of the project. However, it is important to balance benefits offered by this pattern with the potential complexity it could introduce. Factory is a powerful design pattern, but it should be used carefully, especially in small projects, where it might be unnecessary.

Final Thoughts

The Factory design pattern is a fundamental tool to improve code flexibility and maintainability, mostly in contexts where the creation of complex objects and objects that have a variable behavior at runtime is needed. By centralizing the creation logic in a single class, we simplify the client code and improve decoupling between the different parts of the app.

However, it is important to take into consideration the context in which this design pattern is applied. In complex and large projects, Factory could help to reduce coupling and make the application easier to scale. Instead, in small projects that involve objects with few and static properties, this pattern could introduce unnecessary complexity. As well as other design patterns, the appropriate use of the Factory pattern depends on the requisites of the application.

In conclusion, if used wisely, this pattern offers an elegant and powerful way to handle the dynamic creation of objects, ensuring a flexible and easy-to-maintain architecture.

Builder Pattern

The Builder pattern is a creational design pattern that separates the construction of a complex object from its representation, allowing the creation of different representations of an object using the same building process. Practically, Builder allows us to construct objects step-by-step, offering a precise control on every aspect of the object, avoiding the necessity to manage a complex constructor that has many parameters.

***Figure* 3.5**: *The Android mascot as a carpenter*

Use Cases

The Builder pattern is mainly useful when an object needs numerous configuration options, some of which could be optional or have default values. Instead of creating a constructor with a lot of parameters, some of which may never be used in most of the cases, the Builder allows us to construct the object in a clear and clean way, specifying only the option we need.

A recurrent example in modern Android development is the object **`Modifier`**. Most of the composables provided by Jetpack Compose have a property called **`modifier`**, which requires an instance of **`Modifier`**. To add a modifier to a composable instance, we assign a **`Modifier`** object to the dedicated property, and we concatenate the object **`Modifier`** with the properties we want to add to our composable instance.

Mostly, the Builder pattern is used to construct objects that have multiple configuration options. When we have to deal with entities that have a lot of properties, using a constructor with a large number of parameters could be complex and hard to manage. This pattern allows to create the object specifying only the desired properties.

The builder pattern is essential when we work with complex and configurable objects, letting us handle their creation in a clear way. This pattern makes the code more readable, reduces constructor complexity and improves the maintainability of the app.

Structure

The UML diagram illustrated in *Figure 3.6* shows the structure of the Builder pattern, that separates the construction of a complex object from its representation, allowing us to configure individual properties before creating the final object. Every component in this diagram represents a key part in the construction process.

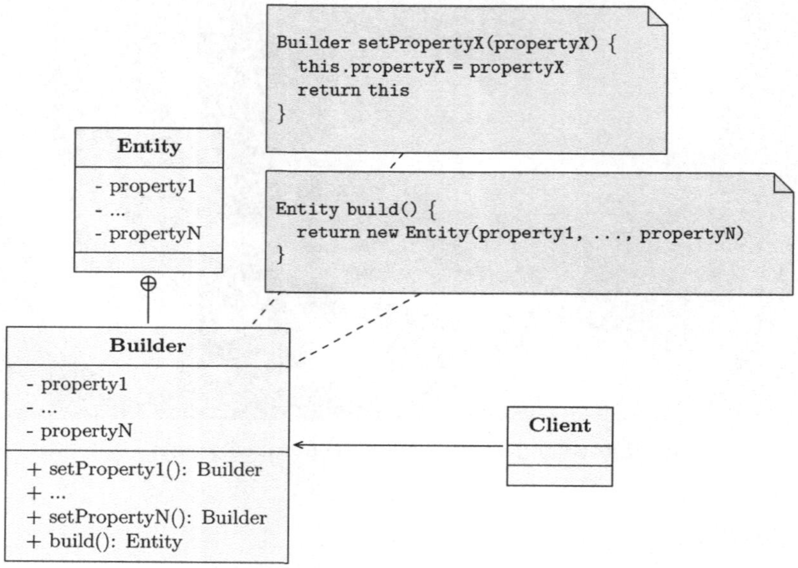

Figure 3.6: *UML diagram of the Builder pattern*

- **`Entity`**: This class represents the final object to be constructed. This class contains all the configurable properties (**`property1`**, ..., **`propertyN`**), that are set during the construction phase by the builder.
- **`Builder`**: This is the design pattern itself. Builder contains the same properties as **`Entity`**, but it is used to set these properties step-by-step. Every setter method (**`setProperty1()`**, ..., **`setPropertyN()`**) returns the Builder itself, allowing us to use chaining. At the end of the process, the **`build()`** method creates and returns the **`Entity`** object configured using the properties configured in the Builder.
- **`Client`**: The client represents the external element, or elements, that uses **`Builder`** to create objects of type **`Entity`**. It interacts only with **`Builder`**, specifying the desired properties and, finally, calling the method **`build()`** to obtain the final object.

The diagram highlights how the Builder pattern allows the creation of complex objects in a fluid way, setting only the desired properties, ensuring that the final object is correctly configured before its usage. This approach favors the readability and the flexibility in the construction of objects that have a lot of properties.

Implementing Builder in Android

Let us now explore how to implement the Builder pattern in Android.

```
class CustomType

class Entity private constructor(
    val property1: CustomType?,
    val propertyN: CustomType?
) {
    class Builder {
        private var property1: CustomType? = null
        private var propertyN: CustomType? = null

        fun setProperty1(property1: CustomType) = apply {
            this.property1 = property1
        }

        fun setPropertyN(propertyN: CustomType) = apply {
            this.propertyN = propertyN
        }

        fun build(): Entity {
            return Entity(property1, propertyN)
        }
    }
}

fun main(){
    val property1 = CustomType()
    val propertyN = CustomType()
    // Here property1 and propertyN of type CustomType can be
customized
    val entity = Entity.Builder()
        .setProperty1(property1)
        .setPropertyN(propertyN)
        .build()
    // Here entity has type Entity
}
```

We start defining a class that represents the complex object that we want to build, and call it **Entity**. This class has two properties, **property1** and **propertyN**, and a private constructor that prevents it from being insatiable from the outside, thus forcing the use of Builder.

The inner class Builder contains several setter methods whose purpose is to set the properties of the class **Entity**, and usually there is a setter for each property, but it is not mandatory. It is important that each method returns the instance of **Entity** to allow the use of *chaining*.

The method **build()** is the core of this design pattern—it creates a new instance of the class **Entity** passing to its constructor the values received in input by the setter methods of the builder.

Examining the method **main()**, we can see how an object of type **Entity** is created using its **Builder**, and we can highlight that if the property is optional, calling the setter method is not mandatory.

```
val entity = Entity.Builder().build()

val entity = Entity.Builder()
    .setProperty1(property1)
    .build()

val entity = Entity.Builder()
    .setPropertyN(propertyN)
    .build()
```

These examples are correct alternatives to create an instance of **Entity**.

Now let us test it. We will see two tests that ensure that the design pattern is implemented correctly.

Test 1:

```
@Test
fun testEntityCreation() {
    val property1 = CustomType()
    val propertyN = CustomType()
    val entity = Entity.Builder()
        .setProperty1(property1)
        .setPropertyN(propertyN)
        .build()
    assert(entity.property1 == property1)
    assert(entity.propertyN == propertyN)
}
```

This test verifies that the object **entity** we created with the Builder pattern has its properties initialized correctly.

In this test, a new object of type Entity is created using the builder and passing to it all of its properties. In this case, the two properties **`property1`** and **`propertyN`**, previously initialized, are passed to the builder. Afterwards, we use the construct assert to verify that the values of the properties of the object **`entity`** are the ones expected to be.

This test is important because it ensures that the builder configures the object's properties in the correct way. If something goes wrong in the property assignment logic, the test will fail, helping in detecting the issue.

Test 2:

```
@Test
fun testEntityPartialCreation() {
    val property1 = CustomType()
    val entity = Entity.Builder()
        .setProperty1(property1)
        .build()
    assert(entity.property1 == property1)
    assert(entity.propertyN == null)
}
```

This second test is basically the same as the previous test, but it sets only one of the two properties of the object.

While the first test initializes all the properties of an object, this test tries to do a partial initialization, which specifies only a part of the object's properties. It verifies that it is possible to create an object of type **`Entity`** setting only some properties, ensuring that the unspecified properties hold the default value (in this case, **`null`**).

This test demonstrates that the Builder pattern can be used in a flexible way, allowing to specify only a subset of the object's properties, leaving the others to their default values. It ensures that the created object is valid even if we do not specify all the properties.

Advantages and Disadvantages

The Builder pattern is a useful tool to handle the creation of complex objects with many optional properties. It centralizes the construction logic, allowing to create objects in a clean and flexible way. However, this pattern also has advantages and disadvantages that we should pay attention to.

Advantages:

- **Incremental construction**: This pattern provides a way to build objects step-by-step, making their creation clear and simple. Instead of using a constructor that has several parameters, every property can be set separately, making the code more readable and tidy.

- **Easy to read and maintain**: The structure of this pattern allows us to concatenate methods when we build objects, and this possibility makes the code more intuitive. This also helps the maintenance, because it is easy to see what properties are setted or not.
- **Flexible parameter management**: The Builder pattern lets us specify only the requested properties, leaving the others optional. This is mainly useful when we work with objects that have a lot of optional parameters. Unlike traditional constructors, it is not mandatory to remember the order of the parameters or passing default values to unused parameters.
- **Object immutability**: The building mechanism offered by this pattern allows us to create immutable objects. Once the object is created, it cannot be changed, unless we add additional methods to do it. This characteristic enhances the security of the code and reduces the chance of errors due to unexpected changes of data.
- **Easy to extend**: Adding new properties to an object that uses the Builder pattern is trivial, we only have to add a new setter to the builder without modifying the existing code. This enhances code flexibility and scalability.

Disadvantages:

- **More complexity**: Even if this pattern makes it simple to create complex objects, it could introduce additional complexity in terms of number of classes or extra code (the Builder class itself). For simple objects, it might be excessive and unnecessary, and the use of a traditional constructor should be preferred.
- **More verbosity**: The use of this pattern requires us to write more code, mostly if we compare it to a traditional constructor. For objects with few properties or for the ones that do not require much configuration, this pattern may be more verbose than it is worth.
- **More memory occupation**: Every time we use the Builder pattern, a new standalone instance of a builder is created, and this may cause a slight increase of memory usage. Even if this is not a significant problem in most of the cases, it could be an issue in application with limited resources.

Thanks to its fluid and flexible structure, the Builder pattern improves the readability and the maintainability of the code, reducing the risk of errors and simplifying the extension of objects. However, for simple objects, the use of this pattern could be excessive, adding unnecessary complexity and verbosity. As always, it is important to carefully evaluate the context in order to maximize the benefits.

The implementation of the Builder pattern in Kotlin simplifies the creation of complex objects, improving code readability and maintainability. The fluent structure provides a flexible and incremental configuration of the object's properties. Tests demonstrate that this design pattern correctly handles the total and the partial creation of objects, ensuring the properties to be correctly initialized.

Final Thoughts

The design pattern Builder is an optimal solution to manage the creation of complex objects, mainly when a lot of optional properties must be defined in a flexible way. The separation of the construction process from the object representation improves the readability of the code and reduces the possibility of errors during the object's creation process. Further, Builder simplifies to add new properties without having to modify the existing constructors.

However, it is important to evaluate the use of this design pattern depending on the complexity of the objects we deal with. For simple objects, it could be too verbose and it could introduce unnecessary complexity. Despite that, if we deal with contexts in which flexibility and immutability are mandatory, the Builder pattern offers a clean and maintainable architecture, making this pattern a powerful tool for the development of complex Android applications.

Dependency Injection

Dependency Injection (DI) is a creational design pattern that makes it easy to manage dependencies between objects, promoting the Inversion of Control (IoC). Instead of allowing the classes to directly create their dependencies, they are "injected" from the outside. This means that the objects that a class needs to run are not instantiated inside it, but they are passed as parameters or provided by a DI framework.

Practically, Dependency Injection separates business logic from dependency management, improving modularity and testability.

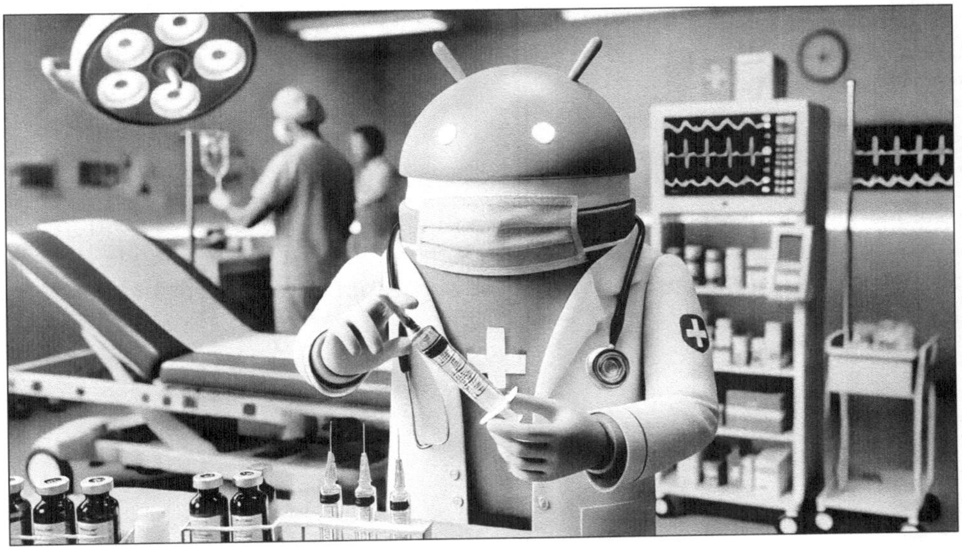

Figure 3.7: *The Android mascot as a doctor*

Use Cases

Dependency Injection is very useful when we have to work in Android development, especially in large applications, where classes must interact with a wide range of services, API, and components. Here are some of its recurrent use cases:

- **Dependency management in ViewModel and Presenter**: In Android, a typical use of DI is the injection of services or repositories in classes such as VIewModel or Presenter. For example, a ViewModel might request a repository to access data. Instead of creating an instance of the repository inside the ViewModel, the repository is injected using this design pattern, improving modularity and testability.
- **Injection of network services or databases**: In many cases, Android applications have to interact with network services (such as REST API client) or local databases (such as Room). Using Dependency Injection, the network client or the database could be injected in every class that needs them. This reduces coupling and allows us to easily replace a service (for example, changing a network implementation) without modifying the business logic in the dependent class.
- **Unit tests and mocking**: DI is fundamental in unit tests. It provides a way to inject mock or fake versions of the dependencies in the classes that need to be tested, making it possible to test the behavior of a single class without depending on real implementations of databases, network services, or other components.

Briefly, this pattern is very useful to improve modularity, testability, and maintainability of Android applications. Injecting dependencies from the outside, we reduce the class coupling, make it easy to update dependencies and components can be tested and maintained easily.

Structure

The following UML diagram shows the structure of the Dependency Injection pattern, in which the dependencies are provided to a client class from the outside, rather than created internally. This approach favors the separation of concerns and improves the code modularity.

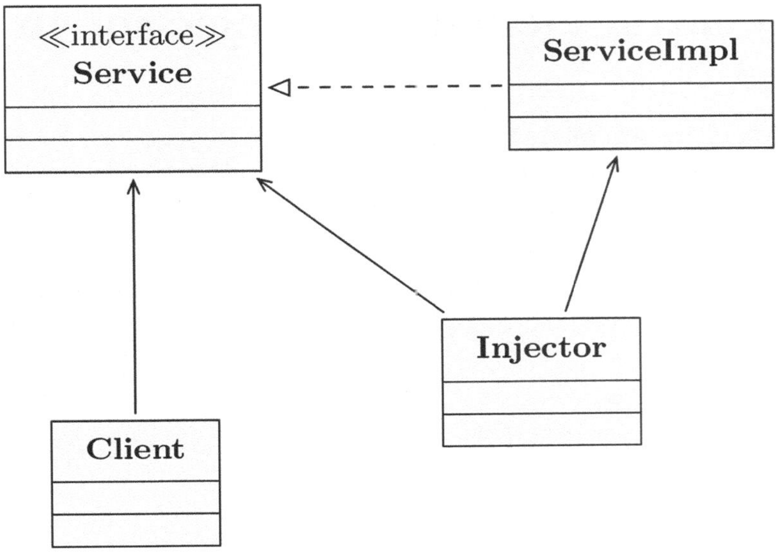

***Figure 3.8**: UML diagram of the Dependency Injection pattern*

- **`Service`**: An interface that defines the contract (the methods) that the concrete implementations of it must respect. In this way, the client interacts only with the interface, without knowing the details of the concrete implementation.
- **`ServiceImpl`**: It is the class that implements **`Service`** and provides the business logic that **`Client`** needs. In other words, it is the concrete implementation of the dependency. While in absence of DI, this class might be directly linked to the client, with this design pattern, this class is kept separated from the client to guarantee flexibility and interchangeability.
- **`Client`**: It is the class that requires the dependency (an instance of **`Service`**). Rather than create and directly manage the dependency, it receives the object needed by the design pattern DI. **`Client`** only interacts with the interface **`Service`**, ensuring loose coupling.
- **`Injector`**: This is the component that is responsible to manage the Dependency Injection. Injector creates the instance of **`ServiceImpl`** and injects it to the **`Client`**.

  There are several injection strategies that can be used–through the client constructor, using setters, or directly into the fields.

The diagram clearly represents how the injector handles the creation and the injection of the dependencies, keeping the client decoupled from the concrete implementations. This approach facilitates code maintainability, allowing us to easily modify or replace dependency without touching the code of the client.

Implementing Dependency Injection in Android

In Android, there are several frameworks that perform Dependency Injection, such as Dagger or Koin, and they are widely used because thanks to them, we do not have to worry about the implementation of this design pattern.

However, it is possible to write our implementation of this pattern. Even if we use frameworks that implement it in our project, it is useful to know how these frameworks work under the hood. The following example shows how to implement Dependency Injection in Kotlin.

```
interface Service {
    fun performAction()
}

class ServiceImpl : Service {
    override fun performAction() {
        // Concrete implementation
    }
}

class Client(private val service: Service) {
    fun execute() {
        service.performAction()
    }
}

class Injector {
    fun inject(): Client {
        val service = ServiceImpl()
        return Client(service)
    }
}

fun main() {
    val injector = Injector()
    val client = injector.inject()
    client.execute()
    // Here ServiceImpl.performAction() has been called
}
```

We start by defining the interface **Service**, that declares the method **performAction()**. Then, we create a concrete implementation of it, **ServiceImpl**, adding some business logic. Now, the class **Client** declares a function **execute()** that calls a method **performAction()** of the service **Service**. Note that **Client** requires an instance of

Service and not **ServiceImpl**. The injection part is performed by **Injector**, which creates a new instance of **ServiceImpl** and passes it as a parameter to the **Client**. The **Client** accepts a **ServiceImpl** instance because **ServiceImpl** implements **Service**. Finally, **main()** can create a new **Client** instance with the required dependencies by calling **injector.inject()**.

Test 1:

```
@Test
fun testDependencyInjection() {
    val injector = Injector()
    val client = injector.inject()
    assert(client.execute() == Unit)
}
```

This test verifies that the client has received a correct instance of service through the injector and the dependency has been injected correctly.

The test creates an instance of **Client** using Injector and checks if the method **execute()** runs correctly.

This test ensures that the Dependency Injection pattern implemented behaves as expected.

Test 2:

```
class MockService : Service {
    override fun performAction() {
        //
    }
}

@Test
fun testDependencyReplacement() {
    val client = Client(MockService())
    assert(client.execute() == Unit)
}
```

This test checks the flexibility of the design pattern we have implemented, performing a replacement of the "real" implementation of the service with a mocked one.

The test injects a mock implementation (**MockService**) to the **Client** and checks if the client executes correctly with the new dependency.

This demonstrates how DI makes the dependency replacement easy in order to test different scenarios.

The implementation of the pattern Dependency Injection in Android simplifies the management of the dependencies and improves code testability and maintainability. With DI, classes are no longer responsible for creating their dependencies, but they receive them from the outside, improving decoupling and favoring the scalability of the app. Tests show how DI allows us to inject different dependencies, making it easy to replace implementations depending on test scenarios and ensuring the correct function of the classes, also when they change dependencies.

Advantages and Disadvantages

Dependency Injection is one of the most used patterns in Android development for managing dependencies between components. The use of DI offers several advantages, mostly in large projects, but it also presents some drawbacks that we must consider.

Advantages:

- **Improves decoupling**: DI separates the business logic of the class from the creation of their dependencies. This reduces coupling between classes, because a class does not know the concrete implementation of their dependencies, but only their interface or the contract that should be respected.
- **Better testability**: Thanks to this pattern, it is possible to inject mocked dependencies during tests. This makes unit tests simpler and reliable, as long as every component can be isolated, without having to depend on concrete implementations or on external components such as databases or network services.
- **Better flexibility and extensibility**: Dependency Injection makes it easy to replace or extend a dependency without modifying the client code. For example, it is possible to change the implementation of a service or passing from a local to a remote database without modifying the business logic of the classes that use these dependencies.
- **Centralized dependency management**: The injector provides a centralized point to manage dependencies. This makes it easy and tidy to check how and when the dependencies are instantiated, and it also reduces the duplication of the code that creates the instances in the whole application.

Disadvantages:

- **Increase of initial complexity**: The adoption of DI introduces a certain level of complexity, especially in small projects. Configuring the injector and handling all dependencies could be seen as an overload when we have only a few components.
- **Debug difficulty**: As long as the dependencies are injected automatically, the execution flow could be less transparent. Debugging might become more complex, because it may not be immediately obvious where the instances of a class come from.

- **Performance overhead**: In more advanced frameworks, such as Dagger or Koin, the complexity of injection could introduce a light performance overhead during the application startup, because dependencies should be resolved and injected. Even if this impact is usually minimal, it should not be a negligible factor in high-performance or realtime apps.
- **Higher learning curve**: For beginner developers, using this pattern could be challenging, especially if they use advanced DI frameworks. The correct configuration and the integration of different components requires a good knowledge of this pattern and the framework adopted.

Dependency Injection offers numerous advantages, mainly in terms of improving decoupling, testability, and flexibility. However, it also involves an increase in complexity, mainly in small projects or when we use complex frameworks. DI is an excellent choice when modularity, maintainability, and testability are a priority, but it is important to balance its benefits with the complexity it introduces, especially in simplex contexts.

Final Thoughts

The design pattern Dependency Injection is a powerful tool to improve modularity, maintainability, and testability of Android applications. Separating the creation of dependencies from their management inside classes, this pattern reduces coupling between components, simplifies the addition of new functionalities and favors the adoption of testing techniques like mocking.

However, as well as other patterns, the implementation of DI should be balanced with respect to the needs of the project. Even if it brings notable advantages in complex applications and large projects, it could introduce an initial complexity, making project setup and debugging harder, mainly for developers who are not familiar with this pattern.

Overall, when applied correctly, Dependency Injection becomes an elegant solution to manage dependencies in a centralized and efficient way, contributing to scalability and robustness of Android apps.

Conclusion

Creational patterns play a fundamental role in developing scalable and maintainable software, providing structured solutions for creation and management of complex objects. In this chapter, we have explored four creational patterns: Singleton, Factory, Builder, and Dependency Injection, each with characteristics and use cases that respond to different problems in the development of Android apps.

Singleton is ideal when we want to guarantee that a class has only one global instance, useful to manage shared resources such as network connection or databases. However, it should be used carefully, as long as it could create testability issues and race conditions in multithreaded environments.

Factory is an efficient choice to centralize the object creation logic, improving code extensibility and modularity. It makes it simple to create different variants of an object, removing the need to know their concrete implementation, but it could introduce complexity when the variants increase.

Builder, instead, is perfect to create complex objects with a large amount of configuration options, allowing us to construct an object step-by-step. This pattern reduces the risk of errors during the creation of objects with a lot of parameters and improves code readability, but it could be excessive for simple objects.

Finally, **Dependency Injection** represents one of the most effective solutions to improve decoupling between classes and improve testability. It allows to inject dependencies from the outside, simplifying to replace components and favoring the inversion of control. However, its implementation could lead to a complexity overload, mainly in smaller projects.

Overall, each of these creational patterns offers essential tools to face different design needs in Android applications. The choice of the right design pattern depends on the specific context and project requirements, but a solid comprehension of each of them brings us to build more robust, flexible, and scalable apps.

In the next chapter, we will explore structural design patterns, which define efficient ways to organize classes and their relationships.

Points to Remember

- **Singleton Pattern**: Ensures that a class has only one global instance and provides a unified access point to that instance.
- **Factory Pattern**: Provides a method to create objects without exposing their construction logic directly.
- **Builder Pattern**: Allows the creation of complex objects step by step, improving readability and maintainability of the code.
- **Dependency Injection (DI)**: Promotes separation of concerns and facilitates testing by avoiding direct object creation within classes.
- **Singleton and Concurrency Management**: If not implemented correctly, the Singleton can introduce race condition issues in multi-threaded contexts.
- **Factory Pattern and the Open-Closed Principle**: The Factory Pattern follows the Open-Closed Principle (OCP), as it allows adding new object classes without modifying the existing code, thus enhancing the application's extensibility.

- **Builder Pattern and Immutable Objects**: The Builder pattern helps create complex objects without using constructors with too many parameters. This is particularly useful for building immutable classes, thus improving code safety.
- **Dependency Injection and Testability**: By using DI, classes can receive their dependencies from external sources, simplifying the use of mock objects to test dependencies without instantiating real objects.
- **When to Avoid Singleton**: Although the Singleton may seem convenient, excessive use can lead to hard coded dependencies and make testing difficult. For shared objects, the best alternative is Dependency Injection.
- **Using Creational Patterns to Improve Modularity**: The combined use of Factory, Builder, and Dependency Injection allows for more modular and reusable code, facilitating separation of concerns and managing dependencies between components of the application.

Multiple Choice Questions

1. What is the main advantage of using the Factory Pattern?
   a. Avoids the creation of complex objects.
   b. Ensures that a class has only one instance.
   c. Improves application performance.
   d. Allows creating objects without specifying their exact class.
2. In which context could the Singleton Pattern be problematic?
   a. When an object with different configurations for each instance is needed.
   b. When it is necessary to guarantee a single shared instance.
   c. When working with repositories.
   d. When using ViewModel in Jetpack Compose.
3. Which creational design pattern is best suited for configuring complex objects with many parameters?
   a. Singleton
   b. Factory
   c. Builder
   d. Dependency Injection

4. Which of the following advantages does Dependency Injection provide in an Android app?
    a. Reduces the need for manual instantiation and improves testability.
    b. Allows reducing the number of Kotlin files in the app.
    c. Increases performance by eliminating the need for repositories.
    d. Completely removes the necessity of using Singleton.
5. For which of these scenarios is the Singleton Pattern most suitable in an Android app?
    a. Creating ViewModel objects.
    b. Managing a single instance of a database or network client.
    c. Dynamically creating complex entities with variable parameters.
    d. Implementing a stateless utility class.

Answers

1. d
2. a
3. c
4. a
5. b

Questions

1. What are the advantages of using the Factory Pattern over directly creating objects with a constructor?
2. How does the Builder Pattern improve code readability and maintainability when working with complex objects?
3. When is it preferable to use Dependency Injection instead of the Singleton Pattern in an Android app?
4. How could the Factory Pattern be combined with Dependency Injection to make the code more flexible and modular?
5. What are the main risks of using the Singleton Pattern in a multi-threaded application?

CHAPTER 4
Structural Patterns

Introduction

The structural design patterns are important to define how classes and objects collaborate inside an Android application. Their main purpose is to make the composition of complex structures easy, keeping the code readable, maintainable, and flexible. In a context like Android development, where the resource management and the interaction between components are critical, the structural patterns help to solve problems related to the integration and control of the resources, and to the dynamic extension of functionalities.

In this chapter, we will explore four of the most relevant structural design patterns:

- **Adapter**: Allows classes with incompatible interfaces to collaborate by adapting a class to the required interface without modifying the original code.
- **Facade**: Provides a simplified interface for interaction with complex systems or modules, reducing the coupling between the client and the internal logic.
- **Proxy**: Controls the access to costly resources or objects, adding functionalities such as caching, authentication, permission checking, or lazy loading.
- **Decorator**: Allows to dynamically extend the behavior of an object, adding extra functionalities in a non-invasive and composable way.

These patterns allow us to address the increasing complexity of an application in an efficient way, improving the resource management and making the code more modular and reusable. By delving into each of them, we will see how to apply them efficiently in the context of Android development, keeping the app architecture clean, solid, and flexible.

By the end of this chapter, the reader will have knowledge of structural design patterns, including their characteristics, implementation, and pros and cons.

Structure

In this chapter, we will cover the following topics:

- Adapter Pattern
- Facade Pattern
- Proxy Pattern
- Decorator Pattern

For each of these topics, we will explore use cases, structure, implementation in Android, advantages, and disadvantages.

Adapter Pattern

The Adapter pattern is a structural design pattern that allows two interfaces, that are incompatible between themselves, to work together. Practically, the Adapter acts as a "translator" between two classes that, without it, would be unable to interact directly, like two people that speak two different languages. This pattern is useful when we have a class that should not be modified, but it must communicate with another class or library.

Figure 4.1: *The Android mascot working as a translator*

Adapter allows us to keep the existing code, adding a new abstraction layer that translates method calls from one interface to another, without altering the original behavior of the classes involved.

Use Cases

The Adapter pattern is mainly useful when we work with external libraries or legacy

API which have incompatible interfaces with respect to our code or other components of our application. We will now explore three typical use cases of this pattern.

- **External library integration**: Imagine that we want to integrate a third-party library that provides a useful service, but it uses a programming interface that is incompatible with your app. Instead of rewriting or modifying the library, we can create an Adapter that translates the calls of your apps to the format requested by the library.
- **Legacy code compatibility**: In large scale applications or systems that evolve over time, it is common that some parts of the code are deprecated or no longer compatible with new interfaces. The Adapter pattern permits to adapt the old code to the new application without the need to rewrite it, translating method calls and maintaining the original behavior.
- **Interaction between different systems**: If two systems must communicate amongst themselves but they use different data formats or protocols, Adapter can be used to get them to cooperate by translating data and commands from one format to another.

The adapter pattern provides a simple mechanism to solve incompatible issues between classes, improving code reusability and making it easier to integrate libraries and external modules without having to do intrusive changes.

Structure

The following UML diagram shows the structure of the Adapter pattern, which acts as a translator from a client and a target class. Since the client cannot directly call the method of the target class–even if the diagram does not show a clear incompatibility, we assume that in our real-use case we have something that prevents us to call a method of the class `Target` from the class `Client`–the adapter allows the client to call the methods of the target through the adapter itself. So, we do not need to modify anything in the target class, because we have an adapter that translates the client's calls.

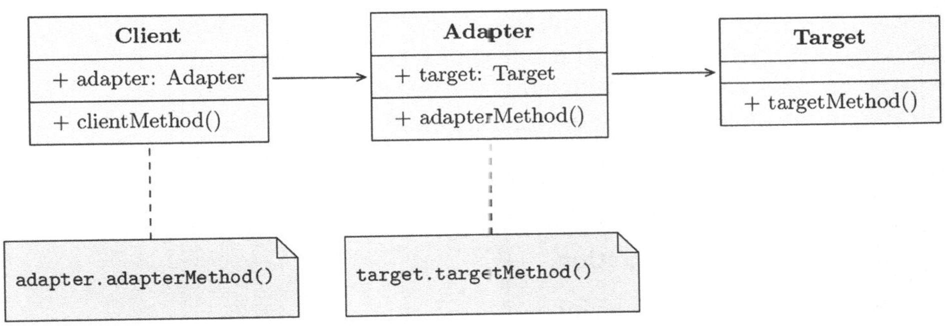

Figure 4.2: *UML diagram of the Adapter pattern*

Now let us dive into the different parts of the diagram:

- **`Client`**: The client represents the class that wants to use the interface of an existing class (**`Target`**), but it is not able to do it due to some incompatibility between them. The client holds an instance of the **`Adapter`** and it calls **`adapterMethod()`**, but it does not interact directly with the target class **`Target`**.
- **`Adapter`**: This class acts as a bridge between the **`Client`** and the **`Target`**. **`Adapter`** holds an instance of **`Target`** and it translates the client's calls (**`adapterMethod()`**) into the appropriate **`Target's`** methods (**`targetMethod()`**). The logic inside **`adapterMethod()`** is responsible to adapt the calls to the correct format requested by **`Target`**.
- **`Target`**: The existing or legacy class with which the **`Client`** wants to interact, but which uses an incompatible interface. The **`Target`** has a method **`targetMethod()`**, which is the one the **`Adapter`** calls to perform the requested action.

This UML diagram shows a clear call flow from the client to the target—the Client calls **`clientMethod()`**, which contains a call to **`adapterMethod()`**. Inside **`adapterMethod()`**, the necessary adaptations are applied before calling **`targetMethod()`**, ultimately reaching the desired result.

This structure lets the client work with classes that are not suitable with respect to its interface, improving flexibility and reusability of the code, without needing to modify the behavior of the existing classes.

Implementing Adapter in Android

The Adapter pattern is particularly useful in Android development when we have to handle situations in which there are classes or interfaces that are not compatible between them. A common example is the adjustment of data coming from a source that needs to be used with UI components, such as RecycleView Adapter. In this case, the adapter acts as a bridge between data and how they are visualized. Luckily, this complex way to render ListViews in Android, using an imperative approach, is being replaced by a clearer, simpler, intuitive, and declarative way provided by Jetpack Compose. Despite this, the old approach is still present in legacy code and large projects, such as AOSP (Android Open Source Project). This is a very clear use case of the Adapter pattern, so it is worth exploring.

What follows is an example implementation of the Adapter pattern in Kotlin.

Suppose we want to adapt an old interface of a legacy system to a new system that uses a different data representation.

```
interface LegacyInterface {
    fun legacyMethod()
```

```
}

// Implementation of Target
class NewSystem {
    fun newSystemMethod() {
        println("Method of the new system in execution")
    }
}

// Adapter class that implements the Legacy interface and adapts
to the NewSystem
class Adapter(private val newSystem: NewSystem) : LegacyInterface {
    override fun legacyMethod() {
        newSystem.newSystemMethod()
    }
}

// Implementation of Client
class Client(private val legacyInterface: LegacyInterface) {
    fun execute() {
        legacyInterface.legacyMethod()
    }
}

fun main() {
    val newSystem = NewSystem()
    val adapter = Adapter(newSystem)
    val client = Client(adapter)

    // Prints "Method of the new system in execution"
    client.execute()
}
```

- **Interface `LegacyInterface`**: Represents the legacy interface that the client wants to use. However, the new system does not support this interface, so the adapter is needed to "translate" the call.
- **Class `NewSystem`**: Is the target class, the more recent system that has a different interface and a method called **`newSystemMethod()`**. This method is the one that should be called by the client but the client is not compatible with this interface.
- **Class `Adapter`**: It implements the legacy interface **`LegacyInterface`** and contains a reference to the class **`NewSystem`**. Inside the method **`legacyMethod()`**, the adapter translates the call in a way that the method **`newSystemMethod()`** of the new system is executed.
- **Class `Client`**: The client knows and uses only the interface **`LegacyInterface`**,

but thanks to the adapter, it can work with the new system without being modified.

Test1:

```
@Test
fun testAdapter() {
    val newSystem = NewSystem()
    val adapter = Adapter(newSystem)
    val client = Client(adapter)

    client.execute()
}
```

This first test verifies that the client can call the legacy method, and that the adapter correctly translates the call to execute the method of the new system **`newSystemMethod()`**.

This test creates a new instance of **`newSystem`** and passes it to the client through the adapter, then it verifies that the client is able to correctly interact with the new system using the legacy interface.

Test2:

```
@Test
fun testAdapterCompatibility() {
    val newSystem = NewSystem()
    val adapter = Adapter(newSystem)

    assert(adapter is LegacyInterface)
}
```

This second test verifies that the adapter is actually compatible with the interface **`LegacyInterface`**, ensuring that it can be used as a replacement for the legacy implementations.

The test uses the **`is`** operator to verify that the instance of the adapter should be considered an implementation of **`LegacyInterface`**.

The Adapter pattern is particularly useful when we work with legacy code or external libraries that use interfaces that are not compatible with our code. In Android, Adapters are often used to adapt data from a source, such as a database or an API call, to UI components, such as a RecyclerView. The ability to keep client and target separated makes the adapter a fundamental partner to handle interaction between different or incompatible systems.

Advantages

The Adapter pattern offers an effective way to make classes collaborate with incompatible interfaces, making it easier to integrate legacy code or third-party libraries.

- **Easy integration with existing code** Adapter makes it easy to integrate new libraries or legacy systems without having to rewrite existing code. This allows to keep the logic unchanged, simplifying the adaptation to new scenery or requirements.
- **Promotes the reusability**: Thanks to this pattern, the existing class can be reused in different contexts, even if their interfaces are not compatible with the other components of the system. This reduces the duplication of code and improves flexibility.
- **Improves code maintainability**: The use of adapter makes it possible to isolate the client code from the detailed implementation of the target class. This improves the separation of concerns, making the code more modular and maintainable. Every modification to the implementation of the target does not impact the implementation of the client, because the client interacts only with the adapter.
- **Class decoupling**: This pattern makes it possible to reduce the strong coupling between classes. The client does not depend on the concrete interface of the target but it interacts through the adapter which deals with translating the calls.

Disadvantages

While the Adapter pattern provides a seamless way to integrate incompatible interfaces, it also introduces certain trade-offs that should be considered.

- **Lack of transparency**: Adapter introduces a new abstraction layer that might make the application flow harder to understand. Developers should be aware that the method calls performed by the client are actually translated into calls of the methods of the target, and this may make the debug more complicated.
- **Performance overhead**: In some cases, the use of this pattern could introduce a little overhead in terms of performance because it adds an additional layer between the client class and the target class.
- **Could hide design flaws**: The overuse of the adapter could be an indicator that the overall application is not well designed. If there are too many adapters, a redesign of the application architecture should be considered to avoid having a code that is too complicated and hard to maintain.
- **Increase of code complexity**: The introduction of this pattern could increase the complexity of the code, mainly when we use a lot of adapters to adapt several interfaces. This could lead to an increase in the number of classes and the logic to handle, making the whole application more complex.

The adapter is a powerful tool to solve incompatibility problems that involve code interfaces, making it easy to integrate new classes and legacy code. However, it should be used with caution to avoid the introduction of performance problems or difficulties in debugging.

Final Thoughts

The Adapter design pattern is a powerful tool capable of solving incompatibility issues that may involve code interfaces, making the code more flexible and reusable. It is particularly useful when we work with legacy systems or third-party libraries because it allows us to adapt existing classes to new contexts without modifying their internal logic.

Adapter improves the modularity and maintainability of the code, separating the logic of the client from the implementation of the target. However, it is important to use it with caution because it might increase complexity and hide design flaws. Too many adapters in a project could be an indication that that project needs an architecture redesign.

Overall, Adapter is an essential design pattern for everybody who works with incompatible interfaces, providing an elegant solution to integrate different systems without sacrificing stability and maintainability of the existing code.

Facade Pattern

The design pattern Facade is a structural design pattern that provides a simplified and unified interface for a complex set of classes. Facade acts like an access point, hiding the complexity of the underlying components and providing a simpler and easy-to-use interface for the client. In other words, Facade deals with orchestrating several operations through multiple and complex components, allowing the client to interact with these components in an easier way.

Figure 4.3: *The Android mascot exposed on a building facade*

The main purpose of this design pattern is to improve the usability of the system, reducing strong coupling from the client and complex internal classes. This pattern is widely used when we deal with libraries, frameworks, or subsystems that include a lot of tangled classes and methods, providing a high-level interface for common operations.

Use Cases

The Facade pattern is useful in any scenario in which we want to simplify the interaction with a complex system. Let us explore some typical use cases:

- **Simplify access to a complex subsystem**: Imagine we have to work with a system that manages several operations, such as a rendering engine or a payment system. Instead of interacting directly with all of these classes, we can create a class that hides the internal details and provides a set of methods that are easier to use for the client. This simplifies the learning curve and makes it easy to interact the subsystem into our application.
- **Abstraction of framework or complex libraries**: Often, when we work with third-party libraries (for example to manage a database, authentication, or network service), the number of classes and interfaces we have to deal with could be overwhelming. A Facade could be used to hide the details of the library and provide a custom interface, tailored to the specific needs of the project, thus simplifying the developers' work.
- **Enforcement of complex operations**: In large applications, several classes could be responsible for single parts of a complex process. For example, in an e-commerce application, the creation of an order can involve inventory management, billing generation, and notifications sending. A Facade can orchestrate all these operations in a single and simple method, hiding complex interactions between the various parts.
- **Reduction of direct dependencies**: This pattern helps to reduce the number of dependencies that the client has with the internal classes. Instead of importing and using many different classes, the client interacts only with the Facade, which acts as a single access point to simplify the interaction.

This design pattern is optimal to simplify the interaction with complex systems or subsystems, providing an access to a single interface that masks the internal complexity. This approach reduces the workload for the developers and makes the application more modular and maintainable.

Structure

The UML diagram of the Facade pattern shows how this pattern acts as a single access point for a complex subsystem. The interface provided by Facade is a high-level simplified interface that hides to the client the complexity and the interaction of the internal classes. This allows the client to interact within the system in an easier way, without worrying about how the different parts of the subsystem are working in detail.

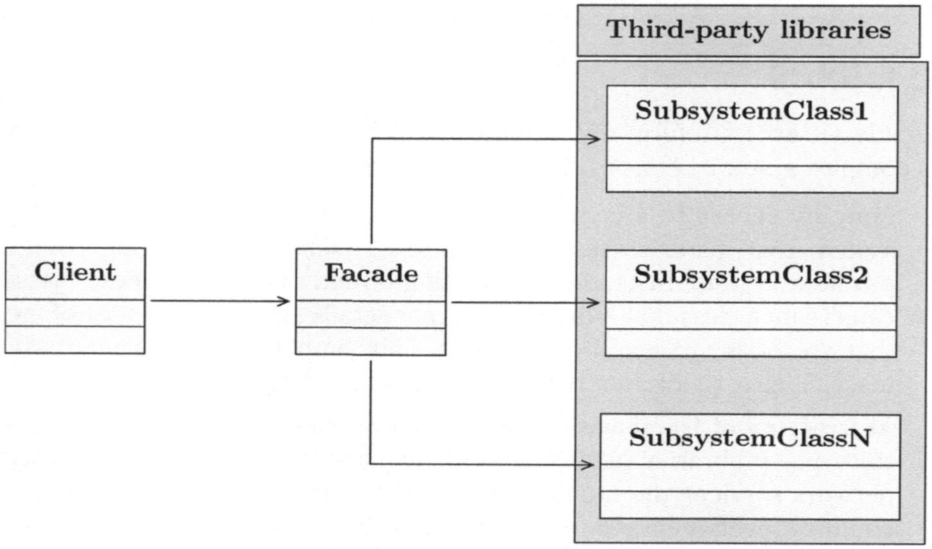

Figure 4.4: *UML diagram of the Facade pattern*

In the diagram illustrated in *Figure* 4.4, we can find the following components:

- **`Client`**: The client is the class or the component that wants to interact with a complex subsystem. However, instead of directly accessing the subsystem's classes, it relies on **`Facade`** to simplify the operations. The client invokes the facade's methods to execute high level operations.
- **`Facade`**: It provides a simplified interface to interact with the subsystem. It contains references to different classes of the subsystem and delegates to these classes the complex logic. The clients interact exclusively with this component, which hides the complexity and coordinates the calls to the internal components.
- **`SubsystemClass` classes**: These classes represent the complex internal logic of the system. Each class is responsible for a single part of the whole complex operation. The client does not interact with these classes, but it is the facade that coordinates the calls to them. The classes in this group can interact with each other, but the client is not aware of it.

A practical example could be, as already mentioned in the previous sections, an e-commerce order management system. The client (the UI, the controller, or the viewmodel) wants to execute a complex operation such as processing an order. Instead of interacting directly with the inventory system, the payment system, and the shipping system, it invokes a high-level method, such as **processOrder()**, on the facade **OrderFacade** that manages all the internal logic, delegating the operation to classes such as **InventoryManager**, **BillingManager**, and **ShippingManager**. We will dive into this example in the next section, where we will see an implementation of this design pattern.

The Facade pattern is useful to simplify the access to complex systems, improving usability and reducing the cognitive load for the developers. By creating a single access point, we reduce the strong coupling between the client and internal classes, improving the maintainability of our application.

Implementing Facade in Android

In the context of an e-commerce application, this design pattern could be used to orchestrate operations related to the management of orders. The goal is to provide a simple interface, hiding the complexity of the internal logic that involves modules such as the management of inventory, payments, and shippings.

In our e-commerce app, when the user completes an order, several modules must collaborate to verify the product availability, process the payment, and organize the shipping. By using Facade, we can simplify this complex logic.

```
class InventoryManager {
    fun checkStock(productId: String): Boolean {
        // Logic to verify the product availability
        println("Checking product availability: $productId")
        return true // For example, the product is available
    }
}

class PaymentService {
    fun processPayment(amount: Double): Boolean {
        // Logic to processing the payment
        println("Processing payment of €$amount...")
        return true // Payment complete
    }
}

class ShippingService {
    fun arrangeShipping(orderId: String) {
        // Logic to organize the shipping
        println("Shipping ready for order: $orderId")
    }
}

class OrderFacade(
```

```
    private val inventoryManager: InventoryManager,
    private val paymentService: PaymentService,
    private val shippingService: ShippingService
) {
    fun processOrder(orderId: String, productId: String, amount:
Double) {
        // Verifies the product availability
        if (!inventoryManager.checkStock(productId)) {
            println("Product not available!")
            return
        }

        // Payment processing
        if (!paymentService.processPayment(amount)) {
            println("Payment field!")
            return
        }

        // Organize the shipping
        shippingService.arrangeShipping(orderId)
        println("Order completed successfully!")
    }
}

// The Client (a ViewModel or Controller in Android)
class OrderViewModel {
    private val inventoryManager = InventoryManager()
    private val paymentService = PaymentService()
    private val shippingService = ShippingService()

    private val orderFacade = OrderFacade(inventoryManager,
paymentService, shippingService)

    fun submitOrder(orderId: String, productId: String, amount:
Double) {
        orderFacade.processOrder(orderId, productId, amount)
    }
}

fun main() {
    // The clients performs the order through the facade
    val orderViewModel = OrderViewModel()
    orderViewModel.submitOrder("ORD123", "PROD456", 99.99)

    // Output:
    // Checking product availability: PROD456
    // Processing payment of €99.99...
```

```
        // Shipping ready for order: ORD123
        // Order completed successfully!
    }
```

It is quite clear that this implementation reflects the components we have seen in the UML diagram, so let us examine them again, but this time from an implementation point of view:

- **Client (`OrderViewModel`)**: The view model or controller represents the client that interacts only with the Facade. In this example, the viewmodel simply calls **`submitOrder()`** which, through the Facade, coordinates all the operations needed to process the order.
- **Facade (`OrderFacade`)**: This class hides the complexity of the interaction between the various modules and provides a simplified interface (**`processOrder()`**) that the client can use to complete the order. Inside it, the Facade verifies the availability of the product, processes the payment, and organizes the shipping.
- **Internal Modules (`InventoryManager`, `PaymentService`, and `ShippingService`)**: We have three distinct modules and each is responsible for a specific part of the order processing. Without the Facade pattern, the client would have to directly handle the complexity of coordinating these components.

Test 1:

```
@Test
fun testProcessOrder() {
    val inventoryManager = InventoryManager()
    val paymentService = PaymentService()
    val shippingService = ShippingService()

    val orderFacade = OrderFacade(inventoryManager, payment
Service, shippingService)

    // Test the complete or the processing
    orderFacade.processOrder("ORD123", "PROD456", 99.99)
}
```

This test verifies that the whole process of performing an order is executed correctly, from the inventory to the shipping.

The test submits an order with all the required details and checks that each module performs its operations in a correct way.

Test 2:

```
@Test
fun testProductUnavailable() {
    val inventoryManager = mock(InventoryManager::class.java)
```

```
    `when`(inventoryManager.checkStock("PROD456")).thenReturn
(false)

    val paymentService = PaymentService()
    val shippingService = ShippingService()

    val orderFacade = OrderFacade(inventoryManager, payment
Service, shippingService)

    // Verifies that the order fails if the product is not
available
    orderFacade.processOrder("ORD123", "PROD456", 99.99)
}
```

This test verifies that the order fails if a product is not available.

The test simulates the case in which the product is not available and checks that the flow of the order interrupts correctly.

In a complex application such as an e-commerce app, the Facade pattern allows the client to handle the whole order processing without having to interact directly with the different models that manage the inventory, the payments, and the shippings, making the code cleaner, modular, and maintainable.

Advantages

Facade pattern is an efficient solution to hide the complexity of internal models and provide an interface that is simpler and intuitive to the client.

- **Reduction of complexity**: This pattern hides the complexity of the logic and the interactions that involve the internal modules, providing a simple interface for the client. This reduces the complexity perceived by the client and makes the interaction with the internal modules more intuitive.
- **Improve maintainability**: Separating the client from internal modules, the pattern Facade allows to modify or update the logic of the modules without impacting the code of the client. This improves the system's maintainability because the internal modification can be performed without requiring changes to the interface used by the client.
- **Decoupling**: The client does not need to know the details on how the internal modules work, reducing the coupling between the client and the internal components. This allows the client to interact only with the Facade, keeping the code cleaner and easier to manage.
- **Flexibility and extensibility**: The Facade could be easily extended to integrate new functionalities. If new modules or services are added, the Facade could be updated to support them without having to modify the client.

- **New developers can join easily**: In large projects, the Facade pattern helps new developers join the team and interact with the application without knowing in depth every internal module. They can simply use the interface provided by this design pattern, saving time and reducing the learning curve.

Disadvantages

Despite its benefits, the Facade pattern comes with some drawbacks that may impact flexibility and control over the underlying system.

- **Hide big complexity**: A risk of using this design pattern is that it could hide too much complexity of the internal modules. This could lead to a lack of comprehension of effective behavior by the developers that interacts only with the Facade. In some cases, it could be necessary to directly access the internal modules to take advantage of the most advanced functionalities.
- **Access point to centralized**: If Facade grows too much in terms of functionalities, it could become a single access point that is too centralized. In other words, this access point may end up handling too many operations. This makes the Facade class hard to maintain and could transform it into a bottleneck for the management of the operations.
- **Additional overhead**: Even if this pattern simplifies the interaction with the internal modules, it could introduce an additional overhead in terms of performance, because the calls have to pass through an additional level of abstraction before reaching the internal modules. Even if the impact of this overhead is generally minimum, it could become relevant in high-performance applications or real-time applications.
- **Lack of flexibility in custom operations**: If Facade provides only high-level operations, it could impede the client to customize or execute tailored operations that request direct access to the internal modules. This could be a limitation in using the application if the client needs to perform operations that are not planned by the Facade.

This design pattern is a powerful tool to simplify the interaction with complex internal modules in an Android application, improving its maintainability and reducing the coupling between the client and internal components. However, it should be used carefully in order to avoid hiding too much complexity or creating an over centralized access point.

Final Thoughts

The design pattern Facade is an efficient approach to simplify the interaction with complex modules inside an Android application. Providing a single access point, the Facade reduces the complexity for the client and makes the application architecture clean and maintainable. In scenarios where different modules must collaborate, such as in the process of order management in an e-commerce app, this pattern permits to orchestrate the operations without exposing the internal logic to the client.

However, it is important to balance the use of Facade with the necessity of maintaining a certain level of flexibility. Hiding too much complexity or centralizing too many operations in the Facade could make the app hard to maintain and limit the access to fine-grained functionalities. When used correctly, this pattern makes it easy to organize the code and integrate new developers or new functionalities. It also reduces the class coupling, making it a key element in well-structured Android applications.

Proxy Pattern

The pattern Proxy is a structured design pattern that provides a substitute or a delegate for another object. Proxy acts as an intermediary that can handle the access to the real object and it can execute additional operations such as caching, authorization management, or access control before delegating the request to the real object. This pattern is useful when we want to have a higher control on the interaction with an object, such as expensive resources or network operations.

Figure 4.5: *The Android mascot surveilling a bank vault*

Proxy can be used to delay the instantiation of an object, provide remote access to a service, or limit access to sensitive resources. It is also useful when designing a framework that requires controlled or restricted access from client code. There are different types of Proxy, such as Virtual Proxy, Remote Proxy, and Protection Proxy, each serving a different purpose but all acting as an intermediary.

Use Cases

This design pattern is particularly useful when we want to add an additional layer of control or optimization before the client accesses an object or a service. Let us see some real use cases:

- **Lazy loading**: In this case, the design pattern is used to delay an instantiation of a complex object until it is actually needed, thus saving resources. For example, if an app must access a high-resolution image from a robot server, a Virtual Proxy can act as the image's delegate. The image is actually downloaded and displayed only when it is going to appear on the device display (or in the viewport).
- **Caching of expensive resources**: In mobile applications, most of the time, it could be very useful to have a Proxy that stores expensive resources in a cache, such as network responses or images. For example, a Proxy can check if an image was already downloaded and stored locally before performing a request to the server. This reduces the usage of mobile data and improves the performance of the application.
- **Access control**: In some situations, we have to consider limiting access to specific resources or functions using authorization methods. A protection proxy can verify the user's credentials or check permissions before allowing access to sensitive resources, such as reading personal data or access to an app's premium function.
- **Remote access**: A Remote Proxy could represent an object that is stored in a remote server. The Proxy acts as an intermediate to simplify the communication between the local client and the remote service, managing operations such as data serialization or network failure handling. This type of proxy is mainly useful in apps that frequently interact with remote API and cloud services.
- **Logging or operations monitoring**: A Proxy can be used to track the operations performed on an object. This could be useful for debug purposes or to analyze how some resources are used. For example, in an Android app that interacts with a database, a Proxy can record every query or operation that is executed on the database to monitor the usage and detect potential inefficiencies.

This pattern is ideal when we deal with a situation in which we want to add a new control, optimization, or security level when we access an object or a service. In Android, this pattern is used often to improve performances, manage expensive resources, and ensure access control in complex scenarios.

Structure

The UML diagram of the Proxy pattern shows how this design pattern acts as an intermediary between the client and the real object. Proxy implements the same interface of the real object, allowing the client to interact with the proxy as if it were interacting directly with the real object. The Proxy can execute additional operations such as caching, logging, access control, or delay the instantiation of the object.

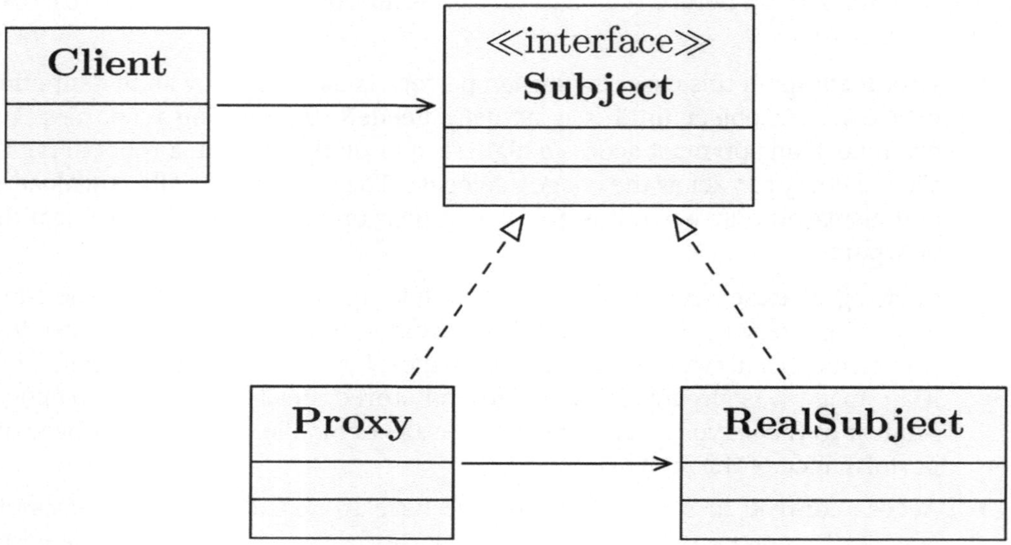

Figure 4.6: *UML diagram of the Proxy pattern*

The preceding diagram is made by the following components:

- **Class `Client`**: As we already know, it is the part of the app that requests the execution of some operations on an object. The client interacts only with the Proxy and it does not know the implementation of the real object.
- **Interface `Subject`**: It defines a common interface that the Proxy and the real object must implement. This ensures that the client can interact with the Proxy and the real object in the same way, without being aware of the difference.
- **`Proxy`**: This is the class that implements the interface **`Subject`** and contains a reference to the real object. Proxy can decide when to create a real object, control the accesses, store results in a cache, or manage the remote communication.
- **`Real Subject`**: This is the class that actually performs the operations requested by the client. The proxy uses it to delegate the client's requests when needed.

The flow of the operation is the following:

1. The **`Client`** invokes a method on the **`Subject.`**
2. The **`Proxy`** receives the request by the client and decides if the operation is to be handled directly or delegated to the **`RealSubject.`**

3. If needed, the **`Proxy`** instantiates the **`RealSubject`** and delegates the requests to it.

Now let us see an example. In an Android app, let us assume that the **Client** represents a UI component that requests data to a remote server. The **Proxy** could be a component that handles the requests to the server and uses the cache to reduce the repeated requests. If data is already saved in the cache, **Proxy** returns them directly; otherwise, it delegates the request to the **RealSubject** that is responsible to retrieve the data from the server.

This UML diagram (*Figure* 4.6) shows clearly how a proxy can control the access to expressive or sensitive resources, executing additional operations before delegating to the real subject.

Implementing Proxy in Android

A common use case in which we can use the Proxy design pattern is to manage the access to network data, optimizing the loading of resources and reducing the bandwidth use. In this example, we will implement a Proxy for the management of images loaded from a remote server, with caching of images in order to improve performance.

```
class Image {
    // Fields and method to hardle image data
}

// Interface that defines the methods to load the image
interface ImageLoader {
    fun loadImage(url: String): Image
}

// Real implementation that handles the loading of images from
the remote server
class RealImageLoader : ImageLoader {
    override fun loadImage(url: String): Image {
        println("Loading of the image from the remote server:
$url")
        return Image()
    }
}

// Proxy that manages image caching in order to optimize loading
class ImageLoaderProxy : ImageLoader {
    private val realImageLoader = RealImageLoader()
    private val imageCache = mutableMapOf<String, Image>()
```

```
    override fun loadImage(url: String): Image {
        // Check if the image is already in the cache
        return if (imageCache.containsKey(url)) {
            println("Image loaded from cache: $url")
            imageCache[url]!!
        } else {
            // If the image is not in the cache, loads it from
the remote server and stores it
            val bitmap = realImageLoader.loadImage(url)
            imageCache[url] = bitmap
            bitmap
        }
    }
}

// Classe client che interagisce con il proxy per caricare le
immagini
class ImageViewModel {
    private val imageLoader: ImageLoader = ImageLoaderProxy()

    fun displayImage(url: String) {
        val image = imageLoader.loadImage(url)
    }
}

fun main() {
    val imageViewModel = ImageViewModel()
    // First request: the image is loaded from the server and
stored in the cache
    imageViewModel.displayImage("https://example.com/image1.png")
    // Second request for the same image: it will be loaded from
cache
    imageViewModel.displayImage("https://example.com/image1.png")
}
```

- **Interface `ImageLoader`**: This interface represents the **Subject**. It defines the method **`loadImage()`** that both the Proxy and the real object **`RealImageLoader`** must implement.
- **Class `RealImageLoader`**: This class actually manages the loading of the images from the remote server. When the Proxy does not have an image cached, it delegates the task of loading it to the **`RealImageLoader`**.
- **Class `ImageLoaderProxy`**: This is the class that really implements the design pattern. Proxy handles the access to the real object, adding caching functionality. Before loading the image, it checks if it is already stored in the cache: if yes, returns it directly, otherwise it loads the image from the server and stores it.

- **Class `ImageViewModel`**: This class represents the client we have seen in the UML diagram. It uses the proxy to load images. It interacts only with the interface **`ImageLoader`** without knowing if the image comes from the cache or from the remote server.

Test

```
@Test
fun testImageCaching() {
    val imageLoader = ImageLoaderProxy()
    // First request: the image should be loaded from the server
    val image1 = imageLoader.loadImage("https://example.com/
image1.png")
    // Second request: the image should be loaded from cache
    val image2 = imageLoader.loadImage("https://example.com/
image1.png")
    // Verifies that the image is the same
    assert(image1 == image2)
}
```

This test verifies that the Proxy loads the image from the server only once and it uses the cache for subsequent requests.

The test calls the method **`loadImage()`** twice with the same URL. The second time, the image must come from the cache, avoiding a new download from the server.

In this example, Proxy has the ability to add the cache functionality without having to modify the logic of the image loading. Just makes the code more efficient and easier to maintain offering a simple interface for the client and optimizing the app performances.

Advantages

Now let us see the advantages and the disadvantages of using this design pattern Proxy, an approach that offers several benefits in terms of control of the access to resources, but which also has some critical issues to consider.

- **Resource optimization**: A Proxy allows to optimize the use of resources, for example, delaying the instantiation of large objects until they are actually needed (lazy loading). This is particularly useful in mobile applications where the computational resources and network capacity are limited.
- **Caching**: The proxy can implement some caching functionalities, storing data locally or resources that are costly to obtain, such as images or network responses. This reduces the loading time and improves the app performances, reducing the necessity to perform repeated access to external resources.
- **Access control**: A proxy can act as a point of control to limit the access to

some objects or services. This is useful when we have to implement security mechanisms, such as permission handling or credential verification, before executing an operation.

- **Remote access abstraction**: In cases in which the service of the object is stored in a remote server, proxy can manage the communication and the request routing between the client and the server, providing a transparent management of the process.
- **Simplification of the client**: This design pattern provides a consistent interface for the client, hiding the complexity of the access to remote or local resources, and allowing the client to interact with the proxy as it is the real object.

Disadvantages

Although the Proxy pattern provides valuable control over resource access, it also introduces certain drawbacks that should be carefully evaluated.

- **Harder debugging**: The new intermediate layer added between the client and the real object could make the debugging more difficult, especially when we deal with logging the operations performed or identify problems related to remote resource management.
- **Additional overhead**: This pattern introduces a new layer between the client and the real object, and that could introduce a slight overhead in terms of performances, especially if proxy performs additional operations such as caching or permission checking.
- **Increase code complexity**: The introduction of a Proxy can complicate the architecture of the application, mainly if it is used excessively or in situations in which it is not strictly needed. It adds an additional layer of abstraction that must be managed and understood.
- **Hard dependency management**: If not handled carefully, Proxy can make the dependency management more complicated, making it difficult to maintain and update the code when the real object or the Proxy itself should be modified or extended.
- **Additional maintenance costs**: The need to update both the Proxy and the real object when the code of the application is updated could bring additional maintenance costs, because both of them must remain synchronized and compatible.

The Proxy pattern offers significant advantages in terms of resource control, caching and access control, but it should be used carefully in order to avoid adding useful complexity to the app architecture.

Final Thoughts

The Proxy design pattern is an extremely useful tool to manage complex or costly resources in an efficient way, improving the memory usage, implementing caching, and providing a secure access control. Thanks to its capacity of hiding the complexity of the real object, Proxy can make the interaction with remote resources more fluid and easier for the client.

However, the introduction of Proxy requires the need to balance the advantage of optimization with a possible growth of architectural complexity and the risk of introducing overhead. It would be important to consider carefully the scenarios in which its application would be appropriate, so that unnecessary abstraction layers that can make the project more complicated, can be avoided.

Summarizing, this design pattern is an optimal choice for those who want to optimize the access to complex resources and to improve security, as long as it is used with caution to keep the code maintainable and performing.

Decorator Pattern

The design pattern Decorator is a structural design pattern that allows extending the behavior of an object in a dynamic way, without modifying its original structure. Unlike inheritance, which requires creating new classes to add functionalities, the Decorator allows to "decorate" an object, adding the new responsibilities through composition. This pattern is useful when we want to extend or modify the behavior of an object during runtime, maintaining the additional logic separated.

Figure 4.7: *The Android mascot while painting his home*

Decorator works by adding a series of "wrapper" objects that all implement the interface of the original object, delegating the operations to it and adding new functionalities. Every decorator can add or modify the behavior of the object without altering the source code.

Use Cases

This design pattern is useful in all of the contexts in which we need to extend the behavior of an object in a flexible and dynamic way, without creating a complex class hierarchy. Here are some practical use cases, especially in the context of Android applications:

- **Extending UI components**: In Android, Decorator could be used to extend the behavior of the components of the user interface, such as a **`TextView`** or a **`Button`**. For example, is it possible to decorate a **`TextView`** to add functionalities such as monitoring of the text digitized by the user or dynamic formatting without having to modify the base component.
- **Input and output handling**: This pattern is often used to extend the classes that manage the input and output of data. In Android, this could include data flow from file or network stream, where it is possible to decorate a reading object to add functionalities such as compression, encryption, or buffering, without modifying the original flow.
- **Adding logging functionalities**: Another common case is the addition of log. Is it possible to decorate an object to track the operations that are executed on it, while keeping the original behavior of the object. For example, we can decorate an instance of **`HttpClient`** to monitor all the network requests performed by the application, without modifying the original object.
- **Customization of a service**: In Android, we could use the Decorator pattern to extend system services or our application components. For example, we can decorate a **`LocationService`** to add extra functionalities, such as position data filtering or notifications, without altering the base service.
- **Adding dynamic behavior**: A practical use of Decorator is adding base components to dynamic configurations or execution conditions. For example, if we have an app that manages payments, we could decorate the payment service in order to add functionalities such as validation or calculation of discounts based on active promotions, without modifying the code of the base service.

Briefly, the design pattern Decorator allows to extend or modify the behavior of the objects in a flexible and non-intrusive way. It is mostly useful when we need to add dynamic functionalities without altering the existing structure of the application.

Structure

The UML diagram of the Decorator pattern shows how this design pattern allows us to dynamically extend the behavior of an object. The client interacts with an object that implements the interface component, that can be the ConcreteComponent or a Decorator class. Every Decorator implements the same interface of the based component, but it can add or modify the behavior calling the method of the original component and adding additional logic.

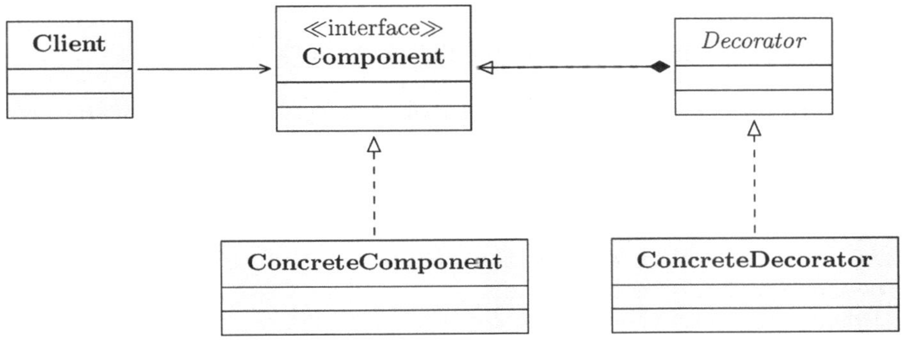

Figure 4.8: *UML diagram of the Decorator pattern*

- **Interface `Component`**: It defines the common interface for all the components, including both the decorated and the undecorated. This interface will be implemented by both the base component (**`ConcreteComponent`**) and the decorators.
- **Class `ConcreteComponent`**: It is the concrete class that represents the original object, that is, the component that will be decorated. It implements the interface **`Component`** and represents the object that receives the additional behavior from the decorators.
- **Abstract class `Decorator`**: This abstract class implements the interface **`Component`** and contains a reference to an object that is a subtype of **`Component`**. The subtypes of **`Decorator`** will extend the behavior of the object, delegating the calls to the component which they are decorating and adding extra functionalities to.
- **Class `ConcreteDecorator`**: It is the concrete class that extends the abstract class **`Decorator`**, adding an additional behavior to the decorated object. It can override the method of the base component to provide additional functionalities.
- **Class `Client`**: As usually, with this class, we indicate any components that interact with the components of the design pattern. The client does not need to know if it is working with a decorated or an undecorated component.

To consider a practical example, imagine that we have a graphical component that draws a text on screen, such a **Textview** in Android. A concrete decorator could be used for adding functionalities such as text formatting, bold or italic, without having to modify the original component. The **Client** can work with the decorated **TextView** without knowing that the text formatting functionality has been added dynamically.

This scheme lets us add new functionalities to existing objects in a flexible way, improving the reusability and maintainability of the code, and avoiding the need to create long hierarchies of inheritance.

Implementing Decorator in Android

Let us now dive into an example of implementation in which we want to decorate an Android TextView with logging functionality. Practically, the logging functionality logs every time the user types some text in the TextView. Without modifying the base class, we can implement a decorator that is responsible to perform this logging action.

```
// Interface that defines the common methods between the base
component and the decorator
interface ViewDecorator {
    fun display()
}

// Base component that implements the visualization behavior of a
simple TextView
class SimpleTextView(private val text: String) : ViewDecorator {
    override fun display() {
        println("TextView shows: $text")
    }
}

// Abstract decorator that implements the interface ViewDecorator
and holds a reference to the component
abstract class TextViewDecorator(private val textView: View
Decorator) : ViewDecorator {
    override fun display() {
        textView.display()
    }
}

// Concrete decorator that adds the login functionality to the
TextView
class LoggingTextView(textView: ViewDecorator) : TextView
Decorator(textView) {
    override fun display() {
        println("Logging: User has typed some text.")
```

```
            super.display()
        }
    }

    // Client class that uses the TextView with the decorator to add
    extra functionalities
    class TextViewClient {
        private val textView: ViewDecorator = LoggingTextView(
            SimpleTextView("Hello, Android!")
        )

        fun renderTextView() {
            textView.display()
        }
    }

    fun main() {
        val textViewClient = TextViewClient()
        textViewClient.renderTextView()

        // Output:
        // Logging: User has typed some text.
        // TextView shows: Hello, Android!
    }
```

- **Interface `ViewDecorator`**: Defines the common method **`display()`** that the base component and the decorators must implement.
- **Class `SimpleTextView`**: It is the base component that represents the simple behavior of the TextView. It implements the method **`display()`** to visualize the text without any additional logic.
- **Abstract Class `TextViewDecorator`**: It is an abstract decorator that implements the interface **`ViewDecorator`** and contains a reference to the base component. Its functionality is to delegate the job to the base component and let the subtypes add new functionalities.
- **Class `LoggingTextView`**: It is a **`ConcreteDecorator`** that extends the behavior of the TextView adding the logging functionality. Before visualizing the text, it logs a message that indicates that the user has typed some text.
- **Class `TextViewClient`**: It represents the client that interacts with interface ViewDecorator. The client uses the decorated **`LoggingTextView`** to add the logging functionality without modifying the behavior of the base **`TextView`**.

Advantages

Now we will analyze the advantages and disadvantages of the design pattern Decorator, a tool that allows adding new functionalities to an object without modifying its original structure.

- **Dynamic addition of functionalities**: The decorator allows to add or modify the behavior of an object during runtime, without the need to modify its base class. This leads to a greater flexibility compared to inheritance, that requires static changes.
- **Flexible composition**: Due to this design pattern, it is possible to combine several decorators to create combinations of functionalities without having to write a new class for each variant. Every decorator can be added or removed based on our needs.
- **Code maintainability and reusability**: As long as every decorator is separated and independent from the original component, it is possible to extend the behavior in a modular way. This promotes the reusability of the decorators in other contexts or components.
- **Reduction of complexity of hierarchies**: Instead of creating multiple subclasses to represent every possible combination of functionalities, the Decorator pattern uses the composition, reducing the necessity of having long hierarchies of classes.
- **Compatibility with the base component**: The Decorator keeps the interface of the original component, ensuring that the decorated object can be used in every context in which the base component is used, without the client knowing about the new functionalities.

Disadvantages

Despite its flexibility in extending object behavior dynamically, the Decorator pattern can introduce complexity and potential trade-offs that need to be considered.

- **Increase of complexity**: Although the Decorator reduces the hierarchies of classes, the introduction of numerous Decorators could lead to an increase of complexity of the execution flow, which becomes harder to understand. Also, it could be harder to track the behavior of the Decorators if they are in a large number.
- **Debugging difficulties**: When we use more Decorators, it could become harder to perform debugging operations to understand which Decorator has modified the behavior of the component in a specific point of the application.
- **Greater number of objects**: The Decorator creates new instances for every additional Decorator, and this could lead to an increase in the number of objects in memory and require more resource management. This could be critical in the context of mobile applications, in which we have limited resources.

- **Strictness of the applying order of Decorators**: The order in which the Decorators are applied could change the final result. If not handled correctly, this could lead to unexpected behaviors that are harder to control, especially when the decorators depend on each other's output.
- **Implicit coupling**: Even if the Decorators add flexibility, they could anyway introduce a certain level of coupling between the Decorators themselves and the components that they decorate. This could make the code harder to maintain in large applications.

Decorator is ideal to use in contexts where flexibility and maintainability are important. However, we need to use it carefully in order to avoid the increase of complexity and difficulties in the debugging of the additional functionalities.

Final Thoughts

The Decorator pattern turns out to be an effective solution when we wish to extend the behavior of an object in a dynamic and flexible way, avoiding the limitation of inheritance. Thanks to its composition, it is possible to add or combine functionalities in a non-invasive way, maintaining the compatibility with the interface of the original component. This makes Decorator mostly useful in contexts such as Android applications, where we want to add functionalities to UI components or services without modifying the base structure.

However, it is important to use this design pattern with caution, since an excessive or poorly organized usage could lead to an increase of complexity, both in terms of the number of object instances, and the comprehension of the execution flow. When used correctly, the Decorator ensures a great flexibility and modularity, contributing to create a better maintainability and reusability of the code in complex applications.

Conclusion

Structural patterns, such as Adapter, Facade, Proxy, and Decorator, perform a crucial role in the organization and management of the complexity of an application, especially in contexts such as Android development, where having a flexible and maintainable architecture is fundamental. These patterns provide practical solutions to face common problems related to interaction between components and resource management.

The **Adapter** pattern allows classes with incompatible interfaces to cooperate, simplifying the integration of modules and libraries without modifying the code. The **Facade** pattern offers a simplified interface for a complex set of modules, reducing the coupling and making the code more readable and maintainable. The **Proxy** pattern allows control of the access to costly resources, implementing functionalities such as caching or lazy loading, while the **Decorator** pattern adds or modifies the behavior of an object dynamically, allowing a flexible composition of functionalities without compromising the original class.

These patterns not only improve code modularity and reusability, but also simplify the evolution of an application, allowing it to extend the functionalities without introducing rigidity or overcomplexity. However, they should be used carefully, since an inappropriate or excessive use could lead to complications in the architecture. In the end, the structural patterns provide the tools we need to keep a clean, flexible, and easy to maintain architecture, making them fundamental to developing robust and scalable Android apps.

Now that we have explored structural patterns, we will move on to behavioral patterns, which focus on communication between objects. In the next chapter, we will examine key behavioral patterns such as Observer, Command, and Strategy.

Points to Remember

- **Adapter** lets classes collaborate with incompatible interfaces, adapting a class to another without modifying the original code.
- **Facade** provides a simplified interface to access complex modules, reducing the coupling between the client and the internal classes.
- **Proxy** manages the access to costly or sensitive resources, implementing mechanisms caching, access control, or lazy loading to optimize performances.
- **Decorator** extends dynamically the behavior of an object, allowing to add functionalities without modifying the base class and maintaining the compatibility with the original interface.
- Structural design patterns improve code maintainability, simplifying the integration between modules, and **reducing the complexity** of inheritance hierarchies.
- Patterns such as Decorator and Adapter **favor composition rather than inheritance**, allowing greater flexibility while adding new functionalities.
- Although structural partners provide a lot of advantages, **they should be used carefully** in order to avoid an excessive increase in complexity or debugging difficulties.
- These design patterns **improve the maintainability and the modularity** of the code, allowing modification to single components without impacting the rest of the application.
- Patterns such as proxy and Facade **allow optimizing resource usage** in Android applications, especially in contexts where the management of network and memory resources is fundamental.

- All these patterns **offer a great flexibility** in handling complex structures, allowing to modify or extend the behavior of the application without introducing strictness in the architecture.

Multiple Choice Questions

1. Which structural pattern allows classes to collaborate with incompatible interfaces?
    a. Proxy
    b. Adapter
    c. Decorator
    d. Facade
2. What is the main purpose of the Facade pattern?
    a. Reducing memory usage
    b. Providing a simple interface for complex systems
    c. Control the access to resources
    d. Adding new functionalities dynamically
3. Which design pattern is commonly used for implementing caching in an Android application?
    a. Adapter
    b. Facade
    c. Proxy
    d. Decorator
4. Which design pattern allows dynamically extending the behavior of an object without modifying the class?
    a. Adapter
    b. Proxy
    c. Decorator
    d. Facade

5. Which is the main advantage of the Proxy pattern with respect to the other structural patterns?
    a. Allowing to control access to costly researchers
    b. Adding functionalities dynamically
    c. Reducing the complexity of the application
    d. Simplify the interface of a system

Answers

1. b
2. b
3. c
4. c
5. a

Questions

1. Explain how the Adapter pattern can be used to integrate a third-party component in an Android app.
2. Describe a scenario in which the Facade pattern simplifies the interaction between a client and a complex system.
3. What are the main disadvantages of using the Proxy pattern in an Android application?
4. How can the Decorator pattern can be used to add functionalities to a UI component in Android?
5. Compare the patterns Adapter and Facade. What are the main differences in their usage?

CHAPTER 5
Behavioral Patterns

Introduction

The behavioral design patterns are fundamental to manage the interaction between objects and how they exchange information or react to events. Unlike creational or structural patterns that concentrate respectively on the object creation and organization, the behavioral patterns define how the object behaves and communicates between themselves.

In the context of Android development, these patterns become essential tools to construct reactive, modular, and maintainable applications, where the management of events and dynamic actions is at the core. In this chapter, we will explore **Observer**, **Command,** and **Strategy**. These patterns provide a powerful solution to keep the code flexible and scalable, while reducing the coupling between components.

These patterns are applicable in a wide range of scenarios, from handling state changes notifications to the implementation of comments and interchangeable behaviors. The purpose is to ensure that the behavior of the applications could be extended or modified without having to rewrite big portions of the code, allowing developers to add new functionalities easily and make the app act accordingly to the user input.

In this chapter, we will explore how each behavioral pattern could be used in Android applications to improve efficiency, modularity, and code clearness, leading to projects that are flexible and maintainable over time.

Structure

In this chapter, we will cover the following topics:

- Observer Pattern
- Command Pattern
- Strategy Pattern

For each of these topics, we will explore use cases, structure, implementation in Android, and their advantages and disadvantages.

Observer Pattern

The Observer pattern is a behavioral design pattern that defines one-to-many relationship between objects, in a way that when an object changes its state, all the other objects which depend on it are automatically notified and updated. This pattern allows the creation of a dynamic notification system, where those interested in the objects (the observers) can register to a subject (the observable) in order to be notified about changes. This pattern is particularly useful when there is a high degree of dependencies between objects.

***Figure 5.1**: The Android mascot doing birdwatching*

In Android development, the Observer pattern is widely used, especially when we have to work with user interfaces that must be updated depending on data changes or system events. This allows decoupling the business logic from the components that depend on it, thus improving the maintainability and the modularity of the code.

Use Cases

The Observer pattern has several practical applications in the development of an Android app, mainly in the following scenarios:

- **Reactive user interfaces**: In Android, the user interface must react to the changes of the data in real time. For example, the use of LiveData or Observable allows the app to automatically notify the Activity or Fragment when the displayed data changes. In modern Android development, this mechanism of updating UI components is a key concept in the new declarative way of building user interfaces of Jetpack Compose. We will mention this approach in the next paragraph.

- **Activity and fragment lifecycle events**: Android provides the Lifecycle framework, which implements the Observer pattern to allow the various components to observe the changes on the lifecycle of an activity or a fragment. This allows us to execute specific operations when they enter a different state such as `onPause()` and `onResume()`.
- **Notifications and global event handling**: This design pattern is useful when we have to manage global events in an Android application. For example, through the `LocalBroadcastManager` or libraries such as `EventBus`, objects can register as observers and receive notifications when specific events occur, such as new data coming or changes in the state of the system.
- **Observable data models**: In architecture such as Model-View-ViewModel (MVVM), ViewModels usually use observables to provide updated data to the views. When data changes, the observers, such as activities or fragments, are notified to update the user interface.
- **Push notifications management**: Push notifications use the concept of Observer. When a push message arrives from a service, such as FMC (Firebase Cloud Messaging), the Android app can notify the various components to handle the event, such as displaying a notification or updating the UI with the new data received.

The Observer design pattern is extremely useful to create reactive and modular Android apps, where state or data changes must be communicated automatically and dynamically to the various components. This improves efficiency and reduces the coupling between components, making the code clear and maintainable.

Observer in Modern Android Development

In modern Android development and Jetpack Compose, the Observer pattern is a built-in mechanism in `State`, `StateFlow`, and `Flow`, as well as composition and recomposition.

During composition, the UI is built based on the current state, while during recomposition, only the parts that are interested by the changes in the state are updated. `Flow` and `StateFlow` further improve this process, providing a structured and reactive way to handle asynchronous data flows. Functions such `collect()` and `collectAsState()` allow us to observe these flows, ensuring that the UI remains synchronized with the state changes, creating a clear and declarative approach of programming that manages the dynamic interfaces in an efficient way.

Structure

The Observer pattern is composed of two main actors–the **subject** (the observable) and the **observers**. The subject holds a list of observers that must be notified every time that the state of the subject changes. The observers are responsible for executing specific actions when they are notified about a change.

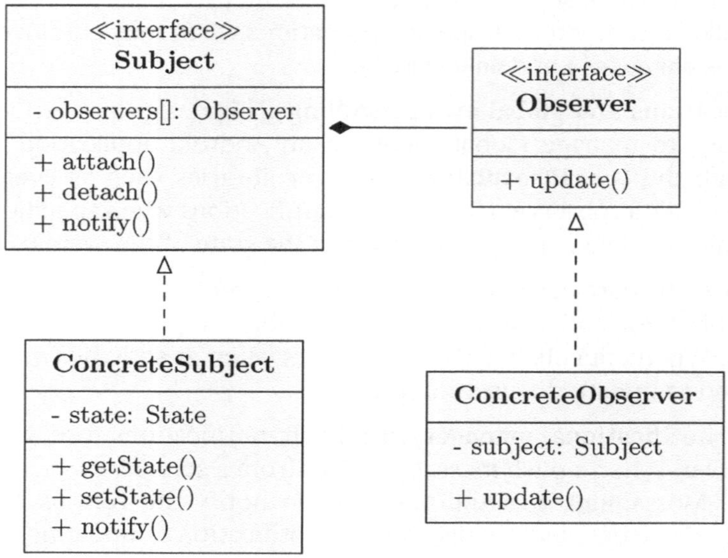

***Figure 5.2**: UML diagram of the Observer pattern*

The UML diagram is made of the following entities:

- **Interface `Subject`**: This is the object that contains the state to observe. It is responsible for registering, removing, and notifying the observers when its state changes. **`Subject`** holds a list of observers and provides the methods to manage that list.
- **Interface `Observer`**: The observers are objects that want to be notified about a subject's state changes. When the subject changes, the observers are notified and they can update their state to respond to the change.
- **Class `ConcreteSubject`**: It is a specific implementation of **`Subject`**. This class holds the observed state and notifies the observers every time the state changes. It could implement specific logic and manage the changes of the state.
- **Class `ConcreteObserver`**: It is a specific implementation of **`Observer`**. This class updates its state depending on the changes of the **`Subject`**. Every ConcreteObserver can implement specific actions that must be executed as a response to the notifications received from the **`Subject`**.

The **`Subject`** contains a list of registered elements of type **`Observer`**. When the state of the **`ConcreteSubject`** changes, it calls the method **`notifyObservers()`** to notify all the registered **`Observer`** elements. Every **`ConcreteObserver`** implements the method **`update()`**, that is called to respond to the state change.

To see a practical example, let us consider an Android application in which the Subject could be an object that manages the data, such as a ViewModel, and the Observers could be activities or fragments that have to update the user interface every time the data changes. The ViewModel uses LiveData, which is an implementation of the design pattern Observer, to hold the observable data, while Activity and Fragments are observers that automatically update themselves when data changes.

This structure allows us to keep the code flexible and reactive, separating the logic of data update from the user interface, thus improving the maintainability of the application.

Implementing Observer in Android

In MAD (Modern Android Development), one of the most common tools to implement the *Observer* design pattern is the use of **`State`** and **`ViewModel`**, which are part of the Android Jetpack framework. **`State`** allows us to observe data changes in a reactive way, while **`ViewModel`** lets the data survive through configuration changes, such as screen rotation.

Following this, we will see a concrete example of the implementation of Observer in Android using **`State`**, **`ViewModel`**, and Jetpack Compose to manage the data and update the user interface when the data changes.

```
class ObserverViewModel: ViewModel() {
    // Observable state
    private val _text: MutableState<String> = mutableStateOf
("Hello, Observer!")
    val text: State<String> = _text

    // Method to update the state
    fun updateText(newText: String) {
        _text.value = newText
    }
}

@Composable
fun ObserverComposable(
    viewModel: ObserverViewModel = viewModel()
) {
    // Observes the state changes in ViewModel
    val textState = viewModel.text.value

    // the Text composable is automatically updated when the
state changes
    Column(
        modifier = Modifier.padding(16.dp),
```

```
            horizontalAlignment = Alignment.CenterHorizontally,
            verticalArrangement = Arrangement.Center
        ) {
            Text(text = textState)
            Spacer(modifier = Modifier.height(8.dp))
            Button(
                onClick = {
                    viewModel.updateText("Hello again, Observer!")
                }
            ) {
                Text("Update Text")
            }
        }
    }
```

- **Class `ObserverViewModel`**: This class is the **subject** of the UML diagram of Observer. Its purpose is to maintain the state as observable, in this case represented by an object **`MutableState`** called **`_text`**. The **`State`** allows the registered observers to be automatically notified when the data changes. The method **`updateText()`** is used to modify the state of **`_text`**, which then notifies the observers. In Jetpack Compose, the composables that observe the state of **`_text`** are automatically recomposed when that state changes.
- **Composable `ObserverComposable`**: The composable observes the changes of **`State`** inside the **`ViewModel`** using the reference **`viewModel.text.value`**, that allows to directly link the value of the state to the UI variable **`textState`**. When the **`ViewModel`** updates the text, the composable **`Text`** is recomposed, showing the new text without having to perform manual updates.

The UI in Jetpack Compose is naturally reactive–every time a **`State`** changes its value, the composables that depend on it are automatically composed, thus implementing the Observer pattern natively.

Test

```
@get:Rule
val composeTestRule = createComposeRule()

@Test
fun testTextUpdatesInCompose() {
    // Set the composable to test
    composeTestRule.setContent {
        ObserverComposable()
    }

    // Verifies the initial text
    composeTestRule.onNodeWithText("Hello, Observer!").assert
Exists()
```

```
        // Simulates the update of the text
        composeTestRule.onNodeWithText("Update Text").performClick()

        // Verifies the new text after the update
        composeTestRule.onNodeWithText("Hello again, Observer!").
    assertExists()
    }
```

The purpose of this test is to verify that the **Text** composable is correctly updated when the state of the **ViewModel** changes.

This test simulates a click on the button that triggers the **updateText()** function, and it verifies that **Text** shows the new content.

The Observer design pattern is a fundamental part of data management in Android development. The framework Android Jetpack implements it in an elegant way with Live Data and ViewModel, but Jetpack Compose has further enhanced its ease of use.

This example shows how Jetpack Compose, due to its declarative and reactive nature, makes it very easy to implement the behavior of Observer, letting us to keep the powerful of this design pattern, while writing less code compared to the approach based on XML layouts.

Advantages and Disadvantages

The Observer pattern is widely used to manage the communication between objects that must be synchronized in a reactive way, without creating strong connections between them. However, as well as the other design patterns, it brings with it advantages and disadvantages that are important to consider.

Advantages:

- **Decoupling**: This pattern separates the subject that generates the events (subject) from the object that receives them (objects), making components less dependent on each other. This decoupling improves the maintainability and flexibility of the code.
- **Reactivity**: It allows us to create reactive and dynamic systems in which the interested objects are automatically updated when the state of the subject changes, without the need to perform polling or manual updates.
- **Easy to extend**: It is simple to add new observers without modifying the subject. We only have to register a new observer that will be notified automatically when the state changes.
- **Native Android support**: Android offers native support for the implementation of this design pattern. Tools such as LiveData, StateFlow, and ViewModel make it easy to manage observable data in reactive user interfaces.

- **Modularity**: Due to the separation of responsibilities between subject and observer, the pattern helps to maintain a modular code, letting us develop and test each part of the app independently.

Disadvantages:

- **Complexity in complex systems**: In systems that have a lot of observers and subjects, the notification management could become complicated. The flow of the updates could become hard to trace, especially if we have a lot of relationships between subjects and observers.
- **Performances**: The continuous dispatch of notifications to many observers could cause an overload, mainly if the state changes occur frequently or if there are many observers registered.
- **Debugging difficulties**: Due to the asynchronous nature of the Observer pattern, it could be difficult to identify the source of issues or bugs, because the updates occur in an indirect and non-linear way.
- **Notification order issues**: The order in which the observers are notified could influence the behavior of the app, and in some specific cases this could cause synchronization problems or unexpected behaviors.
- **Risk of memory leaks**: If these observers are not removed correctly when they are no longer necessary, we risk memory leaks, especially in contexts such as Activity or Fragment. It is important to carefully manage the addition and removal of the observers in order to prevent them from remaining active when they do not have to.

The Observer pattern is a powerful tool to create modular and reactive applications, providing easy notification management. However, its implementation must be handled carefully in complex systems in order to avoid issues with performance, debugging, and memory leaks. If used correctly, it is a fundamental design pattern in Android development, especially when we leverage on constructs such as LiveData and StateFlow.

Final Thoughts

The Observer design pattern is a key element in developing reactive applications as well as in many Android apps, where it is fundamental and that the state changes are reflected dynamically on the user interface. This design pattern allows the code decouples to be modular and easy to extend, as the subjects and the observers are managed independently. Native constructs such as LiveData, ViewModel, and StateFlow perfectly integrate Observer in the Android ecosystem, making it easier to manage the state and the communication between the various components.

However, it is important to keep in mind the potential problems. In complex applications, the management of many observers could introduce complexity and performance issues. Moreover, the notification order and the management of the observers, mainly in lifecycle context such as activities and fragments, should be handled carefully to avoid memory leaks.

In the end, Observer represents one of the most efficient solutions to create reactive user interfaces and keep the code clean and maintainable, especially if implemented using the tools of Modern Android Development.

Command Pattern

The design pattern **Command** is a behavior design pattern that transforms a request or an action to an independent object. This allows us to parametrize the methods with different requests, register the action to be performed or canceled in queue requests, and manage operations in a flexible and reusable way. In other words, this pattern separates the code that generates the requests (invoker) from the code that executes the action (receiver), enclosing every command inside the dedicated object.

Figure 5.3: *The Android mascot working in a control center room*

In Android development, Command is useful to implement actions that can be executed in a way that is flexible and independent of the object that requires them, such as UI actions handling, command mapping in user interfaces, or asynchronous operations management.

Use Cases

- **UI event handling**: In Android, the Command pattern could be used to manage the actions associated with the buttons or events of the user interface. For example, if you have a set of buttons that execute different operations, you can use the Command pattern to map each button to a specific command, improving the flexibility of the code and simplifying the extension of functionalities.

- **Undo/Redo actions**: This design pattern is particularly useful when we have to implement actions such as undo and redo. In an Android app, for example, a drawing app or a text editor app, every operation could be transformed into a command object. This allows us to keep a history of the action executed and cancel or redo the modifications in an orderly way.
- **Asynchronous and background operations**: When we execute asynchronous operations such as network requests or database accesses, the pattern Command allows us to define each operation as an independent object that could be enqueued or executed in background. For example, a series of network requests could be encapsulated in separate commands that handle the execution and the result autonomously.
- **Macro commands**: This design pattern allows us to compose Command Macros, that are grouped sequences of commands. This is useful when we want to execute multiple actions with a single click or a single request. For example, by tapping a button in an e-commerce app we could add a product to cart, send payment requests, and update the UI, all through a Command Macro.
- **Modularization of functionalities**: Another use case of Command is the modularization of the functionalities in a complex application. Implementing actions as commands, we can easily manage the invocation of different functionalities without depending on internal implementations. This makes the code more scalable and easier to maintain, improving the separation of responsibilities.

The pattern Command is particularly suitable when it is necessary to implement flexible, modular, and reusable requests, clearly separating the invocation of the action from its execution. In Android development, this pattern is useful to handle user interactions, asynchronous operations, and functionalities that need flexibility and control.

Structure

The Command design pattern is composed of four main components–the **Command**, the **Receiver**, the **Invoker,** and the **Client**. These elements collaborate in order to execute the requests, which are in the form of object-encapsulated commands and can be executed, enqueued, canceled, or repeated depending on the needs.

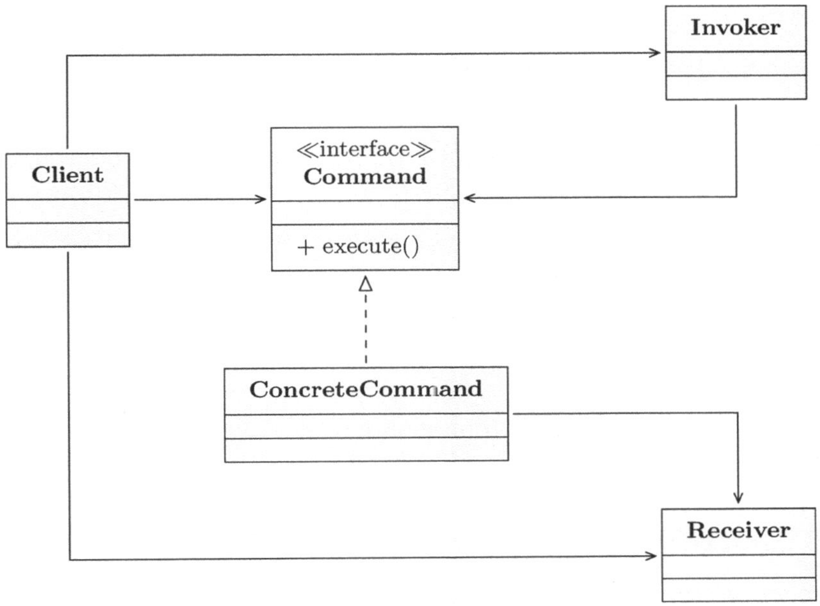

***Figure 5.4**: UML diagram of the Command pattern*

- **Command**: It devices the common interface for all the concrete commands. It contains the method **`execute()`**, which executes the requested action. The concrete commands implement this method to execute specific actions.
- **ConcreteCommand**: It is a class that implements the interface Command and contains a reference to the receiver. It is responsible for executing an action by calling a method on the receiver, and it represents the concrete command that will be executed.
- **Receiver**: It is the object that knows the detailed implementation of the requested action. When the command is executed, the receiver is the entity that actually executes the operation.
- **Invoker**: It is responsible to invoke the commands. It does not execute the action directly, but holds a reference to the command that should be executed and calls the method **`execute()`** on the command when necessary.
- **Client**: It is the entity that configures the command. It creates the object ConcreteCommand, associates the command to the receiver, and passes the command to the invoker.

The flow of the actions in this diagram may seem complicated, and so merits step-by-step description:

1. The client creates an instance of ConcreteCommand and links it to the receiver, which will execute the action.

2. The client passes the command object to the *invoker*.
3. When the action needs to be executed, the invoker calls the method **`execute()`** on the ConcreteCommand object.
4. The ConcreteCommand calls the appropriate method on the receiver to execute the action.

A practical example in Android could be a button to which we associate several actions executed dynamically. The button, which is the invoker in this case, invokes several concrete commands to execute different actions, such as the addition of a product to the cart or send an email, while the receivers actually execute the operations.

This structure makes the code highly flexible and scalable, since it allows us to encapsulate the operations in command objects, making it easy to add new functionalities or undo operations.

Implementing Command in Android

The Command pattern can be used effectively in Android to separate the execution logic of the actions from the user interface, making it easy to handle operations and improving the code flexibility. In this example, we will see how to implement this design pattern in Android using Jetpack Compose to handle the interaction with the user interface, splitting the operations into commands.

Let us suppose we have an Android app with two buttons that execute different actions–one of them adds a product to the cart, while the other one removes it. These actions could be encapsulated in separated, which can be executed dynamically when the user interacts with the buttons.

```
// Interface that defines the execute() method
interface Command {
    fun execute()
}

// Concrete command to add a product to the cart
class AddToCartCommand(private val receiver: CartReceiver) :
Command {
    override fun execute() {
        receiver.addItemToCart()
    }
}

// Concrete command to remove a product from the cart
class RemoveFromCartCommand(private val receiver: CartReceiver) :
Command {
    override fun execute() {
```

```
            receiver.removeItemFromCart()
        }
    }

    // Receiver
    class CartReceiver {
        fun addItemToCart() {
            println("Product added to cart")
        }

        fun removeItemFromCart() {
            println("Product removed from cart")
        }
    }

    // Invoker
    class ButtonInvoker(private var command: Command?) {
        fun setCommand(newCommand: Command) {
            command = newCommand
        }

        fun pressButton() {
            command?.execute()
        }
    }

    @Composable
    fun CommandComposable() {
        // Create the receiver (the cart)
        val cartReceiver = CartReceiver()

        // Create the concrete commands
        val addToCartCommand = AddToCartCommand(cartReceiver)
        val removeFromCartCommand = RemoveFromCartCommand(cartReceiver)

        // Initialize the invoker
        val buttonInvoker = remember { ButtonInvoker(null) }

        Column(
            modifier = Modifier.fillMaxSize(),
            horizontalAlignment = Alignment.CenterHorizontally,
            verticalArrangement = Arrangement.Center
        ) {
            // Button to add a product to the cart
            Button(onClick = {
                buttonInvoker.apply {
                    setCommand(addToCartCommand)
```

```
                pressButton()
            }
        }) {
            Text("Add to cart")
        }

        Spacer(modifier = Modifier.height(16.dp))

        // Button to remove a product from the cart
        Button(onClick = {
            buttonInvoker.apply {
                setCommand(removeFromCartCommand)
                pressButton()
            }
        }) {
            Text("Remove from cart")
        }
    }
}
```

- **Interface `Command`**: This interface defines the method **`execute()`** that the concrete classes must implement while encapsulating the actions that we want to execute (addition or removal of a product).
- **Class `AddToCartCommand` and `RemoveFromCartCommand`**: These are the ConcreteCommands that implement the interface **`Command`**. In **`AddToCartCommand`**, the method **`execute()`** calls **`addItemToCart()`** on **`CartReceiver()`**. In the same manner, **`RemoveFromCartCommand`** calls **`removeItemFromCart()`**.
- **Class `CartReceiver`**: As a **Receiver**, this class gets the action to be performed from the ConcreteCommands, and actually performs these operations. In our scenario, it adds a product to the cart or removes a product from it.
- **Class `ButtonInvoker`**: The invoker holds a reference to a command and executes it when a button is clicked. It is possible to dynamically change the command to execute through the method **`setCommand()`**.
- **Composable `CommandComposable`**: In our UI, we have two buttons that are responsible for two commands–one to add a product to the cart and another to remove it. When the user presses a button, the corresponding command is executed through the invoker.

Advantages and Disadvantages

The Command pattern encapsulates operations as objects, making it easier to parameterize, queue, and undo actions. Let us explore its advantages and disadvantages.

Advantages:

- **Decoupling between invoker and executor**: The pattern Command separates the object that requests the execution of an action (invoker) from the object that actually executes the action (receiver). This decoupling makes the code more flexible and maintainable, allowing us to modify the action without changing the invoker's code.
- **Easy to add new operations**: Adding new operations is easy with Command. The only thing we have to do is to create new concrete commands that implement the interface `Command`, without modifying the existing code. This approach favors the extensibility of the code, allowing us to add new functionality without altering the main architecture.
- **Undo/redo support**: One of the main advantages of this design pattern is its ability to support undo and redo operations. Since every action is encapsulated in a separated command, it is easy to save the previous state and cancel or repeat the actions.
- **Ability to compose macro-commands**: Command allows us to compose multiple commands in a single complex command (also called Macro-Command), letting us execute a series of operations in a single call. This is useful in situations in which we want to execute multiple actions with a single request, such as the addition or the removal of multiple products from the cart in a single operation.
- **Queuing and logging**: The commands could be enqueued or registered for a future execution. This is particularly useful to implement logging systems or to execute actions asynchronously. Actions could be executed also in separate threads, without the invoker having to know the details of the implementation.

Disadvantages:

- **Increase in code complexity**: The use of Command could introduce a certain degree of complexity, mainly if there are a lot of actions and concrete commands. Each operation should be encapsulated in a separated command, and that could lead to an increment in the number of classes and objects created.
- **Memory overhead**: Since every action is represented by a separated object, this design pattern could introduce an overhead in terms of memory usage. This is particularly relevant in mobile applications, where resource management is very important.
- **Boilerplate code**: The implementation of the Command design pattern often requests the addition of boilerplate code, such as the creation of the classes for each concrete command, even for simple actions. This could make the code tougher to read and maintain.

- **Hard management in simple scenarios**: In simple applications, where we have few operations, the use of this pattern could be excessive, adding useless complexity. In cases like this, it could be more efficient to execute the operation directly, without encapsulating them in separated commands.
- **Difficulties in asynchronous environments**: In asynchronous and distributed contexts, it could be complex to keep the consistency between a command invocation and its execution. It is necessary to carefully handle errors of failure during the execution of the command, especially when there are dependencies between multiple commands.

Final Thoughts

The design pattern Command is a powerful tool to manage the operations in a flexible and scalable way, offering numerous advantages in the organization and management of complex actions. Thanks to its capacity to separate the invoker and the receiver (the executor), it allows us to keep the code modular and easy to extend, simplifying the addition of new functionalities or the modification of the existing one. This approach is mainly in the context of Android development, where the management of the user interactions, asynchronous operations, and business logics could be simplified using commands.

However, Command has some drawbacks. In simple applications, the adoption of this pattern could introduce unwanted complexity and overheads, leading to a presence of boilerplate code and an increase in memory usage. It is important to evaluate the context in which we want to use this design pattern, to ensure that the adoption of Command is justified by the application requirements.

In conclusion, Command is an ideal solution to handle complex and modular operations, such as undo/redo functions, Macro-Commands, and dynamic handling of user interactions. If used correctly, it improves the maintainability and flexibility of the code, promoting the separation of responsibilities, and reducing the coupling between application components.

Strategy Pattern

Strategy is a behavioral design pattern that allows us to define a family of algorithms, encapsulate them inside separated classes, and make them dynamically interchangeable. Using this design pattern, we can choose the algorithm to use during runtime, without having to modify the code that uses it, and thus promoting the open/closed principle.

***Figure 5.5**: The Android explaining football tactics*

In Android development, Strategy can be used in situations in which we want to implement different behavior based on dynamic conditions or change the way in which a behavior is executed, without influencing the other parts of the app.

Use Cases

- **Animation handling**: A classic example is the application of different animation to UI elements. Using this design pattern, it is possible to define a series of animation algorithms (such as entry, exit, fade, or zoom animations), and dynamically apply the correct algorithm based on the context (for example, when an activity starts or stops).
- **Sorting algorithms**: If an Android app needs to sort a collection of data in different ways (such as by price, by date, by name), it is possible to use Strategy to encapsulate different sort algorithms. Each sort strategy can be dynamically selected, depending on the user input or another factor, without modifying the client code that requests the sorting.
- **Payment systems**: In an e-commerce app, we can have different payment methods (credit card, PayPal, bank transfer). Each payment method can be implemented as a separate strategy, allowing the system to dynamically choose which to use. This approach keeps the code organized and modular, making it easy to integrate new payment systems in future.
- **Notification management**: In some apps, such as messaging apps or social media apps, there are many ways to notify the user (push notifications, email, SMS). Using this design pattern, every notification method could be an interchangeable strategy, allowing the app to select the best method based on

the user preferences and the context (for example, a push notification during daytime and an email during nighttime).

- **File compression**: If an app has to compress files or data, for example for a backup, several compression strategies such as ZIP, GZIP, or 7zCould be implemented as separated strategies. So, the app can choose the appropriate compression algorithm based on several factors, such as user preferences or required performance.

Structure

The design pattern Strategy is composed of three main elements–the Context, the Strategy (interface or abstract class), and the variants of **ConcreteStrategy**. The relationship between these elements provides Context the ability to use different strategies interchangeably, selecting them at runtime without modifying its code.

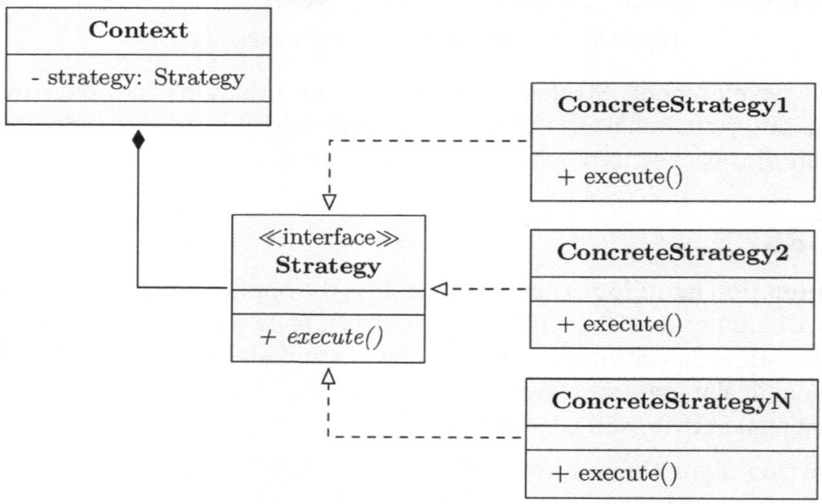

***Figure 5.6**: UML diagram of the Strategy pattern*

- **Interface Strategy**: This component defines the common interface for all the concrete strategies. Each concrete strategy implements this interface with a specific algorithm. This allows Context to use any strategy uniformly.
- **Classes ConcreteStrategy**: These classes implement the interface Strategy and provide specific implementations of the algorithms. Each concrete strategy can be selected dynamically by the Context based on the needs.
- **Class Context**: This class is the one that uses the strategy to execute an operation. It contains a reference to the object Strategy and delegates the execution of the algorithm to the selected strategy. The Context is independent of the concrete implementation of the algorithm, making it easy to modify.

Diagram flow

The Context receives a reference to an object of type Strategy and memorizes it. When an operation is requested to be executed, the Context invokes the method **`execute()`** on the current Strategy. The ConcreteStrategy that has been selected implements the requested algorithm, and the Context executes it calling the method of the Strategy.

Practical example

Let us suppose that we want to have an Android application to calculate the shipping cost of an order. There are several shipping strategies, such as "Standard Shipping", "Premium Shipping", and "International Shipping". Each strategy could be encapsulated in a ConcreteStrategy and selected dynamically based on the shipping type chosen by the user.

Using the pattern Strategy, the Context, which manages the order, can delegate the calculation of the shipping cost to the appropriate Strategy, improving the flexibility of the system and reducing the coupling between the business logic and the calculation algorithm.

Implementing Strategy in Android

The Strategy pattern can be implemented in Android in different contexts, such as managing the user interface, choosing dynamic algorithms, or managing different behaviors based on user input. In this section, we will see how to apply the Strategy pattern in Android, using Kotlin and Jetpack Compose to define a set of interchangeable strategies.

Suppose we want to implement a shipping cost calculation system that varies based on the type of shipping chosen by the user. We have three options—standard shipping, premium shipping, and international shipping. We will use the Strategy pattern to encapsulate each of these options in separate classes and dynamically select them according to the user's choice.

```
// Interface that all the concrete strategies must implement
@UmlInterface("Strategy")
abstract class ShippingStrategy {

    abstract val cost: Double

    // Every class that implements ShippingStrategy must
initialize "cost"
    fun calculateCost(weight: Double): Double {
        return weight * cost
    }
}
```

```
@UmlClass("ConcreteStrategy")
class StandardShipping : ShippingStrategy() {

    override val cost = 5.0

}

@UmlClass("ConcreteStrategy")
class PremiumShipping : ShippingStrategy() {

    override val cost = 10.0

}

@UmlClass("ConcreteStrategy")
class InternationalShipping : ShippingStrategy() {

    override val cost = 20.0

}

@UmlClass("Context")
class Order(private var strategy: ShippingStrategy) {

    fun calculateShippingCost(weight: Double): Double {
        return strategy.calculateCost(weight)
    }

}

@Composable
fun ShippingCalculator() {
    var weight by remember { mutableDoubleStateOf(1.0) }
    var shippingStrategy: ShippingStrategy by remember {
        mutableStateOf(StandardShipping())
    }
    val order = Order(shippingStrategy)

    Column(
        modifier = Modifier.padding(16.dp),
        horizontalAlignment = Alignment.CenterHorizontally,
        verticalArrangement = Arrangement.Center
    ) {
        TextField(
            value = weight.toString(),
            onValueChange = { weight = it.toDoubleOrNull() ?: 1.0
},
```

```
            label = { Text("Package weight (kg)") }
        )
        Spacer(modifier = Modifier.height(16.dp))
        Button(onClick = { shippingStrategy = StandardShipping()
}) {
            Text("Standard Shipping")
        }
        Button(onClick = { shippingStrategy = PremiumShipping()
}) {
            Text("Premium Shipping")
        }
        Button(onClick = { shippingStrategy = International
Shipping() }) {
            Text("International Shipping")
        }
        Spacer(modifier = Modifier.height(16.dp))

        val shippingCost = order.calculateShippingCost(weight)
        val eurFormat = NumberFormat.getCurrencyInstance().apply
{
            maximumFractionDigits = 2
            currency = Currency.getInstance("EUR")
        }
        Text("Shipping cost: ${eurFormat.format(shippingCost)}")
    }
}
```

- **Abstract class `ShippingStrategy`**: Even though this should be an interface, it has been transformed into an abstract class because the implementation of the method **`calculateCost()`** would not have changed in the concrete implementations. But generally, this interface provides a method that every class that implements **`ShippingStrategy`** should define with its specific algorithm to calculate the shipping cost.
- **Classes `StandardShipping`, `PremiumShipping`, `InternationalShipping`**: These classes represent the concrete implementations of the strategies. Although each class should provide its own algorithm to calculate the shipping costs based on the package weight, as explained previously. In this example, the algorithm is the same for all the strategies, so these classes only implement their own unit cost.
- **Class `Order`**: This class implements that which we find as the Context in the UML diagram. Basically, it is responsible to hold the Strategy selected by the user. The Strategy can be dynamically changed.
- **Composable `ShippingCalculator`**: The UI allows the user to insert the package weight and select the shipping strategy. Based on the user choice, the shipping strategy is set and the shipping cost is calculated and displayed in real time.

The power of recomposition of Jetpack Compose lets us get rid of functions for updating the strategy, such as **`setShippingStrategy()`**.

The design pattern Strategy is an optimal way to implement interchangeable behaviors in Android, improving the maintainability and flexibility of the code. With Jetpack Compose, it is possible to build a dynamic user interface, allowing the user to select from different strategies without having to modify the behavior of the Context or duplicate the code. This approach simplifies the management of the algorithms, which can vary based on different conditions or user preferences.

Advantages and Disadvantages

The Strategy pattern enables dynamic selection of algorithms by encapsulating them as independent objects. This promotes flexibility and maintainability, but also introduces certain trade-offs. Let us examine its benefits and drawbacks.

Advantages:

- **Algorithm flexibility and interchangeability**: Strategy provides a way to separate the algorithm logic from the execution logic, allowing us to dynamically change the algorithm to use without modifying the code in the Context. This makes the code easy to extend, since new strategies can be added without modifying the existing code.
- **Compliance with the open/closed principle**: This pattern provides a way to add new strategies as new classes, without having to alter the behavior of the existing one. In that way we have a set of classes that are open to extension but closed to modification, which is what is stated by the open/closed principle.
- **Maintenance made easy**: The maintainability of the code is improved because Strategy encapsulates the algorithms in separated classes. Each algorithm is isolated in a specific class, and this makes it easy to debug, update, or replace single strategies without altering other parts of the app.
- **Reduction of conditional complexity**: This design pattern eliminates the use of big conditional structures (**`if-else`** or **`switch`**) that dynamically select the algorithm to execute. This makes the code simpler, more readable, and modular.

Disadvantages:

- **Increase of the number of classes**: One of the main disadvantages of Strategy is the high number of classes that it introduces. Each algorithm or behavior must be implemented as a separate strategy, which can lead to a proliferation of classes in complex projects.
- **Configuration complexity**: The management and selection of the strategies could add complexity, especially if it is not implemented correctly. The client

code has to dynamically handle which strategy to select, and it could be hard to understand what strategy is currently used.

- **Instances overhead**: If the strategies are instantiated frequently with complex algorithms, they could increase the overhead in terms of memory and performances, which is a crucial point in Android applications.
- **Poor code reusability**: If the strategies are too specific, it could be hard to reuse them in other contexts and projects. To improve reusability, it is important to design the strategies in a way that they can be generalized or used in different scenarios.

Final Thoughts

The design pattern Strategy is an elegant and flexible solution to manage interchangeable behaviors, mainly in situations in which the algorithms and the business logic can drastically vary based on runtime conditions. The encapsulation of the algorithm inside separate classes allows us to respect the open/closed principle, promoting code extensibility and maintainability without introducing conditional complexity.

However, it is important to consider the possible disadvantages linked to the increasing number of classes and to the handling of strategies. In simple projects, the adoption of this design pattern could be excessive, while in complex applications it could provide the modularity we need to keep the code scalable and reusable.

In conclusion, the pattern Strategy is a fundamental tool to design flexible, modular, and easy-to-extend apps. In any case, however, it is crucial to evaluate the context of use in order to maximize the benefits without introducing unwanted complexity.

Conclusion

In this chapter, dedicated to behavioral design patterns, we have explored three fundamental tools to design Android apps that are modular and easy to extend. Every design pattern that we have discussed solves specific problems about the management of the communication and the modification of the objects in a dynamic way.

We started with the pattern Observer, highlighting its usefulness in creating reactive applications, where state changes are automatically reflected in the corresponding objects. The pattern has proved its application in context such as user interface management, using native tools like `LiveData` and `StateFlow`, to simplify the synchronization between the business logic and the UI.

Then, we explored the pattern Command, that allows us to encapsulate requests or actions in separated objects. This approach is useful to implement undo/redo actions, asynchronous operation and even decompose complex user interactions. In Android,

Command allows us to maintain the code flexibly and cleanly, separating the invocation of an action from its execution.

The pattern Strategy brings additional benefits, offering an elegant solution to handle interchangeable behaviors. We have seen how it can be applied in scenarios such as the management of different algorithms (sorting, payment methods, shippings). The ability to dynamically change the strategy without influencing the rest of the system makes it ideal to improve the extensibility and maintainability of the code.

In the chapter, we have highlighted how the use of these patterns reduces the complexity of the codes and promotes the adoption of best practices, such as the compliance of SOLID principles, the open/closed principle in particular. These patterns favor the separation of concerns, making the code less dependent and thus more maintainable and adaptable to future requirements.

Overall, the behavioral design patterns offer solid structures to develop scalable, modular, and reactive Android applications. Using them consciously allows us to create elegant solutions, reducing complexity, and ensuring that the apps remain flexible and ready for future evolutions.

In the next chapter, we will shift our focus to architectural patterns, which provide high-level guidelines for structuring applications.

Points to Remember

- **Observer** allows us to link a subject to multiple observers, dynamically notifying all the observers when a state change occurs on the subject.
- **Command** separates the action from the object that requests it, allowing to perform operations like undo/redo and to memorize performed actions.
- **Strategy** allows to define different algorithms that are interchangeable, allowing the user to choose which one to use at runtime without modifying the context that uses them.
- The behavioral patterns reduce the coupling between classes, allowing them to interact in a more flexible way and maintaining mutual independence.
- Implementing these patterns removes the necessity to use big conditional blocks (**`if-else`** or **`switch-case`**), simplifying the code and making it more modular.
- Behavioral design patterns promote modularity, allowing to add new functionalities without altering the existing code, thus improving the app's scalability.
- These patterns adhere to the *open/close* principle, enabling the extension of the code through the addition of new behaviors, without having to modify the existing classes.

- They enable an optimal asynchronous operations handling, such as background data loading, while keeping the user interface fluid and reactive.
- They are useful to handle dynamic operations related to the user interface, such as event responses or interactions that request an adaptable behavior.
- They improve the resource management in mobile applications, optimizing the action handling and reducing the memory consumption.

Multiple Choice Questions

1. Which design pattern allows us to dynamically change the algorithm used by an object?
   a. Observer
   b. Command
   c. Strategy
   d. All of them
2. Which behavioral design pattern is optimal to implement undo/redo operations?
   a. Strategy
   b. Command
   c. Observer
   d. All of them
3. What is the main purpose of the Observer pattern?
   a. Encapsulate algorithms
   b. Handle asynchronous operations
   c. Automatically notify state changes
   d. Separate the invocation of an action from its execution
4. Which of the SOLID principles is adhered to by the Strategy pattern?
   a. Single responsibility principle
   b. Dependency inversion principle
   c. Open/closed principle
   d. Liskov substitution principle

5. In which context is the pattern Command more useful?
   a. Separate actions and commands
   b. Dynamically modify the user interface
   c. Create asynchronous operations
   d. Organize dynamic layouts

Answers

1. c
2. b
3. c
4. c
5. a

Questions

1. Explain how the pattern Strategy can be used to improve the flexibility of an Android application.
2. How does the pattern Command make it easy to implement undo/redo operations?
3. Describe the pattern Observer and show how it can be used to update the user interface in real time.
4. What are the advantages of using the pattern Command with respect to a simple implementation of the commands using `if-else` and `switch`?
5. How do the behavioral design patterns favor the adherence to SOLID principles?

References

1. **The Observer Pattern in Java | Baeldung** - https://www.baeldung.com/java-observer-pattern
2. **Observer Design Pattern - Observer Pattern in Java - HowToDoInJava** - https://howtodoinjava.com/design-patterns/behavioral/observer-design-pattern/
3. **Observer Design Pattern in Java - Tutorial** - https://vogella.com/tutorials/DesignPatternObserver/article.html
4. **Understanding the Command Design Pattern** - https://ajayiyengar.com/2017/04/11/understanding-the-command-design-pattern/
5. **Command Design Pattern - GeeksforGeeks** - https://www.geeksforgeeks.org/command-pattern/
6. **Command Pattern in Java: Empowering Flexible Command Execution** - https://java-design-patterns.com/patterns/command
7. **Strategy Design Pattern - GeeksforGeeks** - https://www.geeksforgeeks.org/strategy-pattern-set-1/
8. **Strategy Design Pattern** - https://howtodoinjava.com/design-patterns/behavioral/strategy-design-pattern/

Chapter 6
Architectural Patterns

Introduction

Architectural design patterns are fundamental building blocks for creating modular, maintainable, and scalable Android applications. These patterns define structures and data flows that separate the business logic and the presentation logic, thus simplifying the development and making the code better organized. In an ecosystem such as Android, where the interactions between the user interface and data are frequent and complex, a well-defined architecture is essential to maintain the consistency of the code and keep the application reactive.

Each of the design patterns such as **Model-View-Controller (MVC)**, **Model-View-Presenter (MVP)**, **Model-View-ViewModel (MVVM)**, **and Model-View-Intent (MVI)** offer a unique approach to managing the data flow and the interaction between the app components. While MVC has been one of the first approaches to structure the code in Android, more recent patterns such as MVVM and MVI leverage the modern functionalities of Kotlin and Jetpack Compose, ensuring more precise control of the state and better user interface reactivity.

These patterns provide a solid base for projects of every complexity and have become essential tools for Android developers, helping them to keep the code clear and performant. The choice of the architectural pattern depends on the specific needs of the project, the testability and modularity requirements, and the complexity of the user interface.

Through this overview of architectural design patterns, we will explore how each of them can respond to these development needs and contribute to improving the development of high-quality Android applications.

Structure

In this chapter, we will cover the following topics:

- Model-View-Controller (MVC) Pattern
- Model-View-Presenter (MVP) Pattern

- Model-View-ViewModel (MVVM) Pattern
- Model-View-Intent (MVI) Pattern

For each of these topics, we will explore use cases, structure, implementation in Android, advantages, and disadvantages.

Model-View-Controller (MVC) Pattern

Model-View-Controller (MVC) is one of the older and most-widely used design patterns in software development. Created to modularize the code, it divides the responsibilities into three main components: the **Model**, which manages the data and the business logic; the **View**, which deals with the user interface, and the **Controller**, which acts as an intermediary between the Model and the View. This pattern keeps a clear distinction between the presentation logic and the business logic, making it easy to maintain and update the code.

In Android, MVC was initially adopted as a reference architecture, but over time it has proved to have limited use when dealing with complex applications, mainly in terms of keeping the Controller lean and avoiding the View from depending too much on the Model. Despite these limits, MVC remains useful for simple applications or scenarios in which the user interface and the business logic are relatively simple.

Use Cases

- **Small-scale applications or prototypes:** This design pattern is optimal for simple applications or prototypes, where it is necessary to quickly develop functionalities without having to manage a complex state. The separation of responsibility between Model, View, and Controller speeds up the development and makes the code structure immediately clear.
- **CRUD applications**: MVC is effective in CRUD apps (Create, Read, Update, Delete), where the user interface directly interacts with the data through simple operations of creation, reading, update, and cancellation. The Controller handles the user requests and updates the View based on the Model, making the flow simple and direct.
- **Interfaces that require small presentation logic**: This design pattern is suitable for apps with interfaces that require minimal presentation logic or lightweight data models. For example, data visualization apps or simple dashboards could be structured with MVC without generating a Controller that is too complex.
- **Applications that require direct handling of user interactions**: In certain apps, a dedicated component is needed to process user inputs and coordinate updates. MVC could be a good choice, because it allows this component, the Controller, to manage user inputs, update the data (Model), and notify the user interface (View).

Model-View-Controller is a good choice for applications that do not require intensive state or interaction management. However, for more advanced and reactive applications, it may be better to use patterns such as Model-View-ViewModel (MVVM) or Model-View-Intent (MVI).

Structure of MVC

We have already introduced the three-component separation of MVC–Model, View, and Controller. This separation helps to maintain the organization of the code, with each component responsible for managing a specific aspect of the application. Here is an overview of the structure and the role of each component.

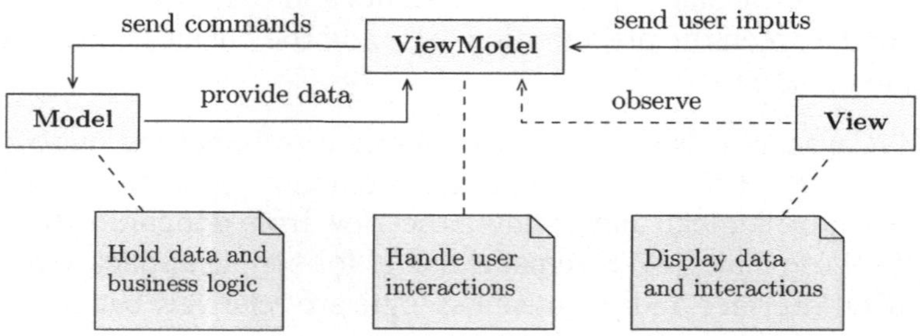

Figure 6.1: *UML diagram of Model-View-Controller* (MVC)

- **Model**: It contains the business logic and manages the application data. It is responsible for access to external resources such as databases or APIs and represents the source of truth for the application state.

  The Model does not interact directly with the View, but it communicates only with the Controller, which requests or updates the data. When the state of the model changes, the Controller is responsible for notifying the View, which updates itself.

- **View**: It corresponds to the user interface and it is responsible for two actions– displaying the data to the user and collecting his interactions. It does not contain business logic but is exclusively concerned with presentation logic and user interaction.

  The View is updated by the controller and receives from it the information needed to display the data from the Model. Any input or event that is generated by the user is sent from the View to the Controller.

- **Controller**: It is the mediator between the Model and the View, and it is responsible for handling the presentation logic. It intercepts user commands through the View, computes the required logic, and updates the Model or the View accordingly.

The structure of MVC clearly separates the responsibility of the data management (Model), the presentation logic (Controller), and the user interface (View). This separation simplifies the code management for small and medium applications, thus improving modularity and making it easy to modify the code, in particular, the business logic and the presentation logic, without interfering with other parts of the app. However, this structure could be less efficient for complex applications, where the Controller could become hard to manage, presenting too much code linked to the presentation logic and user interactions.

Implementing MVC in Android

Even if MVC is not commonly used in modern Android applications, it is worth seeing an implementation of it. It can be combined with Jetpack Compose to manage the view reactively. In this implementation, the Model represents the data and the business logic, the View is built with Jetpack Compose to show the UI, and the Controller acts as an intermediary to handle user interactions and update the state.

Here is an example of using MVC in an application that shows a list of users, giving the user the ability to update them by tapping a button.

1. **Implementation of the Model**

The Model represents the data and the business logic of the application. It includes data classes and the repository for the management of external resources.

```
data class User(val id: Int, val name: String)

class UserRepository {
    fun fetchUsers(): List<User> {
        // Simulation of a network call
        return listOf(User(1, "Mike"), User(2, "John"))
    }
}
```

The **`UserRepository`** manages access to data, fetching a list of users, for example, from an API or a dummy data source.

2. **Implementation of the View**

The View in MVC is the user interface of the application, and this is responsible for data visualization and user interaction handling. In traditional Android development, the View was represented by an Activity or a Fragment.

```
class UserListActivity : AppCompatActivity() {

    private lateinit var controller: UserController

    override fun onCreate(savedInstanceState: Bundle?) {
```

```
        super.onCreate(savedInstanceState)
        setContentView(R.layout.activity_user_list)

        controller = UserController(this)
        controller.loadUsers()
    }

    fun displayUsers(users: List<User>) {
       // Logic to display the list of the users, for example
using a RecyclerView
    }
}
```

The **UserListActivity** contains the logic to set the UI and display the list of users. In this case, it delegates to the Controller the logic for fetching the data, and it only displays them with the method **displayUsers()**.

3. **Implementation of the Controller**

The Controller is responsible for the presentation logic. It manages the interaction between the View and the Model, coordinating the logic of the application.

```
class UserController(private val view: UserListActivity) {

    private val repository = UserRepository()

    fun loadUsers() {
        val users = repository.fetchUsers()
        view.displayUsers(users)
    }
}
```

The **UserController** receives a **UserListActivity** as a parameter to update the View when needed. The method **loadUsers** calls the repository to obtain the data and then calls **displayUsers** to update the user interface.

In this implementation of MVC, the separation between View, Controller, and Model is clear and makes it easy to manage the presentation logic and the data. However, in more complex applications, MVC could be a limitation, since the risk is that the Controller becomes too heavy, forcing us to switch to newer and more efficient architectural design patterns.

Advantages and Disadvantages

This design pattern offers several advantages for organizing the code and improving the modularity of the application. However, there are also some disadvantages, especially in more complex applications. Here is an overview of the main pros and cons of MVC.

Advantages:

- **Separation of responsibilities**: MVC clearly separates the business logic (Model), the presentation logic (Controller), and the UI (View). This makes it easy to manage and maintain the code since each component has a well-defined role.
- **Testing made easy**: The separation between business logic and user interface allows us to test the Model and the Controller apart from the View. This improves the quality of the code and makes it easier to detect and fix potential bugs.
- **Modularity and reusability**: MVC promotes code reusability because the Model can be used in different Views or applications. Additionally, modifying the View or the user interface is simpler, since these modifications do not require taking action on the Model or the Controller.
- **Parallel development**: Since the business logic and the user interface are separated, different developers could work at the same time on the Model, the View, and the Controller without interfering with each other, accelerating the development process.

Disadvantages:

- **Controller complexity**: In complex applications, the controller could become too heavy, since it manages both the presentation logic and the interaction with the Model. This phenomenon, known as "God Controller", makes it hard to test and maintain.
- **Strong coupling View-Controller**: The View depends on the Controller for updating the user interface based on the modification of the Model. This coupling could reduce the flexibility and make it harder to change the modes of interaction between View and Model without having to make changes also in the Controller.
- **Scalability problems**: MVC could be less effective in applications that have complex states or reactive interfaces, such as the ones that require continuous UI updates. In these cases, the pattern tends to generate code that is less maintainable with respect to modern architectures such as MVVM or MVI.
- **Dependency on the View**: Since the view is responsible for the user input handling and communication with the Controller, every change in the user interface requires a change in the View itself. This could cause an increment of the specific code of the view, mainly in applications that have complex UIs.

Final Thoughts

The pattern Model-View-Controller (MVC) continues to represent a valid option for organizing the code in a clear and modular way, especially in small or medium-sized applications. Its structure divides the responsibilities between the Model, which handles the business logic and the data, the View, which deals with the user interface, and the Controller, which acts as a mediator, ensuring that every component deals with a specific part of the application.

MVC offers advantages in terms of modularity, testability, and reusability, in addition to allowing parallelization of the development of the business logic and the user interface. However, in more complex applications, this design pattern could be less efficient–the Controller tends to overload itself with responsibilities, and the management of dynamic states becomes more complicated.

Wrapping up, MVC is particularly indicated for simple projects, where the state management is limited and the simplicity of the architecture is an advantage. In more advanced contexts, MVC could be overtaken by architectures such as MVVM or MVI, which offer more sophisticated management of the state and greater flexibility for complex and reactive applications.

Model-View-Presenter (MVP) Pattern

Model-View-Presenter (MVP) is an architectural design pattern born as an evolution of MVC to further separate presentation logic from the View and improve the code testability. In MVP, the **Model** handles the data and business logic, the **Presenter** coordinates the interaction between the Model, and the **View** and contains the presentation logic, while the View is responsible only for presenting the data and sending user inputs to the Presenter. This pattern is designed to reduce the complexity of the View while maintaining the presentation logic of the Presenter, and this makes it easier to write unit tests for the business logic.

MVP has been widely used in Android development, mainly in applications that require good modularity and testability. Even though it is less prevalent today due to the introduction of more advanced patterns such as MVVM, MVP remains a good choice in context in which a clear separation between the logic and the UI is required, and when the Presenter needs to control the View.

Use Cases

- **Applications with complex presentation logic**: MVP is ideal for apps that require structured presentation logic since the Presenter deals with directly handling the data and transforming them to be ready to be displayed by the View. For example, it is suitable for apps that display charts or finance apps where the data presentation requires specific calculations or manipulations.
- **Highly testable applications**: Since this design pattern isolates the business logic from the presentation of the View, it is possible to test the Presenter independently, without having to rely on the user interface. This makes MVP

an excellent choice for applications that require complete test coverage, such as banking or healthcare apps.

- **Advanced handling of user interaction**: MVP is useful for apps that require advanced user interactions, such as social media or instant messaging apps. The Presenter could directly manage data flows that are coming from user interactions, keeping the view lightweight and without complex logic.
- **Applications with multiple views of the same content**: In apps where the same business logic is used in more than one screen, the Presenter could be reused in different Views without modifications. This is useful for e-commerce apps or catalogs, where the same product management logic is shown in different sections of the app.

MVP is particularly useful for apps that require precise control of the presentation logic, a high degree of testability, and modularity on the UI. Even if it is less widespread than partners such as MVVM, MVP offers a solid architecture for complex and modular projects.

Structure of MVP

The design pattern Model-View-Presenter (MVP) divides the responsibilities into three main components–Model, View, and Presenter. In this architecture, the presenter takes the role of the intermediary between the Model and the View, managing the business logic in the presentation logic. The view is only responsible for displaying the data and sending user inputs to the Presenter, thus maintaining a clear separation between the user interface and logic.

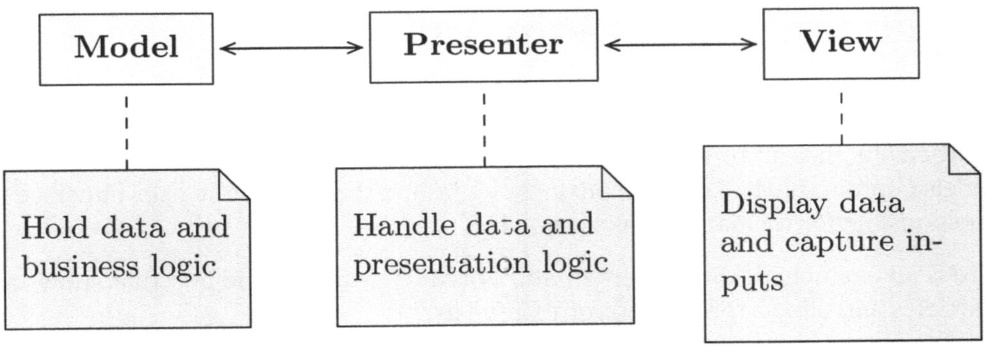

Figure 6.2: *UML diagram of Model-View-Presenter (MVP)*

- **Model**: It manages the application data and the business logic. It is responsible for access to a database, API or other data source. The model doesn't interact directly with the View and does not know anything about it, and it communicates only with the Presenter.

The model provides the requested data to the Presenter and notifies it about updates that require changes to the user interface.

- **View**: It deals with the presentation of the data to the user. It is responsible only for UI and the interactions with the user. The View has no business logic and receives data already processed by the Presenter.

  The View sends user inputs to the Presenter, such as taps on UI elements or text inputs, and receives comments from the Presenter about what to display. This relationship makes the View lighter and easier to manage.

- **Presenter**: It is the core of MVP since it contains the presentation logic and acts as an intermediary between the Model and the View.

  The Presenter obtains the data from the Model, processes them, and sends them to the View for visualization. On the other hand, the Presenter receives the user inputs from the View, manages the response logic, and updates the Model or the View based on the needs.

The structure of MVP maintains a strict separation between presentation and business logic. The Presenter takes the central role, handling the logic, and maintaining control of the interaction flow from the Model and the View, and vice versa. This approach lets us write unit tests for the presentation logic, without depending on the View and improves the modularity and maintainability.

However, since the Presenter manages the whole presentation logic, it could become more complex in large applications, requiring care during the management of responsibilities and the data flow.

Implementing MVP in Android

In order to implement MVP in Android, we follow the partition of the responsibilities into Model, View, and Presenter, keeping the business logic, separate from the user interface. In this architecture, the presenter manages the presentation logic, the Models contain the data and the business logic, and the View is the user interface that is responsible for the data visualization.

Here is an example of the implementation of MVP in an Android app that shows a list of articles and allows the user to refresh the list.

1. **Implementation of the Model**

The Model contains the application data and the logic to access and update these data. In this case, we use a repository that simulates the access to a list of articles.

```
data class Article(val id: Int, val title: String)

class ArticleRepository {
```

```
    private val articles = mutableListOf<Article>(
        Article(1, "Article 1"),
        Article(2, "Article 2")
    )

    fun getArticles(): List<Article> {
        return articles
    }

    fun addArticle(article: Article) {
        articles.add(article)
    }
}
```

2. **Definition of the View**

The View is represented by an interface that defines the methods that the Presenter uses to update the UI. This approach makes the View testable and independent of the Activity or Fragment.

```
interface ArticleView {
    fun showArticles(articles: List<Article>)
    fun showError(message: String)
}
```

3. **Implementation of the Presenter**

The Presenter is responsible for the presentation logic. It receives the data from the Model and sends it to the View while avoiding direct interaction between the Model and the View. The Presenter is completely separated from the UI, and this fact makes it easily testable.

```
class ArticlePresenter(private val view: ArticleView, private val
repository: ArticleRepository) {

    fun loadArticles() {
        val articles = repository.getArticles()
        if (articles.isNotEmpty()) {
            view.showArticles(articles)
        } else {
            view.showError("No article found")
        }
    }

    fun addArticle(title: String) {
        val newArticle = Article(repository.getArticles().size +
1, title)
        repository.addArticle(newArticle)
        loadArticles()
```

```
        }
    }
```

In this Presenter, **`loadArticles()`** fetches the data from the repository and updates the View. The method **`addArticle()`** adds a new article and then refreshes the list to update the UI.

4. **Implementation of the View**

The Activity implements the interface of the View and passes the user input to the Presenter. The Presenter, on his side, deals with updating the UI by calling the methods defined in the interface **`ArticleView`**.

```
class ArticleListActivity : AppCompatActivity(), ArticleView {

    private lateinit var presenter: ArticlePresenter
    private lateinit var repository: ArticleRepository

    override fun onCreate(savedInstanceState: Bundle?) {
        super.onCreate(savedInstanceState)
        setContentView(R.layout.activity_article_list)

        repository = ArticleRepository()
        presenter = ArticlePresenter(this, repository)

        // Loads the articles
        presenter.loadArticles()

        // Button to add a new article
        findViewById<Button>(R.id.addArticleButton).setOnClick-
Listener {
            presenter.addArticle("New Article ${repository.get
Articles().size + 1}")
        }
    }

    override fun showArticles(articles: List<Article>) {
        // Shows the list of the articles
        articles.forEach { article ->
            Log.d("ArticleListActivity", "ID: ${article.id},
Title: ${article.title}")
        }
    }

    override fun showError(message: String) {
        Toast.makeText(this, message, Toast.LENGTH_SHORT).show()
    }
}
```

In **ArticleListActivity**, we implement **ArticleView** and define the methods **showArticles** and **showError** to manage the user interface. The Activity passes the user interaction to the Presenter, which then updates the View.

Advantages and Disadvantages

MVP offers numerous advantages to modularize the code and improve the testability of the application, but it also comes with some disadvantages, mainly in complex applications. Here is an analysis of the main pros and cons of MVP.

Advantages:

- **Separation of the presentation logic**: MVP isolates the presentation logic on the Presenter, keeping the View simpler and focused only on the UI. This makes the maintainability easier and reduces the coupling between the View and the Model.
- **Improved testability**: The presentation logic resides on the Presenter, which does not depend on the View and thus is easy to test with unit tests. This allows us to test the functionalities of the app without having to interact directly with the UI.
- **Greater modularity**: The View and the Presenter are completely separate, allowing us to easily replace or update the user interface without modifying the presentation logic or the business logic. This approach makes MVP particularly suitable for medium or large projects, where it is important to keep each component well-defined.
- **Development parallelization**: Since the Presenter handles the logic and the View manages only the UI, it is possible to split the workload between different developers. A team could deal with the UI, while another team works on the logic and the Presenter, accelerating the development process.

Disadvantages:

- **Potential complexity of the Presenter**: In complex applications, the Presenter could become too complex if it assumes too many responsibilities. This is known as "God presenter", which reminds us of the "God Controller" we discussed in the previous section.
- **Needs for interfaces**: In order to separate the View and the Presenter, we usually need to declare interfaces to define the methods of communication. This could generate boilerplate code and increase the complexity of the code, especially in small-sized projects.
- **Much boilerplate code**: Following what has been explained in the previous point, we can conclude that the needs of interfaces force us to introduce boilerplate code that we could avoid if we switch to more advanced patterns such as MVVM or MVI.

- **UI state management difficulties**: In applications that require frequent and dynamic updates on the user interface, the Presenter is forced to constantly handle the state changes and synchronize them with the View. This could make the code more complex and difficult to maintain, especially if we have to deal with reactive UIs.

Final Thoughts

The design pattern Model-View-Presenter (MVP) stands out as a solid choice for applications that require a clear separation between presentation logic and user interface. MVP promotes modularity and testability while keeping the code well-organized and easy to maintain. The presentation logic, which is isolated in the Presenter, allows us to reduce the coupling between the View and the Model, making it easy to update and test the different components of the app.

However, MVP could become complex in very dynamic applications or large projects, where the Presenter risks assuming too many responsibilities. In this context, the code could become hard to manage, requiring careful attention to maintain the Presenter lean and well-structured. Also, the use of the interfaces and the quantity of boilerplate code makes MVP less suitable for small apps or scenarios in which the management of the application state is relatively simple.

In conclusion, MVP remains a versatile and reliable design pattern, which is particularly suitable for apps with complex presentation logic and a strong need for testability. If we adopt the right precautions, we can build a solid base for modular and easy-to-extend applications, promoting a good separation of responsibilities between the components.

Model-View-ViewModel (MVVM) Pattern

The design pattern Model-View-ViewModel (MVVM) represents one of the most used architectures in Modern Android development, especially thanks to its capacity to separate business logic from the presentation logic of the user interface. In MVVM, the three main components, the Model, the ViewModel, and the View, work together to ensure efficient data management and fluid communication with the UI.

The **Model** represents the business logic and handles the data. The **ViewModel** acts as an intermediate between the Model and the View, holding and transforming the data in a way that the View can observe and react to data changes without depending directly on the Model. Finally, the **View** observes the changes in the ViewModel to update itself automatically.

In Android development, the MVVM pattern is particularly suitable, thanks to the support of components such as LiveData and ViewModel, which are part of Android

Jetpack, that allow us to handle states and data in a reactive and persistent way. MVVM offers a modular structure that is optimal for complex and large projects.

Use Cases

MVVM is useful for a large variety of common scenarios in Android development, including:

- **Applications with complex states**: MVVM is ideal for applications with complex states that require frequent updates, such as instant messaging or social network apps. The ViewModel allows keeping the updating logic separate from the View, reducing the complexity and improving modularity.
- **Data persistence management**: Thanks to the support of Android Jetpack, this design pattern simplifies data saving during configuration changes, like screen rotations. The ViewModel preserves the state, ensuring that the data remains intact without having to reload it from the source.
- **Reactive apps with complex UI**: MVVM is useful in a context in which the UI must react to the data change in real-time, such as finance or sports apps that show data constantly being updated. Using LiveData, Flow, or StateFlow, and observers, the View updates automatically when the model emits new data.
- **Testing the business logic**: This pattern clearly isolates the logic of the View, making it easier to write unit tests for the ViewModel. This is particularly useful in apps that require complex business logic and that must be highly reliable.

The MVVM architecture is optimal for apps that require sophisticated management of states, a real-time data flow, and a reactive and updated user interface, while keeping the properties of stability and modularity.

Structure of MVVM

The design pattern Model-View-ViewModel, as we have seen, is made of three main components that collaborate to separate the business logic and user interface, while maintaining the application modular and reactive.

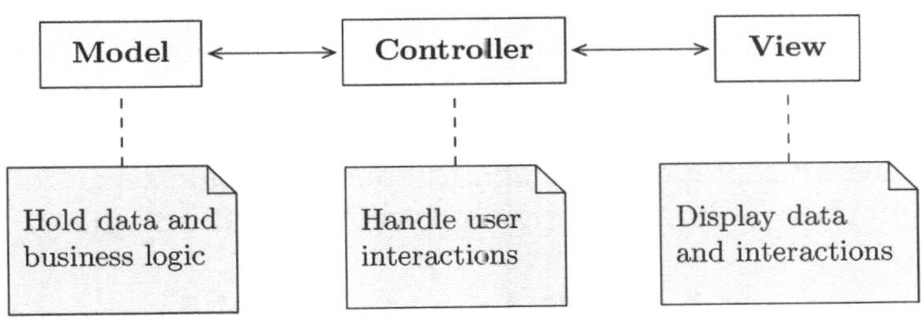

Figure 6.3: UML *diagram of Model-View-ViewModel* (MVVM)

- **Model**: This component represents the business logic and manages the application data. It could contain access to a database, a network API, or any other data source. The model is completely independent of the View and the ViewModel and does not know or interact with any of these components. The Models provide data through a repository or other data sources that the ViewModel could then observe and use to update the View.
- **ViewModel**: This component is the link between the Model and the View. It contains data objects used by the View and the logic to manage them, observing and transforming the data from the Model in a format that is suitable for the View. In Android, the ViewModel is supported by the component **`ViewModel`**, which is part of the Jetpack library, that is able to keep the state even during configuration changes.

  The ViewModel uses components such as LiveData or Flow to emit updates that the View observes to update the user interface.
- **View**: This component represents the user interface that has the purpose of observing the data and the states managed by the ViewModel, but it does not contain any business logic. The view is represented by UI components such as Activity or Fragments, and it contains the composable items provided by the Jetpack Compose library, or custom composables that we can define using the **`@Composable`** annotation.

The relations between these three components are not very complicated, but it is important to understand the direction of communication between each couple of components.

- The Model is the component that is completely independent. It manages the data and the business logic of the application, without taking care of the ViewModel and the View, thus maintaining a loose coupling.
- The ViewModel interacts with the Model to obtain or update the data, and it is not aware of the View.
- The View observes the ViewModel, reacting to any change in the data or state that the ViewModel exposes. Additionally, the view can update the data or state of the ViewModel based on user interactions.

This structure maintains the code as highly modular—the View is responsible for data presentation, the ViewModel handles the data interaction logic, and the Model manages the data itself. This isolation simplifies the changes and improves the maintainability while keeping the presentation logic and the business logic separate, and ensuring that the user interface is always reactive and synchronized with the up-to-date data.

Implementing MVVM in Android

The implementation of MVVM in Android is made simple by the Jetpack libraries and Kotlin because they provide built-in components such as ViewModel and data types like StateFlow, which allow us to manage the state reactively and maintain the separation between business logic and user interface. In this section, we will see how to implement the three main components of MVVM– Model, ViewModel, and View– in an Android app.

Suppose we want to create a simpler application that displays a list of articles downloaded from an API.

1. **Implementation of the Model**

The Model is responsible for data handling. We can define:

1. a class **Article** that defines the properties of an article
2. a class **ArticleRepository** to access the data
3. a class **ArticleDataSource** that interacts with an API or a local database

```
data class Article(
    val title: String,
    val content: String
)

// DataSource to obtain data from a simulated API
object ArticleDataSource {
    // Simulate a network call to fetch articles from an API
    fun fetchArticles(): List<Article> = listOf(
        Article(
            title = "How to Train Your Coffee Mug",
            content = "Sit. Stay. Hold my brew."
        ),
        Article(
            title = "Secrets of the Lazy Cat",
            content = "Sleep. Eat. Repeat."
        ),
        Article(
            title = "Guide to Napping Anywhere",
            content = "Step 1: Find a cozy spot."
        )
    )
}

// Repository that uses DataSource to fetch data
class ArticleRepository(private val dataSource: ArticleData-
Source) {
    fun getArticles(): List<Article> = dataSource.fetchArticles()
}
```

2. **Implementation of the ViewModel**

The ViewModel is the connection between the Model and the View. It receives the data from the **ArticleRepository** and exposes them through StateFlow in a way that the View can observe them and react automatically to their changes.

```
class ArticleViewModel : ViewModel() {
    private val repository = ArticleRepository(ArticleDataSource)

    // StateFlow that exposes the list of articles
    private val _articles = MutableStateFlow<List<Article>>
(emptyList())
    val articles: StateFlow<List<Article>> get() = _articles

    init {
        fetchArticles()
    }

    private fun fetchArticles() {
        // Obtains the data from the Repository and sets it in
the StateFlow
        _articles.value = repository.getArticles()
    }
}
```

In this example, the ViewModel uses the Repository to obtain the data and expose it through a StateFlow object, making the list of articles observable by the View.

3. **Implementation of the View**

The View is responsible for data presentation and user interaction. In Android, The View might be an Activity or a Fragment, and using Jetpack Compose, we will have a hierarchy of composables that react to data changes through the mechanism of recomposition.

```
@Composable
fun Article(article: Article) {
    Column(
        modifier = Modifier.padding(4.dp)
    ) {
        Text(text = article.title)
        Text(text = article.content, color = Color.Gray)
    }
}

@Composable
fun ArticleListScreen(viewModel: ArticleViewModel = viewModel())
{
```

```
    val articles: List<Article> = viewModel.articles.collect
AsState(emptyList()).value

    Column(
        modifier = Modifier.padding(16.dp),
    ) {
        Text(
            modifier = Modifier.padding(4.dp),
            text = "Articles",
            style = MaterialTheme.typography.headlineMedium
        )
        articles.forEach {
            Article(it)
        }
    }
}
```

Here, we can clearly see the power of Jetpack libraries—the function **`viewModel()`** can instantiate the desired ViewModel, in our case **`ArticleViewModel`**, using type inference. Then, the function **`collectAsState()`** transforms **`StateFlow`** into an observable that triggers the recomposition when changed.

LiveData, Flow, or StateFlow

In the MVVM architecture, the ViewModel is responsible for managing and exposing data to the UI in a lifecycle-aware manner. To achieve this, it relies on observable data types that notify the UI of changes automatically. LiveData, Flow, and StateFlow are three alternatives to implement observable data in the ViewModel. However, each of them has its own characteristics. Let us see what they are in order to be able to choose the right one, based on our needs.

- **LiveData**: It was the main construct in Android for observable data management before the introduction of Flow and StateFlow. Even if it is still valid, it is limited to Android development and is not Kotlin-native. LiveData is less flexible for performing complex data transformations and it is more indicated to handle the lifecycle of Activities and Fragments.
- **Flow**: It is part of the Kotlin Coroutines and represents an asynchronous data stream. It has been introduced to replace approaches such as RxJava and offers easy and Kotlin-native asynchronous operations management. Flow is suggested for short-term data flows (such as network requests) and it is extremely flexible to perform transformation and combinations of data.
- **StateFlow**: It is based on Flow and it has been created to handle persistent states that change over time. It is similar to LiveData but more versatile. StateFlow is an ideal choice for data that must persist and update in real-time, such as the state of the user interface in MVVM. Unlike LiveData, StateFlow performs well

in complex threading environments and supports cold data management. Cold data is data that does not remain active if there are observers for them, and this makes StateFlow more efficient.

So... what is the right choice? It depends on many factors, but generally, we might prefer Flow and StateFlow because they are more updated and versatile than LiveData, since they are directly integrated into the Kotlin Coroutines, making them more flexible and testable.

In modern Android applications, StateFlow is generally preferred for the persistent UI state, while Flow is ideal for asynchronous and reactive data flows.

Advantages and Disadvantages

The pattern MVVM brings numerous pros to the development of Android applications, improving modularity and UI reactivity, even if it comes with some complexities. Let us see, in detail, the advantages and disadvantages of this design pattern:

Advantages:

- **Separates business logic and user interface:** With MVVM, the application logic is isolated into the ViewModel, reducing the code in the View, which will contain only the code that describes the presentation. This improves the modularity and allows us to modify or update the interface without interfering with the business logic and vice versa.
- **Makes testing business logic easier**: The separation of the ViewModel makes it easier to test business logic independently from UI. This allows us to ensure that the behavior of the app is correct before being integrated into the user interface.
- **Supports configuration changes**: The pattern MVVM is particularly useful on Android because it takes advantage of the ViewModel to preserve data through configuration changes, such as screen rotation. This reduces the necessity of reloading the data or manually handling the state of the View.
- **Reactive and automatically updated UI**: By using reactive components such as LiveData or Flow, MVVM allows the View to automatically update based on state changes in the ViewModel. The View becomes leaner and the UI reacts in real time to data or state changes.

Disadvantages:

- **Requires a good knowledge of reactive components**: MVVM could be hard to master for beginners because it requires the knowledge of concepts such as LiveData, ViewModel, and reactive programming. This learning curve may be an initial barrier, especially for those coming from more traditional architectures.
- **Introduction of boilerplate code**: MVVM could lead to creating boilerplate code, such as the definition of observers and the integration of data flows. In

simple applications, this approach can be overwhelming and make the code more complex than it really needs to be.

- **Complexity with multiple data sources**: When an app uses data that are coming from different sources and complex flows, the synchronization between ViewModel and View could be hard to manage. This could lead to complex state management or to the need to solve possible conflicts or overlappings between data sources.
- **Possible increase in memory usage**: MVVM requires careful handling of the memory since the ViewModel can hold data no longer used, risking using resources unnecessarily. It is important to implement sweep and release mechanisms to avoid this problem, especially on mobile devices.

This design pattern offers a powerful and flexible architecture for complex and reactive Android applications, improving modularity, testability, and state handling. However, its implementation requires careful planning and good knowledge of Android development tools, in order to avoid unnecessary complexity and unwanted resource usage.

Final Thoughts

The design pattern MVVM stands out as one of the most effective architectures for developing modular, testable, and reactive Android applications. We can clearly say that it is the industry standard now. The clear separation between the Model, the ViewModel, and the View ensures that the business logic is separated from the presentation logic, improving the maintainability and reducing the coupling between components.

Thanks to the integration with the Jetpack libraries and Kotlin native data types, such as StateFlow and ViewModel, MVVM makes it easy to manage the state, even in complex scenarios and it guarantees that the data remains available during configuration changes. Additionally, this design pattern promotes a reactive user interface—the View reacts automatically to state changes that occur in the ViewModel, providing a fluid and always up-to-date user experience.

Even though it has a higher learning curve and comes with some boilerplate code, the benefits offered by MVVM make it an extremely valid architecture for applications that require modularity and scalability. If used correctly, this design pattern allows us to create solid applications that are ready to keep the properties of maintainability and scalability over time.

Model-View-Intent (MVI) Pattern

MVI is an emerging architectural design pattern that is reactive and unidirectional, designed to handle the data flow in a clear and structured way, reducing the coupling between business logic and presentation. In MVI, the View observes a unique application state, identified as the Model, and the Intents, which represent the user actions, update this state. Each Intent generates a new state, making the app behavior predictable and easy to test.

MVI differs from other patterns, such as MVVM, for its unique approach to the unidirectional data flow. Every change is propagated in only one direction, improving the predictability and thus making the debugging easier. MVI is particularly useful in applications with a complex state logic, where the management of the global state is crucial, such as systems that need undo and redo actions.

In the context of Android development, MVI integrates well with tools like Kotlin Coroutines, and Flow, making a powerful and flexible design pattern for modern applications, where handling the state and the interactions is essential to create a reactive and fluid user interface.

Use Cases

MVI is particularly effective in contexts in which it is important to manage complex states and ensure that each change is traceable and reproducible. Here are some typical use cases in which this pattern proves to be very useful:

- **Apps with complex state management**: MVI is ideal for apps that have to keep a consistent and easy-to-monitor application state. For example, applications such as e-commerce or social media apps, in which the state can change frequently based on user interactions and server responses.
- **Undo/Redo functionalities**: Due to unique state management, this design pattern makes it easy to implement undo/redo actions. Each Intent produces a new state, so the app can "go back" or "go forward" between the previous state and the next state, which is useful in applications such as text editors or drawing apps.
- **Apps with complex user interactions**: Applications that require constant and reactive response to user interactions, such as messaging apps or games, benefit from the unidirectional flow of MVI. Each Intent generates a new state, ensuring that the interface is synchronized with the expected behavior.
- **Real-time data API management**: Apps that consume APIs in real-time, such as trading or finance apps, can use MVI to update the state of the interface without interfering with other data flows, ensuring that every API update is reflected correctly in the Model observed by the View.

In general, this design pattern is mainly suitable for applications that require a clear and predictable management of the state and that derive benefits from a unidirectional flow of data to maintain the consistency between business logic and user interface.

Structure of MVI

The pattern MVI presents a structure that is characterized by unidirectional communication–data flows in only one direction through Model, View, and Intent. This architecture ensures that every change in the state is traceable and that the View stays synchronized with the Model, making it easy to manage the application state and perform the debugging operations.

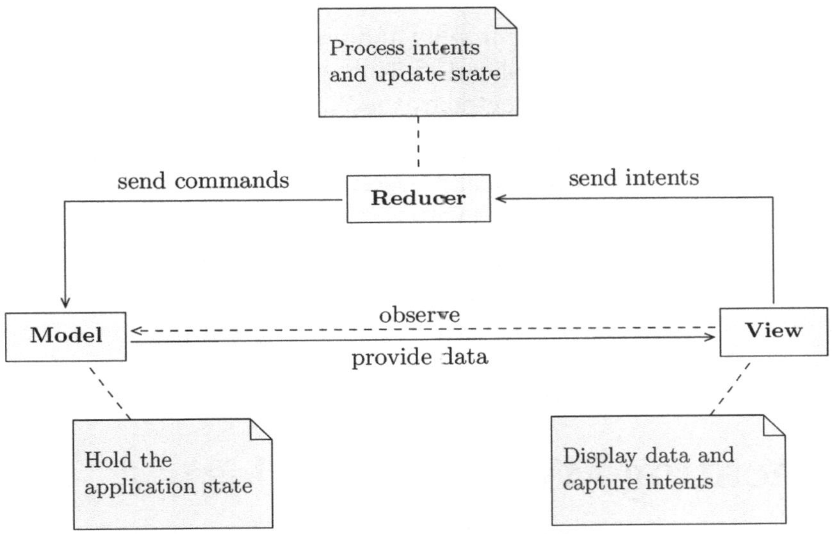

***Figure 6.4**: UML diagram of Model-View-Intent*

- **Model**: It represents the state of the application. The model is a data structure that contains all the information needed to represent the state of the View at a given time. For example, in a news app, the Model could include a list of articles, a loading flag, and an error message.

  The Model is updated by the Reducer in response to Intents from the user or system events.

- **View**: It is the user interface and is responsible for displaying data contained in the Model and reacting to user interactions. The View does not directly manipulate the Model, but it sends the Intents to the Reducer, which processes the Intents, and updates the state.

  So, the View is a purely visual representation of the Model–when the model changes, the View is automatically updated to reflect the new state.

- **Intent**: These represent the actions or intentions of the user. Intents can include operations such as "loading data", "show details", or "report an error". They are independent of the logic of the View and do not act directly on the Model.

Intents are processed by the Reducer, which then determines the update of the Model. This process is by a unidirectional flow, in which the View does not interact directly with the Model.

Now let us explore the relations between these components:

- The View sends the Intent through the Reducer as a response to the user actions (for example, a tap on a button). The Reducer interprets these Intents and determines the new state of the Model.
- The Reducer processes the Intents and updates the Model, which represents the whole status of the application. This ensures that the Model is always in a consistent state that is reflected by the View.
- The View observes the Model (usually through flows like StateFlow or LiveData) and updates itself automatically based on state changes, keeping the user interface always synchronized with the Model.

The structure of MVI ensures a unidirectional data flow and a high level of control over the state of the application. The Reducer acts as an intermediary between the Intent and the Model, while the View is a visual representation of the state. This approach favors predictability, modularity, and the possibility of performing unit tests since the business logic is centralized in the Model and is not directly dependent on the View.

Implementing MVI in Android

The implementation of the pattern MVI in Android requires the use of reacting components to ensure a unidirectional data flow. MVI is based on three main components–Model, View, and Intent. Each Intent represents an action that modifies the state of the Model, and the View updates itself by observing the state.

Resuming the example from the previous section of MVVM, let us create a simple application that displays a list of articles fetched from an API, but this time we will have the possibility to refresh the list through an Intent triggered by the user.

1. **Implementation of the Model**

The Model is a representation of the state of the application. This state can contain the list of articles and other information, such as a possible error message or a loading state.

```
data class Article(
    val title: String,
    val content: String
)

data class ArticleState(
    val articles: List<Article> = emptyList(),
```

```
        val isLoading: Boolean = false,
        val error: String? = null
    )
```

2. **Implementation of the Intents**

The Intents represent the user interactions, which are the actions that could be triggered by the user, such as updating the list or displaying an error message. Intents define the possible actions without depending directly on the View.

```
    sealed class ArticleIntent {
        object LoadArticles : ArticleIntent()
        data class ShowError(val message: String) : ArticleIntent()
    }
```

In this example, the Intent **`LoadArticles`** is triggered when the user requests the loading of the article list, while **`showError`** displays possible error messages.

3. **Implementation of the Reducer**

The Reducer is responsible for managing the flow of Intents and updating the Model. We use StateFlow to hold and update the state observable by the View.

```
    class ArticleReducer {

        private val _state = MutableStateFlow(ArticleState())
        val state: StateFlow<ArticleState> get() = _state

        fun processIntent(intent: ArticleIntent) {
            when (intent) {
                is ArticleIntent.LoadArticles -> loadArticles()
                is ArticleIntent.ShowError -> showError(intent.message)
            }
        }

        private fun loadArticles() {
            _state.value = _state.value.copy(isLoading = true)

            // Simulates a network call or a data source to obtain
    data
            val articles = listOf(
                Article(
                    title = "How to Train Your Coffee Mug",
                    content = "Sit. Stay. Hold my brew."
                ),
                Article(
                    title = "Secrets of the Lazy Cat",
                    content = "Sleep. Eat. Repeat."
                ),
```

```
                Article(
                    title = "Guide to Napping Anywhere",
                    content = "Step 1: Find a cozy spot."
                )
            )

            _state.value = _state.value.copy(articles = articles,
isLoading = false)
        }

        private fun showError(message: String) {
            _state.value = _state.value.copy(error = message,
isLoading = false)
        }
    }
```

In this Reducer, **processIntent()** handles the different Intents sent from the View, such as the loading of the articles or the display of an error. The model is updated and the state emitted from StateFlow is observed by the View.

4. **Implementation of the View**

The View observes the state provided by the Reducer and sends Intents as a response to user interactions. We will build a view using three composables: **ArticleListScreen**, **ErrorView**, and **ArticleList**.

```
@Composable
fun ArticleListScreen(reducer: ArticleReducer) {
    val state = reducer.state.collectAsState().value

    Column(
        modifier = Modifier.padding(16.dp),
        horizontalAlignment = Alignment.CenterHorizontally
    ) {
        // Build the UI based on the current state
        when {
            state.isLoading -> CircularProgressIndicator()
            state.error != null -> ErrorView(state.error) {
                reducer.processIntent(ArticleIntent.LoadArticles)
// Retry Intent
            }

            else -> ArticleList(articles = state.articles)
        }

        // Button to trigger the intent
        Button(
```

```
            onClick = { reducer.processIntent(ArticleIntent.
LoadArticles) }
        ) {
            Text(text = "Load Articles")
        }
    }
}

@Composable
fun ArticleView(article: Article) {
    Column(
        modifier = Modifier.padding(4.dp)
    ) {
        Text(text = article.title)
        Text(text = article.content, color = Color.Gray)
    }
}

@Composable
fun ArticleList(articles: List<Article>) {
    // Shows the list of the articles
    Column {
        Text(
            modifier = Modifier.padding(4.dp),
            text = "Articles",
            style = MaterialTheme.typography.headlineMedium
        )
        articles.forEach {
            ArticleView(it)
        }
    }
}

@Composable
fun ErrorView(error: String, onRetry: () -> Unit = {}) {
    // Shows the error and allows to perform a retry
    Column(horizontalAlignment = Alignment.CenterHorizontally) {
        Text(
            text = "Error: $error",
            color = MaterialTheme.colorScheme.error
        )
        Button(onClick = onRetry) {
            Text("Retry")
        }
    }
}
```

We use `collectAsState()` to transform the StateFlow exposed by the Reducer into an observable state that Compose can observe. Depending on the state the View will choose the right component to display between `CircularProgressIndicator`, `ErrorView`, and `ArticleList`. Finally, there is a button that allows the user to trigger the Intent `ArticleIntent.LoadArticles` to refresh the list of articles.

Jetpack Compose perfectly integrates with MVI since it automatically reacts to state changes, simplifying the unidirectional data flow, making the MVI Architecture more fluid and maintainable. With Compose, we do not need to manually handle the lifecycle of the components, and the UI stays synchronized with the Model in a natural way, improving the development experience and the readability of the code.

Advantages and Disadvantages

The design pattern MVI offers numerous advantages, in particular for applications that have complex states and dynamic interactions, but it also has some disadvantages that are worth considering.

Advantages:

- **Unidirectional data flow**: MVI handles a unidirectional data flow between Model, View, and Intent, making the behavior of the app more predictable and simplifying the debug. This flow allows us to easily trace the state changes and ensure that the View always correctly reflects the Model.
- **Clear state management**: With this design pattern, the state of the app is centralized in the Model and updated only through the Reducer, and this makes it easy to maintain consistency and identify the current app state at every moment. This is useful also for complex applications or applications that require the management of undo/redo operations.
- **Improved testability**: Thanks to the sharp separation between View and business logic, MVI allows us to test the Model and the Reducer independently from the View, increasing the reliability of the code and simplifying the test automation.
- **Improved loose coupling**: The View does not directly depend on the Model, but it only interacts with the Reducer through Intents, promoting a modular architecture and making every component independent of others.

Disadvantages:

- **Steep learning curve**: MVI requires a good knowledge of reactive programming and data flows, in particular Kotlin Coroutines and StateFlow. For beginners, it could be hard to adapt to this unidirectional flow.
- **Boilerplate code and complexity**: The implementation of Intent and the management of the Model could introduce a lot of boilerplate code, mainly

in simple applications, where this design pattern could be less suitable if compared to simpler patterns like MVVM.

- **High state complexity with a lot of Intents**: If we have numerous Intents and states, the Model could become hard to manage, requiring attention to avoid cycles or dependencies between intents.
- **Higher memory usage**: MVI tends to preserve the whole state of the application, and this could result in higher memory usage, especially in applications with a lot of persistent data. We can deal with this drawback only if we carefully manage the usage of memory and resources.

Model-View-Intent is a powerful design pattern, in particular for applications that require clear and reactive state management. However, its complexity and the boilerplate code could make it less suitable for simple projects or for developers with poor experience in reactive programming.

Final Thoughts

The design pattern Model-View-Intent (MVI) is emerging as a powerful architecture to manage Android applications that contain complex states and have frequent interactions. Thanks to the unidirectional data flow, MVI allows to maintain a clear separation between business logic and user interface, reducing the coupling and improving the modularity of the code. The centralized management of the state makes the behavior of the app predictable, making it easy to debug and maintain it.

MVI is particularly useful for applications that require a high level of control of the state and reactive responses to user input, such as finance apps, social media apps, e-commerce apps, and games. However, due to the steeper learning curve and greater complexity, MVI is recommended for highly structured projects, where the advantages of state handling overcome the costs in terms of additional code and resources.

In conclusion, MVI represents an excellent choice for those who are looking for a modern and reactive architecture, capable of ensuring flexibility and scalability, allowing at the same time to maintain a well-defined workflow through the different components of the application.

Conclusion

In this chapter, we discussed four of the most common architectural design patterns for Android development–**MVC**, **MVP**, **MVVI,** and **MVI**. They offer solid foundations to build Android applications, improving code management, testability, and maintainability. Each pattern responds to specific design and operational needs, allowing the developers to choose the architecture that best suits the complexity of the app, the test and modularity requirements, and the nature of the user interaction.

Model-View-Controller (MVC) is a simple and ready-to-use choice for small applications, with relatively linear data flow, and where testability is not a critical requirement. However, for more complex applications, MVC could be a limitation.

Model-View-Presenter (MVP) represents a good evolution for applications that require a clearer separation between business and presentation logic since it improves testability and gives us the possibility to maintain a lightweight View. However, in more dynamic apps, the Presenter could become a bottleneck if not managed correctly.

Model-View-ViewModel (MVVM) and **Model-View-Intent (MVI)** are the ideal patterns for modern and reactive applications, especially thanks to their integration with Kotlin Coroutines and the API of Jetpack, such as Flow and StateFlow, which give us also the possibility to build a reactive UI declaratively using Jetpack Compose. These patterns offer us efficient state management and promote the use of unidirectional data flow, improving the loose coupling and ensuring that the user interface is always synchronized with the Model.

To summarize, the architectural design patterns not only simplify the structure and the maintainability of the code but also improve the development experience and the quality of the final product. The choice of the best pattern to use requires an evaluation of the application needs and the resources of the development team, allowing us to make the most of the potential of the architecture to create stable and scalable Android applications.

In the next chapter, we will explore network patterns.

Points to Remember

- **Model-View-Controller (MVC)** was one of the first architectural design patterns used in Android, suitable for simple applications. The View sends the input to the Controller, which manages the business logic through the Model, and then updates the View.
- **Model-View-Presenter (MVP)** improves the separation of the presentation logic, centralizing it into the Presenter. It is suitable for applications that require high testability and modularity.
- **Model-View-ViewModel (MVVM)** is supported by tools such as LiveData and StateFlow, making it easy to manage the state and the synchronization of the UI with the Model in a reactive way.
- **Model-View-Intent (MVI)** ensures a unidirectional data flow, improving predictability and promoting loose coupling between components. It is ideal for applications with complex states.
- All these patterns offer a clear separation between business logic and interface, simplifying the management and the maintainability of the code.

- Patterns such as MVP and MVVM promote testability, since they isolate the presentation logic from the View, allowing us to test the code independently.
- Architectural design patterns make it easy to integrate and modify the components, making the code modular and reusable.
- Patterns such as MVVM and MVI are particularly suitable for large-scale applications since they allow an advanced management of the state and the interactions.
- Patterns having a unidirectional data flow, such as MVI, make debugging easy and reduce the risk of errors since its unidirectional data flow makes the behavior of the app more predictable
- The choice of the right architectural pattern to use depends on the complexity of the application, the testing requirements, and the need for a reactive interface, ensuring a solid base for the management of the code.

Multiple Choice Questions

1. Which design pattern is known for its unidirectional data flow that makes it easy to manage the application state?
   a. MVC
   b. MVP
   c. MVI
   d. MVVM
2. Which design pattern has a component that is mainly responsible for managing the presentation logic?
   a. MVVM
   b. MVC
   c. MVI
   d. MVP
3. Which design pattern takes advantage of LiveData and State-Flow to keep the View synchronized with the status of the Model?
   a. MVP
   b. MVVM
   c. MVC
   d. MVI

4. Which design pattern is suitable for simple applications?
    a. MVC
    b. MVP
    c. MVVM
    d. MVI
5. Which of the following is the most recent design pattern?
    a. MVC
    b. MVP
    c. MVVM
    d. MVI

Answers

1. c
2. d
3. b
4. a
5. c

Questions

1. What are the main advantages of using an architectural pattern such as MVVM rather than MVC in modern Android applications?
2. How does the design pattern MVI handle the unidirectional data flow and what are the benefits of this characteristic?
3. Explain how MVP could improve the testability of an Android application with respect to MVC.
4. Which consideration should we make when choosing between MVP and MVVM for an Android application that requires high reactivity and dynamic updates of the UI?
5. How does the architectural design pattern contribute to the modularity and the maintainability of the code in a complex application?

References

1. **Android Architecture Patterns - GeeksforGeeks** - https://www.geeksforgeeks.org/android-architecture-patterns/
2. **MVC - MDN Web Docs Glossary: Definitions of Web-related terms** - https://developer.mozilla.org/en-US/docs/Glossary/MVC
3. **MVP (Model View Presenter) Architecture Pattern in Android with Example - GeeksforGeeks** - https://www.geeksforgeeks.org/mvp-model-view-presenter-architecture-pattern-in-android-with-example/
4. **Introduction to Model View View Model (MVVM) - GeeksforGeeks** - https://www.geeksforgeeks.org/introduction-to-model-view-view-model-mvvm/
5. **Model-View-ViewModel (MVVM)** - https://learn.microsoft.com/it-it/dotnet/architecture/maui/mvvm
6. **Stateful Android Apps With MVI (MODEL – VIEW – INTENT) | by Burak iren | Huawei Developers | Medium** - https://medium.com/huawei-developers/stateful-android-apps-with-mvi-architecture-model-view-intent-d106b09bd967
7. **Model-View-Intent (MVI) Pattern in Reactive Programming: A Comprehensive Overview - GeeksforGeeks** - https://www.geeksforgeeks.org/model-view-intent-mvi-pattern-in-reactive-programming-a-comprehensive-overview/
8. **Android MVI (Model-View-Intent) Architecture – Example code | by Krishan Madushanka** - https://krishanmadushankadev.medium.com/android-mvi-model-view-intent-architecture-example-code-bc7dc8edb33
9. **MVVM vs. MVI - Understand the Difference Once and for All** - https://www.youtube.com/watch?v=b2z1jvD4VMQ

Chapter 7
Concurrency, Network, and, Security Patterns

Introduction

Modern Android development requires solutions that address the challenges of concurrency management, data access, and sensitive information protection. Concurrency, network, and security patterns provide the foundations for ensuring high performance, reliability, and security, thus contributing to the improvement of the user experience and the maintainability of the code.

- The **Concurrency Patterns**, such as Thread Pool and Producer-Consumer, are mandatory to handle intensive operations without compromising the smoothness of the user interface. Thanks to these patterns, it is possible to coordinate parallel tasks and optimize the use of the resources.
- The **Network Patterns**, represented by Repository and Caching, provide tools to access and manage the data in a structured and efficient way. These patterns not only improve the performance and the reactivity of the app but also ensure a smooth user experience, even in non-optimal network conditions.
- The **Security Patterns**, such as Encryption, Authentication, and Authorization are essential tools to protect user data and provide controlled and secured accesses. Their implementation ensures compliance with the security regulations and reinforces the user's trust in the application.

This chapter explores each of these patterns, showing how to implement them in Android using modern tools and technologies. Understanding and applying these patterns is crucial if we want to develop robust, scalable, and secure apps that are ready to face the challenges of contemporary mobile development.

Structure

In this chapter, we will cover the following topics:

- Concurrency Patterns
  - Thread Pool
  - Producer-Consumer
- Network Patterns
  - Repository
  - Caching
- Security Patterns
  - Encryption
  - Authentication and Authorization

Concurrency Patterns

In Android, concurrency is crucial to ensure a seamless user experience, since heavy tasks such as data downloading and image processing must not block the main thread or UI thread.

Two of the most common concurrency patterns are **Thread Pool** and **Producer-Consumer**–the former uses a fixed set of threads to execute tasks in parallel, while the latter coordinates two entities to produce and consume data. We are going to examine them in this section.

These patterns provide fundamental tools for optimizing concurrency in Android, ensuring efficient resource handling, a better reactivity of the app, and a clear separation of responsibilities between concurrent tasks. Using modern libraries such as Kotlin Coroutines, we are able to implement these patterns in an idiomatic and secure way.

Thread Pool

Thread Pool is a concurrency pattern designed for efficiently handling the execution of multiple threads in parallel. In Android, where resources such as CPU and memory are limited, this pattern is fundamental to optimize the execution of activities that require intensive computation, avoiding thread overload. Rather than creating new threads for each activity, Thread Pool keeps a fixed set of reusable threads, reducing the cost of creation and destruction of the threads.

This design pattern is particularly useful in contexts where a lot of tasks must be executed in parallel, such as image loading, network request handling, or background database operations. In Android, the use of Thread Pool allows us to improve the reactiveness of the app, getting rid of long activities that would block the main thread. Frameworks such as Kotlin Coroutines and classes such as **Executors** provide powerful tools to implement this pattern easily and effectively.

Implementing Thread Pool in Android

In Android, Thread Pool can be implemented using the class **Executors**, which is provided by the Java standard library. This class allows us to create a customizable pool of threads, optimizing the management of concurrent tasks. In a modern approach, we can combine Kotlin Coroutines and **Dispatchers** to obtain similar results.

Example using `Executor`:

Here is an example of the implementation of Thread Pool to execute background operations using **Executors**.

```
class ThreadPoolExample {
    // Create a pool with 4 threads
    private val threadPool = Executors.newFixedThreadPool(4)

    fun executeTask(task: Runnable) {
        threadPool.execute(task)
    }

    fun shutdown() {
        threadPool.shutdown()
    }
}

fun main() {
    val threadPoolExample = ThreadPoolExample()

    for (i in 1..10) {
        threadPoolExample.executeTask {
            println("Execution of task $i on thread ${Thread.
currentThread().name}")
        }
    }

    threadPoolExample.shutdown()
}
```

Example using Kotlin Coroutines:

With Kotlin Coroutines, the use of **Dispatchers.IO** or a customized thread pool further simplifies the implementation.

```
fun main() = runBlocking {
    val customDispatcher = Executors.newFixedThreadPool(4).
asCoroutineDispatcher()

    repeat(10) { index ->
        launch(customDispatcher) {
            println("Execution of task $index on thread thread
${Thread.currentThread().name}")
        }
    }

    (customDispatcher.executor as ExecutorService).shutdown()
}
```

Comparing the two implementations:

The first implementation, which uses **`Executors`**, is more flexible to directly manage the threads, but it requires manual action for shutting down the threads and error handling. The other implementation, which is based on Kotlin Coroutines, is more idiomatic for Android and compatible with modern libraries. Additionally, it supports cancellation and scope control through **`CoroutinesScope`**.

Advantages and Disadvantages

Advantages:

- **Efficiency in thread management**: Thread Pool re-uses the existing threads. This improves efficiency, especially in applications with several concurrent tasks.
- **Control on resource usage**: It limits the number of threads executing concurrently at a given time, preventing CPU overload and ensuring that the app remains reactive, especially on mobile devices.
- **Simplicity in task management**: It centralizes the execution of tasks, allowing us to easily assign them to the pool of threads without worrying about the creation and direct management of the threads.

Disadvantages:

- **Complexity in error and timeout handling**: If a task that is inside the pool fails or blocks, it could be hard to handle the error without influencing the other tasks. Explicit management of errors is needed.
- **Non-optimal pool configuration**: Setting the thread pool size too low or too high could lead to inefficiencies, such as performance slowdowns or resource waste.
- **Possible deadlocks**: If a thread waits for a busy resource that is locked by

another thread of the pool, we could end with a deadlock that blocks the execution of all the tasks. This requires attention in the design phase.

Producer-Consumer

The Producer-Consumer is a concurrent design pattern we can use to handle the communication between two entities–the **Producer**, which generates data or events, and the **Consumer**, which processes the data. The pattern uses a shared queue to temporarily store the data generated, allowing the Producer and the Consumer to operate independently. This approach ensures an orderly and controlled task flow, avoiding overloads and conflicts between the two processes.

In Android, the pattern Producer-Consumer is particularly useful in scenarios in which the continuous data flow must be handled in an asynchronous way, such as the reading of data from a network, background events processing, or frame-by-frame graphic rendering. Using structures such as **`BlockingQueue`** or **`Channel`**, it is possible to implement the pattern in an efficient and scalable way.

Implementing Producer-Consumer in Android

The pattern Producer-Consumer could be implemented in Android in a modern and clean way using **`Channels`** provided by Kotlin Coroutines. **`Channels`** allow us to use synchronous and secure handling of the data flow between a producer and a consumer, reducing the risk of issues such as deadlocks and UI blocks.

Here is a practical example:

```
fun main() = runBlocking {
    // Shared queue with a maximum capacity of  10 elements
    val channel = Channel<String>(10)

    // Producer Coroutine
    val producer = launch {
        for (i in 1..10) {
            val item = "Item $i"
            channel.send(item) // Add the element to the channel
            println("Producer: Product $item")
            delay(500) // Simulates a production activity
        }
        channel.close() // Close the channel when the job is
finished
    }

    // Consumer Coroutine
    val consumer = launch {
        // Remove and consume the elements from the channel
```

```
            for (item in channel) {
                println("Consumer: Consumato $item")
                delay(1000) // Simulates a consumption activity
            }
        }

        producer.join() // Wait for Producer termination
        consumer.join() // Wait for Consumer termination
    }
```

- **Channel**: We created a **`Channel<String>`** with the capacity of 10 elements that act as a shared queue between the Producer and the Consumer.
- **Producer Coroutine**: It generates the elements and adds them to the **`channel`** using **`channel.send(item)`**, then uses a delay to simulate a production time and finally closes the **`channel`** with **`channel.close()`** once the production is completed.
- **Consumer Coroutine**: It consumes the elements of the **`channel`** using a **`for`** loop, processing each element. Also here, delay simulates consumption time.

The Coroutines are executed asynchronously, allowing the Producer and the Consumer to operate independently, but using the **`Channel`** as a synchronization medium.

Why use Channels? Although there are alternative and traditional approaches such as **`BlockingQueue`**, that are part of Java, we recommend using **`Channels`** because they come with Kotlin Coroutines, offering a modern and scalable way to implement these design patterns.

Advantages and Disadvantages

Advantages:

- **Producer-Consumer decoupling**: The two entities work independently using a shared queue, improving the loose coupling between them. This makes the system more flexible and modular.
- **Optimized data flow handling**: The queue acts as a buffer, allowing the Producer and the Consumer to operate at different speeds without losing data or causing blocks.
- **Efficient resource handling**: The pattern allows for redistribution of the workload between multiple producers and consumers, optimizing resource usage and improving performances.

Disadvantages:

- **Synchronization overhead**: The need to manage a shared and synchronized queue introduces an overhead that might reduce the performance in applications with a high workload.

- **Potential saturation of the queue**: If the Consumer is not fast enough in processing the elements produced, the queue could saturate, leading to slowdowns or data loss, depending on the implementation.
- **Higher code complexity**: Implementing the pattern requires careful error and exception handling, in addition to careful management in complex scenarios, such as a safe and data-preserving reaction of the app in case of errors.

Network Patterns

Network patterns are very important to efficiently manage access to data from remote sources, such as REST API or remote databases, and to ensure a fluid and reactive user experience. Two of the most relevant patterns in this category are Repository and Caching, often used to optimize the data flow in an Android app.

- The **Repository** design pattern centralizes access to data, providing a unified interface for the business logic.
- The **Caching** design pattern temporarily memorizes data that are frequently requested, reducing the necessity to perform repeated access to the remote data sources.

The combination of Repository and Caching allows us to develop robust reactive Android apps, offering an optimal balance between speed of data access, reliability, and resource management. With the help of modern tools such as *Retrofit*, *Room*, *Kotlin Coroutines*, and advanced caching libraries, these patterns represent the base for efficient and scalable data management in applications of any complexity.

Repository

Even if it is not a pure network design pattern, the Repository is used alongside network logic to abstract access to the data, both local and remote, in a centralized way. This design pattern acts as an intermediary between the business logic and data source, such as network API, local databases, or file systems. This pattern allows us to centralize the logic of access data, reducing code duplication and simplifying the business logic.

In Android, a Repository is fundamental to managing data that comes from different sources, it provides an interface that is consistent with business logic, and it is able to decide autonomously which data source to use and how to combine them. Additionally, using frameworks such as Kotlin Coroutines and Flow, and libraries such as Retrofit and Room, we can let the Repository handle reactive and asynchronous data flows, improving the modularity and the maintainability of the code.

Implementing Repository in Android

The Repository design pattern is a common approach to managing access to data in Android, providing a unified interface to the business logic, which is independent of where the data comes from (API, local database, cache, and more). By using libraries such as Retrofit, Room, and Kotlin Coroutines, is it possible to implement a Repository in an efficient and modern way?

Here is a practical example of an implementation of a Repository that combines data from a REST API and a database.

1. **Definition of the entity data type**

```
data class User(
    val id: Int,
    val name: String,
    val email: String
)
```

2. **Definition of the remote data source (API)**

```
interface ApiService {
    @GET("users")
    suspend fun getUsers(): List<User>
}
```

3. **Definition of the local data source (database)**

```
@Dao
interface UserDao {
    @Query("SELECT * FROM user")
    suspend fun getAllUsers(): List<User>

    @Insert(onConflict = OnConflictStrategy.REPLACE)
    suspend fun insertUsers(users: List<User>)
}

@Entity
data class UserEntity(
    @PrimaryKey val id: Int,
    val name: String,
    val email: String
)
```

4. **Implementation of the Repository**

```
class UserRepository(
    private val apiService: ApiService,
    private val userDao: UserDao
) {
```

```
    fun getUsers(): Flow<List<User>> = flow {
        // Try to fetch data from the local database
        val localUsers = userDao.getAllUsers()
        if (localUsers.isNotEmpty()) {
            emit(localUsers.map { it.toUser() })
        }

        // Fetch data from API
        try {
            val remoteUsers = apiService.getUsers()
            emit(remoteUsers)

            // Save data on the local database
            userDao.insertUsers(remoteUsers.map { it.toUser
Entity() })
        } catch (e: Exception) {
            // In case of error, return only local data
            emit(localUsers.map { it.toUser() })
        }
    }

    // Mappers to convert UserEntity to User and vice versa
    private fun UserEntity.asUser() = User(id, name, email)
    private fun User.asUserEntity() = UserEntity(id, name, email)
}
```

- **Remote data source (API)**: Data is fetched from a REST API using Retrofit.
- **Local data source (database)**: Data is stored and fetched from a local database using Room.
- **Repository**: It combines the two data sources, using the database as a cache for remote data, and additionally handling network errors.

Caching Pattern

The Caching pattern is an essential design technique used to improve the performance of an application, reducing the workload on the main data source, such as a network API or a remote database. This technique improves the user experience because it makes the user get the data faster, eventually saving network traffic. In Android, caching is widely used in the management of resources such as images, network data, or frequently requested content. Its implementation consists of rapidly accessing data stored without having to retrieve them every time from slow or costly sources, such as APIs or remote databases.

There are two main caching types:

- **Memory caching**: It is ideal for temporary and frequently used data, memorized in the RAM for fast access. **`LruCache`** is an Android-native solution to implement this technique.

- **Disk caching**: It is used for persistent data that must survive the app lifecycle. Solutions such as Room, which we have just seen in the previous section, allow us to archive data in a structured way.

Caching is not only an optimization technique but also a key element to improve the app's reliability. For example, in scenarios of limited connection, caching allows us to provide preloaded or previously saved data to the user, ensuring continuity of use and avoiding compromising the user experience.

However, Caching introduces some complexities, such as obsolete data invalidation handling, and the balance between available memory and the amount of cache data. Libraries such as *HttpOk* for the caching of HTTP responses, or *Glide* and *Coil* for the image handling, simplify many of these challenges.

In conclusion, Caching is a powerful design pattern that can significantly improve the performance, reactivity, and reliability of an Android app if it is implemented correctly. The choice between memory caching and disk caching, or a combination of both, depends on the specific requirements of the application and the available resources. By exploiting modern libraries and following best practices, the Caching pattern could become a competitive advantage for the apps or every complexity.

Security Patterns

Security patterns are fundamental tools to provide data protection and safe management in access to Android applications. In a world that is increasingly connected, where apps frequently process sensitive data such as credentials, personal information, and financial transactions, it is essential to adopt strategies that minimize the risks of vulnerability and provide compliance with regulations such as GDPR.

Two of the most used and relevant security patterns are:

- **Encryption**: This pattern protects the data, transforming them in a format that is readable only by who has a decryption key. It is essential to protect the data stored locally or sent via the network, preventing unauthorized access in case of loss of the device or network attacks. In Android, tools such as the **Android Keystore System**, **`EncryptedSharedPreferences`**, or advanced libraries such as **Tink** simplify the implementation of the Encryption.
- **Authentication and Authorization**: Authentication verifies the identity of the users, while Authorization controls what resources are functionalities they can access. These processes can be implemented with technologies such as **OAuth 2.0**, **JWT (JSON Web Tokens)**, and **BiometricPrompt API**. They guarantee secure and controlled access, providing a smooth and protected user experience.

These patterns work together to build robust, reliable, and secure applications. The adoption of Encryption and modern techniques for authentication and authorization not only protects the user data but also reinforces trust in the security of the app. This approach is essential to address the challenges of an increasingly complex and interconnected digital environment.

Encryption

The Encryption pattern is a fundamental tool to protect sensitive data inside Android applications. This design pattern ensures that data which is stored locally or forwarded through the network is protected from unauthorized access, by transforming it into an unreadable format for anyone who does not have the decipher key. The adoption of Encryption is crucial to satisfy security standards, such as the European GDPR, and protect user privacy.

In Android, Encryption is applied in several scenarios:

- **Data stored locally**: Files, shared preferences, or databases could be encrypted using libraries such as `EncryptedSharedPreferences` or `SQLCipher`.
- **Data transmission**: During network communications, the use of secure protocols such as HTTPS and end-to-end Encryption is mandatory to ensure data integrity and confidentiality.
- **User Authentication**: Sensitive elements such as access tokens or passwords must be always encrypted before being stored or transmitted.

Native Android tools, such as the Android Keystore System, offer secure mechanisms to generate and manage Encryption keys without these ever being directly exposed to the application code. Additionally, libraries such as Tink by Google simplify the implementation of the Encryption process, providing secure and optimized solutions.

The adoption of Encryption is not only a technical choice but a mandatory requirement to protect the users and enhance their trust in the app. When implemented correctly, this design pattern ensures that data remains secure even in case of loss of the device or malicious attacks.

Implementing Encryption in Android

Let us now see how to implement the Encryption design pattern in the different scenarios we have introduced in the earlier sections.

1. **Encryption of locally stored data: `EncryptedSharedPreferences`**

The `EncryptedSharedPreferences` is a native solution to protect sensitive data that are stored in the `SharedPreferences`.

```
fun getEncryptedSharedPreferences(context: Context): Shared
Preferences {
    val masterKey = MasterKey.Builder(context)
        .setKeyScheme(MasterKey.KeyScheme.AES256_GCM)
        .build()

    return EncryptedSharedPreferences.create(
        context,
        "encrypted_prefs",
        masterKey,
        EncryptedSharedPreferences.PrefKeyEncryptionScheme.
AES256_SIV,
        EncryptedSharedPreferences.PrefValueEncryptionScheme.
AES256_GCM
    )
}

// Usage
val encryptedPrefs = getEncryptedSharedPreferences(context)
encryptedPrefs.edit().putString("secure_key", "secure_value").
apply()
val value = encryptedPrefs.getString("secure_key", null)
println(value) // Output: secure_value
```

2. **Encryption of locally stored files: Cypher and Android Keystore**

Files that are stored locally can be encrypted using a secure key that is generated and stored in the Android Keystore.

```
// Generate a keystore key
fun generateKey(alias: String) {
    val keyGenerator = KeyGenerator.getInstance(KeyProperties.
KEY_ALGORITHM_AES, "AndroidKeyStore")
    keyGenerator.init(
        KeyGenParameterSpec.Builder(
            alias,
            KeyProperties.PURPOSE_ENCRYPT or KeyProperties.
PURPOSE_DECRYPT
        )
            .setBlockModes(KeyProperties.BLOCK_MODE_GCM)
            .setEncryptionPaddings(KeyProperties.ENCRYPTION_
PADDING_NONE)
            .build()
    )
    keyGenerator.generateKey()
}

// Encrypt a file
```

```
fun encryptData(alias: String, data: ByteArray): Pair<ByteArray,
ByteArray> {
    val keyStore = KeyStore.getInstance("AndroidKeyStore")
    keyStore.load(null)
    val secretKey = keyStore.getKey(alias, null) as SecretKey

    val cipher = Cipher.getInstance("AES/GCM/NoPadding")
    cipher.init(Cipher.ENCRYPT_MODE, secretKey)

    val iv = cipher.iv // Initialization vector
    val encryptedData = cipher.doFinal(data)

    return Pair(iv, encryptedData)
}

// Decrypt a file
fun decryptData(alias: String, iv: ByteArray, encryptedData:
ByteArray): ByteArray {
    val keyStore = KeyStore.getInstance("AndroidKeyStore")
    keyStore.load(null)
    val secretKey = keyStore.getKey(alias, null) as SecretKey

    val cipher = Cipher.getInstance("AES/GCM/NoPadding")
    cipher.init(Cipher.DECRYPT_MODE, secretKey, IvParameter-
Spec(iv))

    return cipher.doFinal(encryptedData)
}

// Usage
val alias = "secureKeyAlias"
generateKey(alias)
val data = "Sensitive data".toByteArray()
val (iv, encryptedData) = encryptData(alias, data)
val decryptedData = decryptData(alias, iv, encryptedData)
println(String(decryptedData)) // Output: Sensitive data
```

3. **Encryption of network communication: HTTPS and TLS**

In order to protect the data transmitted through the network, we have to check that all the network requests use HTTPS. Libraries such as Retrofit automatically configure HTTPS if the endpoint supports it. It is possible to verify the SSL certificates to provide an additional level of security.

4. **Use of Tink for an advanced Encryption**

The library Tink by Google simplifies the Encryption providing high-level APIs. It is useful in Context scenarios that require advanced standards of security.

```
// Configure Tink
AeadConfig.register()

// Generate a key and obtain an AEAD instance
val keysetHandle = KeysetHandle.generateNew(AeadConfig.AES256_GCM)
val aead = keysetHandle.getPrimitive(Aead::class.java)

// Encrypt the data
val plaintext = "Sensitive data".toByteArray()
val associatedData = "Metadata".toByteArray()
val ciphertext = aead.encrypt(plaintext, associatedData)

// Decrypt the data
val decryptedText = aead.decrypt(ciphertext, associatedData)
println(String(decryptedText)) // Output: Sensitive data
```

The implementation of the Encryption pattern in Android provides several tools to protect the data in memory, on the disk and during transmission. Using native or third-party libraries such as **`EncryptedSharedPreferences`**, Android Keystore, and Tink, it is possible to implement scalable and secure solutions that are able to ensure privacy and security for user data.

Authentication and Authorization

Authentication and Authorization are two fundamental pillars to ensure the security and access management in Android applications. Both of these patterns work together to identify users and check their permissions, in order to protect data and sensitive information.

- **Authentication**: It is the process of verifying the user's identity. In an Android app, this can be done through several methodologies, such as credentials (email and password), biometric authentication (fingerprint or facial recognition), or single sign-on (SSO) using a third-party provider, such as Google or Facebook.
- **Authorization**: It is the process that determines which resources or actions a user can access. Once he has authenticated himself, the user receives specific permissions based on his role and access level. For example, a standard user may view only his data, while an administrator is able to manage the data of all the users.

In Android, the implementation of Authentication and Authorization relies on modern technologies such as **OAuth 2.0**, **JWT (JSON Web Tokens)**, and integrated authentication providers, such as **Firebase Authentication**. Additionally, there are native tools, such as **BiometricPrompt API**, that offer advanced solutions for secure authentication.

These processes are essential to protect personal data and ensure compliance with regulations such as the GDPR. Implementing Authentication and Authorization in an effective way improves overall security and inspires user trust while maintaining control over who has access to what and when.

Implementing Authentication and Authorization in Android

The implementation of Authentication and Authorization in Android can be done using the modern tools and libraries cited in the previous section. Here is an overview of the main techniques we can use to manage these processes.

1. **Authentication with Firebase**

Firebase Authentication offers a simple and scalable solution to manage the authentication through credentials (email/password), Google sign-in, and other providers.

To configure it:

1. Add Firebase to your project following the official documentation.
2. Enable the desired authentication methods on the Firebase Console.

Example with email and password

```
class AuthManager(private val auth: FirebaseAuth) {

    fun signIn(email: String, password: String, onComplete:
(Boolean) -> Unit) {
        auth.signInWithEmailAndPassword(email, password)
            .addOnCompleteListener { task ->
                onComplete(task.isSuccessful)
            }
    }

    fun signUp(email: String, password: String, onComplete:
(Boolean) -> Unit) {
        auth.createUserWithEmailAndPassword(email, password)
            .addOnCompleteListener { task ->
                onComplete(task.isSuccessful)
            }
    }

    fun signOut() {
        auth.signOut()
    }
}
```

Usage

```
val authManager = AuthManager()

authManager.signIn("user@example.com", "password123")
{ isSuccessful ->
    if (isSuccessful) {
        // Notify the user the message "Authentication
successful!"
    } else {
        // Notify the user the message "Authentication failed."
    }
}
```

2. **Biometric Authentication with BiometricPromptAPI**

The BiometricPrompt API allows us to integrate biometric authentication (fingerprint or facial recondition) in a simple and secure way.

Example

```
@Composable
fun BiometricAuthentication(
    onAuthSuccess: () -> Unit,
    onAuthError: () -> Unit
) {
    val context = LocalContext.current
    val lifecycleOwner = LocalLifecycleOwner.current

    // Get the main executor and create a BiometricPrompt instance
    val executor = ContextCompat.getMainExecutor(context)
    val biometricPrompt = remember {
        BiometricPrompt(
            context as FragmentActivity,
            executor,
            object : BiometricPrompt.AuthenticationCallback() {
                override fun onAuthenticationSucceeded(result:
BiometricPrompt.AuthenticationResult) {
                    super.onAuthenticationSucceeded(result)
                    onAuthSuccess()
                }

                override fun onAuthenticationError(errorCode:
Int, errString: CharSequence) {
                    super.onAuthenticationError(errorCode,
errString)
                    onAuthError()
                }
```

```
            }
        )
    }

    // Create a PromptInfo instance to configure the biometric
prompt
    val promptInfo = remember {
        PromptInfo.Builder()
            .setTitle("Biometric Authentication")
            .setSubtitle("Verify your identity")
            .setNegativeButtonText("Cancel")
            .setAllowedAuthenticators(BIOMETRIC_STRONG or DEVICE_
CREDENTIAL)
            .build()
    }

    // Use a DisposableEffect to observe the lifecycle and
authenticate when the activity resumes
    // This ensures that the biometric prompt is shown when the
activity is in the foreground
    // and is automatically dismissed when the activity is paused
or destroyed
    DisposableEffect(key1 = lifecycleOwner) {
        val observer = LifecycleEventObserver { _, event ->
            if (event == Lifecycle.Event.ON_RESUME) {
                biometricPrompt.authenticate(promptInfo)
            }
        }
        lifecycleOwner.lifecycle.addObserver(observer)
        onDispose {
            lifecycleOwner.lifecycle.removeObserver(observer)
        }
    }
}
```

Usage

```
val biometricAuth = BiometricAuthentication(
    onAuthSuccess = {
        // Notify the user the message "Authentication
successful!"
    },
    onAuthError = {
        // Notify the user the message "Authentication failed."
    }
)
```

3. **Authorization with OAuth 2.0**

OAuth 2.0 provides a method to implement secure Authentication and Authorization through access tokens. In Android, this is commonly implemented with libraries such as **`Auth0`** or using WebViews for authorization flows.

Example with Auth0

```
class OAuthManager(context: Context) {
    private val account = Auth0(context)

    fun login(onSuccess: (String) -> Unit, onFailure:
(AuthenticationException) -> Unit) {
        WebAuthProvider.login(account)
            .withScheme("demo") // Configura il tuo scheme
            .start(context as Activity, object : Callback<Creden-
tials, AuthenticationException> {
                override fun onFailure(exception: Authentica-
tionException) {
                    onFailure(exception)
                }

                override fun onSuccess(credentials: Credentials)
{
                    onSuccess(credentials.accessToken)
                }
            }
            )
    }
}
```

To configure it, we need to add the library Auth0 to our project and configure the domain and the client ID on the Auth0 console.

The implementation of Authentication and Authorization in Android combines native tools and third-party libraries to cover common scenarios such as logging in with email and password, biometric authentication, and access through OAuth 2.0. Each method offers specific advantages to improve the security and the user experience, ensuring, at the same time, compliance with the data protection regulations.

Conclusion

In this chapter, we have explored some of the fundamental patterns that make Android apps efficient, scalable, and secure. Each category of these patterns addresses specific challenges of the development, providing established solutions to improve the user experience and the robustness of the code.

Concurrency Patterns including Thread Pool and Producer-Consumer demonstrate effective strategies for handling asynchronous operations, taking full advantage of system resources and ensuring smoothness to the user interface. These patterns help to manage intensive activities without blocking the main thread, which is a crucial requirement for responsive applications.

Network Patterns such as Repository and Caching combine to provide optimized and structured access to the data. Repository centralizes and abstracts the logic to access the data, while Caching improves the performance and ensures data availability, even in poor connectivity scenarios. Together, these patterns offer a solid base to handle the data flow efficiently and smartly.

Security Patterns, in particular Encryption, Authentication, and Authorization, protect sensitive data and manage accesses safely. Encryption safeguards the data stored or transmitted, while Authentication and Authorization control who can access what. These patterns reinforce user trust, ensuring compliance with security standards.

Combining these patterns allows us to create modern Android applications that not only respond to technical requirements but also offer high performance, security, and efficient data management. The adoption of these practices helps developers design apps that are not only functional but also reliable and ready to face the challenges of the digital world.

Although the focus of this chapter has been on exploring categories of patterns that we have not seen in the previous chapter of the book, we have started to see how different design patterns can be combined. In the next chapter, we will deeply see what we can achieve by combining patterns.

Points to Remember

- **Thread Pool:** Allows us to manage concurrent tasks creating a fixed set of reusable threads, optimizing the use of the resources and improving the performance of the application.
- **Producer-Consumer**: It coordinates the production and consumption of data through a shared queue, allowing for asynchronous and balanced processing between producers and consumers.
- **Repository pattern:** It abstracts access to the data centralizing the logic. To do so, it combines local and remote data sources for efficient and maintainable data handling.
- **Caching:** It improves the performance of memorizing the data that are frequently requested, thus ensuring a smooth user experience also in conditions of poor network availability.
- **Encryption:** It protects the data, transforming it into an unreadable format

that can be decrypted only by using a decryption key. It provides security for files, databases, and network communications.

- **Authentication and Authorization:** Authentication verifies the identity of the user, and why the authorization controls the access to the resources, ensuring a safe and customized management of users.
- **Kotlin Coroutines:** They represent an essential tool to implement concurrency patterns such as Thread Pool and Producer-Consumer in a modern and idiomatic way.
- **EncryptedSharedPreferences:** This class provides a native way to protect sensitive data that are stored in the `SharedPreferences`, using advanced encryption algorithms.
- **Android Keystore System:** It allows us to generate and manage encryption keys in a secure environment, protecting the keys from direct access to the application code.
- **OAuth 2.0 and BiometricPromptAPI:** They provide advanced methods to implement Authentication and Authorization, ensuring secure access to the apps using secure tokens and biometric authentication.

Multiple Choice Questions

1. What is the main advantage of using the pattern Thread Pool?
    a. It increases the maximum number of threads available.
    b. It reduces the cost of creation and destruction of the threads.
    c. It ensures the sequential execution of the tasks.
    d. It makes the code less maintainable.
2. Which of these represents a typical use case of the pattern Repository?
    a. Memorize sensitive data in an unreadable format.
    b. Synchronize the threads in a shared queue.
    c. Implement a two-factor authentication.
    d. Combine local and remote data sources in a centralized way.
3. What is the purpose of the pattern Caching?
    a. Protect the data from authorized access.
    b. Improve the performance by memorizing frequently accessed data.

   c. Automate data synchronization between multiple devices.

   d. Provide a secure pipeline for network requests.

4. Which of these Android tools is used to generate and manage encryption keys?

   a. LruCache

   b. Retrofit

   c. Android Keystore System

   d. Firebase Authentication

5. Which of the following sentences correctly describes Authentication and Authorization?

   a. Authentication verifies user identity, while Authorization assigns the resources.

   b. Authentication assigns permissions to the users, while Authorization verifies their credentials.

   c. Both deal with protecting the data stored on the device.

   d. Both serve exclusively for controlling physical access.

Answers

1. b
2. d
3. b
4. c
5. a

Questions

1. Describe how the pattern Thread Pool works and explain how it can improve the performance of an Android app.
2. What are the main advantages of using the Repository pattern for data handling in applications? Provide a practical example.
3. What are the scenarios of Android development in which the pattern Caching is particularly useful? Mention at least two use cases.

4. Describe how the Android Keystore System works and why it is important for the security of the apps.
5. What is the main difference between Authentication and Authorization? Provide a practical example of how they are used together.

References

1. **ThreadPool in practice. A thread pool is a managed collection... | by Nodrex | Medium** - https://medium.com/@nchumbadze/threadpool-in-practice-7d07f169d9a8
2. **Thread Pools in Java - GeeksforGeeks** - https://www.geeksforgeeks.org/thread-pools-java/
3. **Design Patterns for Concurrent Programming : Producer-Consumer pattern | by Niraj Ranasinghe | Medium** - https://medium.com/@nirajranasinghe/design-patterns-for-concurrent-programming-producer-consumer-pattern-39193cac195a
4. **Repository Design Pattern - GeeksforGeeks** - https://www.geeksforgeeks.org/repository-design-pattern/
5. **Caching Design Pattern - GeeksforGeeks** - https://www.geeksforgeeks.org/caching-design-pattern/
6. **Android Keystore system | Security** - https://developer.android.com/privacy-and-security/keystore
7. **EncryptedSharedPreferences | Android Developers** - https://developer.android.com/reference/androidx/security/crypto/EncryptedSharedPreferences
8. **FULL Guide to Encryption & Decryption in Android (Keystore, Ciphers and more)** - https://www.youtube.com/watch?v=aaSck7jBDbw
9. **Authentication vs. Authorization** - https://auth0.com/docs/get-started/identity-fundamentals/authentication-and-authorization
10. **Authentication and Authorization in Android: Securing Your App and User Data | by Sujatha Mudadla | Medium** - https://medium.com/@sujathamudadla1213/authentication-and-authorization-in-android-securing-your-app-and-user-data-72973b70d00e

CHAPTER 8
Combining Patterns

Introduction

It is well-known that design patterns are powerful tools in modern Android development but their true strength is realized when they are combined together. In this chapter, we will explore how the synergy between different patterns lets us address complex problems, thus improving code structure and optimizing the performance of the apps.

Usually, a single design pattern is not sufficient to face the real challenges of a project. For example, a pattern like **Repository** can simplify the access to the data, but only by combining it with the **Caching** pattern we are able to truly optimize the performance and provide offline access. On the other hand, the use of **MVVM** alongside **Observer** allows us to create smooth user interfaces which stay synchronized with the underlying data.

Through a selection of useful combinations, such as **Dependency Injection + Factory** and **Proxy + Encryption**, this chapter will demonstrate how complementary patterns can improve modularity, security, and maintainability of the code. Additionally, we will study practical scenarios and concrete implementations to illustrate the advantages of each approach.

Combining patterns is not only a matter of efficiency but also creativity and problem-solving. This chapter will provide the tools and necessary examples for taking full advantage of these combinations, raising the quality of our Android development.

Structure

In this chapter, we will cover the following topics:

- Benefits of Combining Design Patterns
- Common Pattern Combinations in Android
  - Repository + Caching
  - MVVM + Observer
  - Dependency Injection + Factory

- Adapter + Decorator
- Other Combinations

Benefits of Combining Design Patterns

The combination of design patterns is a practice that allows us to exploit their complementary characteristics to solve complex problems and optimize the architecture of our apps. In Android, where apps require high performance, modularity, and maintainability, the combined use of design patterns provides meaningful advantages that go beyond the application of a single pattern.

Now let us study the main benefits of combining design patterns in Android applications.

- **Complexity reduction**: Combining design patterns helps us to reduce the complexity of code architecture of the project. For example, using Facade to simplify the access to complex subsystems and Adapter to adapt the different interfaces significantly reduces the number of dependencies between the components.
- **Synergy between patterns**: Some patterns are designed to work better together rather than independent of each other. For example, Repository naturally integrates with Caching in order to improve the access to the data, while balancing efficiency and reliability. Instead, Model-View-ViewModel (MVVM) and Observer provide a reactive approach that keeps the UI synchronized with the data, simplifying the management of complex states.
- **Scalability and flexibility**: The combined use of design patterns ensures a structure that can grow easily with the application. An example is the combination of Dependency Injection and Factory, which allows us to replace or update components without having to rewrite big portions of the codebase.
- **Greater reusability**: The separation of concerns through the combination of patterns improves the reusability of the components. For example, using Builder with Strategy makes it possible to configure complex objects while maintaining a behavioral logic that is interchangeable.
- **Maintainability and testability**: The combination of patterns reduces the coupling between the components, making it easy to maintain and test them. For example, a centralized Singleton that uses a Factory to create objects simplifies the unit tests, thereby allowing to mock the dependencies.

Combining design patterns is a good practice to better face the challenges of Android development. These benefits reflect on building robust, flexible, and maintainable applications that are also adaptable to the evolving requirements of the project.

Common Pattern Combinations in Android

In the Android development process, design patterns rarely work independently. The daily challenges of development, such as data management, performance optimization, and security, require solutions that combine multiple patterns in order to obtain the best results. These combinations not only face specific problems, but improve the modularity, scalability, and maintainability of the code.

In this section, we will explore some of the most common combinations of design patterns that are used in modern Android development. Each combination is designed to address practical needs and provides a concrete example of how design patterns can work together to solve complex problems.

The combinations include:

- Integration of Repository and Caching for optimized data management.
- The use of MVVM and Observer to build smooth and intuitive user interfaces.
- The joint application of Dependency Injection and Factory for dynamic and flexible dependency management.
- Other useful combinations, such as an Adapter with a Decorator, simplify the integration with third-party libraries and improve the existing functionalities.

This section offers a practical guide to understanding how to combine design patterns effectively, providing examples that show real scenarios and concrete advantages. The ability to integrate multiple patterns into the design of an app is a fundamental know-how to create elegant and scalable solutions.

Repository + Caching

The combination of Repository and Caching is one of the most common in Android development. These patterns work together to optimize access to the data, improve performance, and ensure a seamless user experience, even in scenarios of poor connectivity.

An example of a typical use case is an e-commerce application that shows a list of products. Data can be stored in the cache to ensure fast access, while they are periodically updated using a network API.

- When the user opens the app, the product data is fetched from the local cache, that is, the memory or the internal storage.
- If the data is not present in the cache or it is outdated, the Repository requests it to the network API.

- The new and updated data are stored in the cache for future use.

```
class ProductRepository(
    private val memoryCache: MemoryCache<String, List<Product>>,
    private val apiService: ApiService,
    private val database: ProductDatabase
) {

    suspend fun getProducts(): List<Product> {
        // Fetch from memory
        memoryCache.get("products")?.let {
            return it
        }

        // Fetch from local database
        val localProducts = database.productDao().getAllProd-
ucts()
        if (localProducts.isNotEmpty()) {
            memoryCache.put("products", localProducts)
            return localProducts
        }

        // Fetch from network
        val remoteProducts = apiService.getProducts()
        database.productDao().insertAll(remoteProducts)
        memoryCache.put("products", remoteProducts)
        return remoteProducts
    }
}
```

Advantages:

- **Improved performance**: The caching mechanism reduces the number of network requests, making the app faster and more reactive.
- **Offline access**: Data stored locally allows users to access them even without an internet connection.
- **Modularity**: The repository abstracts the logic of data access, keeping the code well-organized and testable.

Disadvantages:

- **Synchronization management**: We need to make sure that the cache and data sources are updated, and this could lead to an increase in complexity.
- **Memory consumption**: The caching might occupy a relevant amount of resources in devices with low RAM capacity.
- **Cache invalidation**: It is necessary to implement strategies to remove outdated data from the cache.

The combination of Repository and Caching represents a perfect example of how design patterns can work together to improve the user experience and the quality of the code. This approach is particularly useful for applications that require fast, reliable, and scalable access to data.

MVVM + Observer

The combination of MVVM (Model-View-ViewModel) and Observer is the heart of modern Android development, especially if we use Jetpack Compose or StateFlow. This combination allows us to build reactive and intuitive user interfaces, where each change in the data is reflected automatically on the UI, simplifying the management of the states.

The pattern MVVM separates the business logic (Model), the presentation logic (ViewModel), and the user interface (View), thereby promoting modularity and testability. The Observer, on the other hand, is used to automatically notify the View every time that the data in the ViewModel changes.

Together, these patterns allow us to:

- Automatically update the UI as a response to the state changes.
- Reduce the boilerplate code, thanks to the bindings.
- Separate the responsibilities between business logic and user interface.

As an example, we will now see the classical To-Do list:

1. The list of the activities is held in the ViewModel as an observable flow, such as a **`LiveData`** or **`StateFlow`** object.
2. The View subscribes to the updates of the ViewModel using the Observer.
3. When a new activity is added by the user, the ViewModel updates the data, and the Observer deals with notifying the View to update the UI.

ViewModel

```
class TaskViewModel : ViewModel() {
    private val _tasks = MutableStateFlow<List<String>>
(emptyList())
    val tasks: StateFlow<List<String>> = _tasks

    fun addTask(task: String) {
        val updatedTasks = _tasks.value.toMutableList().apply {
add(task) }
        _tasks.value = updatedTasks
    }
}
```

View with Jetpack Compose

```
@Composable
fun TaskListScreen(viewModel: TaskViewModel) {
    val tasks by viewModel.tasks.collectAsState()

    Column {
        tasks.forEach { task ->
            Text(text = task)
        }

        Button(onClick = { viewModel.addTask("New Task") }) {
            Text("Add Task")
        }
    }
}
```

Advantages:

- **Automatic updates**: The changes in the data are automatically reflected on the UI, improving the user experience.
- **Separation of concerns**: MVVM separates the presentation logic from the UI, making the code more modular and testable.
- **Less boilerplate code**: The Observer removes the need to manually update the UI, simplifying a lot of the implementation.

Disadvantages:

- **Learning curve**: The initial configuration of MVVM and Observer can be tricky for beginner developers.
- **Binding overhead**: Using observable flows for each data could introduce overload, especially in applications with many updates.
- **Hard debugging**: Automatic UI updates can make it difficult to track data flows.

The combination of MVVM and Observer is essential for developing modern Android apps, in particular with Jetpack Compose and reactive flows such as LiveData or StateFlow. This approach not only simplifies the management of the UI but also ensures a clear separation between business logic and presentation, improving the code maintainability and user experience.

Dependency Injection + Factory

The combination of Dependency Injection (DI) and Factory is a powerful solution to manage the dynamic creation and injection of complex objects. This approach not only simplifies the code but also improves the flexibility and testability of the application.

The pattern Dependency Injection allows us to provide to a component his dependency on the outside, improving modularity and promoting loose coupling. On the other hand, Factory deals with the creation of objects, centralizing and abstracting the building logic.

Combining these two partners, we can:

- Delegate to the factory the complexity of object creation.
- Using *DI* to dynamically provide objects created by the Factory, makes the configuration and the tests easier.

Let us see a practical example. Now we will take into consideration an application that uses different network clients based on its configuration (for example, Retrofit for REST API or a WebSocket Client for real-time communications). Factory creates the clients, while *DI* provides them with the components that require these.

Factory

```
interface NetworkClient {
    fun connect()
}

class RetrofitClient : NetworkClient {
    override fun connect() {
        println("Connecting via Retrofit")
    }
}

class WebSocketClient : NetworkClient {
    override fun connect() {
        println("Connecting via WebSocket")
    }
}

class NetworkClientFactory {
    fun createClient(type: String): NetworkClient {
        return when (type) {
            "rest" -> RetrofitClient()
            "websocket" -> WebSocketClient()
            else -> throw IllegalArgumentException("Unsupported
client type")
        }
    }
}
```

Dependency Injection

```
class NetworkModule(private val factory: NetworkClientFactory) {
    fun provideNetworkClient(type: String): NetworkClient {
        return factory.createClient(type)
    }
}
```

Usage

```
val factory = NetworkClientFactory()
val networkModule = NetworkModule(factory)

val restClient = networkModule.provideNetworkClient("rest")
restClient.connect() // Output: "Connecting via Retrofit"

val websocketClient = networkModule.provideNetworkClient
("websocket")
websocketClient.connect() // Output: "Connecting via WebSocket"
```

Advantages:

- **Separation of concerns**: The Factory centralizes the creation of the objects, while DI simplifies the injection of dependencies in the components.
- **Easy to test**: DI allows us to provide mocks or stubs to the component, improving the testing phase.
- **Loose coupling**: Combining Factory and DI lets us avoid the hard coding of the dependencies, making the code more readable and maintainable.

Disadvantages:

- **Initial overhead**: Configuring a Factory and a DI requires time and might be complex for newcomers.
- **Increase in project complexity**: The introduction of these patterns might introduce complexity, especially if we have to deal with small projects.
- **External library dependencies**: In some cases, DI is managed by frameworks such as Dagger-Hilt or Koin. Developers must have a knowledge of these tools in order to use them.

The combination of Dependency Injection and Factory is useful in applications that want to be modular and scalable. This approach improves the management of the dependencies and allows us to dynamically configure complex subjects, making the code more maintainable and easier to test. It is a mandatory solution for projects that need advanced flexibility and modularity.

Adapter + Decorator

The combination of Adapter and Decorator is an effective solution if we want to adapt and enrich the app's functionalities dynamically, without modifying the existing code. This approach is particularly useful in Android applications that integrate third-party libraries or legacy modules, where we need to adapt the interfaces and add custom behaviors.

The Adapter pattern deals with making an incompatible interface able to communicate with other existing parts of the application. The Decorator pattern, instead, dynamically adds functionalities to an existing object, while keeping the original interface.

If we combine these two patterns, we can achieve the following results:

- Adapt the interface of a third-party library to easily integrate into our application.
- Dynamically extended functionalities of the adapted objects without modifying the original code.

An application that uses a logging library that does not satisfy all the requirements of our project can be an example. The Adapter can transform the library interface to make it compatible with our application, while the Decorator can add functionalities such as log printing on a file or a remote server.

Adapter

```
interface Logger {
    fun log(message: String)
}

class ThirdPartyLogger {
    fun logToConsole(msg: String) {
        println("Third-party log: $msg")
    }
}

class LoggerAdapter(private val thirdPartyLogger: ThirdParty
Logger) : Logger {
    override fun log(message: String) {
        thirdPartyLogger.logToConsole(message)
    }
}
```

Decorator

```
class FileLoggerDecorator(private val logger: Logger) : Logger {
    override fun log(message: String) {
        logger.log(message)
```

```
        saveToFile(message)
    }

    private fun saveToFile(message: String) {
        println("Saved to file: $message")
    }
}
```

Usage

```
val thirdPartyLogger = ThirdPartyLogger()
val adapter = LoggerAdapter(thirdPartyLogger)
val decoratedLogger = FileLoggerDecorator(adapter)

decoratedLogger.log("Log message")
// Output:
// Third-party log: Log message
// Saved to file: Log message
```

Advantages:

- **Flexibility**: The combination of these patterns allows us to interact with existing libraries or extend their functionalities without modifying the original code.
- **Modularity**: The separation of Adapter and Decorator guarantees a clear and modular design.
- **Code reusability**: The same Decorators can be applied to different implementations of the Adapter.

Disadvantages:

- **Complexity increase**: As with most design pattern combinations, the Adapter-Decorator might introduce an additional level of complexity, especially for small projects.
- **Performance**: Decorating multiple times the same object can lead to the introduction of a small overhead, which is a downgrade in terms of performance.
- **Third-party dependencies**: The need to adapt the interfaces could result from non-optimal choices regarding external libraries.

The combination of Adapter and Decorator is a powerful solution that allows us to integrate and improve third-party libraries or legacy modules in our Android applications. This approach allows us to adapt incompatible interfaces and dynamically extend functionalities while keeping the code well-organized and easy to maintain. It is particularly useful in scenarios in which flexibility and customizations are key requirements.

Other Combinations

In addition to the most common combination of design patterns, there are other combinations which, even if less frequently used, are extremely effective in solving specific problems in Android development. These combinations allow us to face complex scenarios elegantly, improving the modularity, maintainability, and scalability of the code.

Let us briefly explore five additional combinations of design patterns.

Facade + Adapter

Purpose: The pattern Facade simplifies the interaction with complex modules, while the Adapter adapts incompatible interfaces in order to integrate them with other parts of the app.

Use case: An app that uses third-party APIs, each with a different response format, might use Facade to provide a single access point, while the Adapters translate the responses in the desired format.

Practical example: A news app that aggregates data fetched from multiple RSS APIs, converting formats with Adapter and offering a simplified interface through Facade.

Strategy + Factory

Purpose: Using Factory to create configurable objects and Strategy to define their dynamic behavior. These combinations allow us to manage behavior variation in a flexible way.

Use case: An app to manage lists can use Factory to create objects that represent different sorting parameters (for example, alphabetically, by test), and Strategy to apply the desired algorithm based on user preferences.

Practical example: A task management app that uses different sorting methods to display the activities in a customized way.

Builder + Strategy

Purpose: Builder creates complex configurable subjects, while Strategy determines the corresponding behavior. This combination separates the creation logic from the behavioral logic, promoting modularity.

Use case: Configure network requests with Builder in order to define parameters such as header and body, and Strategy to choose among different authentication methods (for example, JWT or OAuth).

Practical example: A document management app that lets the user customize the network requests to synchronize files in the cloud.

Singleton + Factory

Purpose: Centralize the creation of objects with a Singleton that uses a Factory to manage complex instances.

Use case: Manage a single network client inside an application that has many modules that require different API connections. The Singleton ensures a single instance, while the Factory creates a configuration for each service.

Practical example: An e-commerce app that uses a Singleton for the network client and a Factory to configure requests to the catalog, orders, and payments.

Proxy + Encryption

Purpose: Proxy controls user access, while Encryption protects sensitive data during access or network transmission. This combination is ideal to ensure security and control.

Use case: Sensitive file protection inside an app, where Proxy verifies the authorizations to access and Encryption encrypts the files during saving or transmission.

Practical example: A password management app that uses Proxy to authenticate the user before accessing the encrypted data saved on the device.

These combinations of design patterns demonstrate how the patterns can work together to address specific needs, offering elegant and scalable solutions. Their use allows us to improve the architecture of the apps, making them more modular, secure, and maintainable. Even if they are less common than the ones that we have seen previously in this chapter, they represent valuable tools for developers who want to optimize every aspect of their projects.

Conclusion

This chapter has shown the importance and the power of combining design patterns in Android development. Working with complimentary patterns allows us to address complex problems in a structured way, optimizing not only the functionalities of the applications but also their properties of scalability, modularity, and maintainability.

We have explored common combinations such as Repository + Caching, ideal for efficient data management, and MVVM + Observer, which makes user interfaces smooth and dynamic. Additionally, we have seen the effectiveness of more sophisticated approaches, such as Dependency Injection + Factory and Proxy + Encryption, which are useful to simplify dependency management and improve security.

The combinations presented demonstrate that the smart use of the patterns can solve specific problems without excessively increasing the complexity of the code. However, it is essential to adopt these approaches in a balanced way, avoiding situations of over-engineering that could unnecessarily complicate the project.

In conclusion, the art of combining the same pattern is a fundamental skill for modern Android developers. Experimenting and mastering these combinations allow us to create robust, elegant applications that are ready to face the challenges in a technological world that is continually evolving. The ability to choose and integrate the right patterns not only improves the architecture of the apps but also represents a step forward in the development of high-quality software.

Since the combination of design patterns could have a negative impact on application performance, we will take a more in-depth look at this aspect in the next chapter.

Points to Remember

- **Combining patterns improves flexibility**: Combining complementary patterns allows us to solve context problems and improve the modularity of our Android apps.
- **Repository + Caching**: This combination centralizes access to data and improves the performance of storing data frequently requested, ensuring a smooth user experience, including offline experience.
- **MVVM + Observer**: It is ideal to build reactive interfaces. This combination keeps the data of the UI synchronized with the app's state.
- **Dependency Injection + Factory**: It handles the dynamic creation of complex objects and simplifies the configuration and the testability of the code.
- **Adapter + Decorator**: It is perfect to integrate third-party libraries which have interfaces not compatible with our app and add dynamic functionalities without having to modify the original code.
- **Facade + Adapter**: This combination simplifies the access to complex subsystems and enables incompatible interfaces to work together.
- **Builder + Strategy**: It separates the configuration of complex objects from the behavioral logic, thus promoting reusability.
- **Proxy + Encryption**: It combines access control with sensitive data protection. It is ideal to ensure security for applications that deal with confidential information.
- **Avoid over-engineering**: Even if combining patterns offers powerful solutions, it is important to apply them only where needed, in order to avoid excessive code complexity.

- **Choosing the right partners is crucial**: Integrating patterns efficiently requires experience and a clear comprehension of project requirements, balancing simplicity and functionality.

Multiple Choice Questions

1. What is the main advantage of the combination Repository + Caching?
   a. Improves code modularity.
   b. Ensures data availability offline.
   c. Reduces the complexity of the system.
   d. Increases the maximum number of available threads.
2. Why do we use MVVM in combination with Observer?
   a. To improve the modularity of interfaces.
   b. To reduce the memory consumption.
   c. To simplify the access to data.
   d. To automatically update the UI as a response to state changes.
3. What does Dependency Injection provide when it is combined with Factory?
   a. A good grade of testability for complex objects created dynamically.
   b. The optimization of network requests.
   c. Asynchronous tasks management.
   d. The ability to easily integrate third-party libraries in the app.
4. Which of these combinations is ideal to integrate and extend third-party libraries that have incompatible interfaces?
   a. Singlet + Factory
   b. Adapter + Decorator
   c. Builder + Strategy
   d. Proxy + Encryption
5. Which of these combinations is better suitable to ensure security for sensitive data?
   a. Facade + Adapter
   b. Repository + Caching

c. Proxy + Encryption

d. Builder + Strategy

Answers

1. b
2. d
3. a
4. b
5. c

Questions

1. How does the combination of Repository and Caching improve the performance and user experience in an Android application? Provide a practical example.
2. Explain how MVVM and Observer work together to create a reactive data flow between the ViewModel and the UI. What are the advantages of this approach?
3. Describe a practical use case in which Dependency Injection and Factory can be combined to improve modularity and testability.
4. When is it best to use the combination Adapter + Decorator? Explain, providing an example, how these patterns can make it easy to integrate third-party libraries.
5. Proxy and Encryption are usually used together to improve security. What are the main challenges to the implementation of this combination in Android apps?

CHAPTER 9
Performance Considerations

Introduction

In the world of Android development, the performance of an application represents a fundamental element to ensure a smooth and satisfying user experience. A slow app, which consumes too many resources or freezes frequently, is at risk of being rapidly abandoned by users, for the low quality of their functionalities. This chapter is dedicated to performance optimization, a crucial aspect in modern Android app design.

We will start by analyzing the most common problem that can compromise performance, such as memory leaks, inefficient CPU usage, and unresponsive UI. Subsequently, we will dive into optimization techniques and unused object detection. We will see how design patterns such as Command, Producer-Consumer, and Repository + Caching can be applied to reduce the CPU workload and improve the overall efficiency of the applications.

Finally, we will explore advanced profiling and measurement tools, such as Android Studio Profiler, to identify bottlenecks and optimize every aspect of the app. Using a combination of techniques, design patterns, and tools, this chapter will provide a practical guide to improve the performance of our apps, ensuring authority and optimal functionality, as well as a better user experience.

Structure

In this chapter, we will cover the following topics:

- Common Performance Issues in Android
- Memory Management and Optimization
- Design Patterns to Reduce CPU Usage
- Improve App Responsiveness
- Profiling and Measurement Tools

Common Performance Issues in Android

The performance of an Android application is fundamental to ensure a smooth and satisfying experience to the users. However, there are many common problems that could compromise the reactivity of the app, increase loading time, and consume resources inefficiently. Recognizing and addressing these problems is the first step towards the development of well-performed Android applications. Let us now explore, one by one, these common problems.

Memory Leaks

One of the most common problems in Android development are memory leaks, which occur when an object that is no longer used remains in memory due to unallocated pointers. These problems can cause an overuse of RAM and, in some cases, an app crash.

Common causes:

- Activities and fragments incorrectly deallocated.
- Improper use of listeners or callbacks that hold useless references.
- Inefficient handling of static objects or singletons.

Unresponsive UI

The user interface that does not respond immediately to the user's commands is often the result of long operations executed on the main thread. This problem can manifest itself in:

- Lags during UI rendering.
- Jerky animations or delayed interactions.
- Timeouts that cause problems perceivable by the user.

Common causes:

- Execution of network requests or I/O operations on the main thread.
- Handling of a huge quantity of data without delegating the management to a background thread.
- Missing use of modern tools such as Coroutines or WorkManager.

Excessive Resource Usage

The excessive use of resources, such as CPU, GPU, battery, or memory is one of the most significant problems that can affect Android applications. This problem not only compromises the app performance, but also reduces the battery life and negatively influences the user experience, especially on old and low-power devices.

Common causes:

- Frequent polling instead of push notifications.
- Unoptimized rendering cycles or unnecessary animation repetitions.
- Unnecessary or too frequent network requests.

Inefficient Use of Graphic Memory

Android applications that handle a lot of images or graphical resources could suffer from slowdowns if these are not optimized. Loading images without proper downscaling or keeping too many resources in memory could lead to crashes or poor performance.

Common causes:

- Missing image resizing, which should be adapted to the device resolution.
- Missing use of image optimization libraries such as Glide or Coil.
- Continuous allocation of bitmaps without recycling.

These performance problems are very common in Android development and can have a significant impact on the user experience. However, with a good knowledge of the causes and the use of the right tools and design patterns, it is possible to mitigate or even avoid them. In the following sections, we will deepen strategies and useful patterns to face these issues.

Memory Management and Optimization

Efficient memory management is one of the most important things if we want to ensure the performance of an Android application. An improper use of the memory can lead to slowdowns, memory leaks, and crashes. Optimizing the memory means reducing the consumption of resources, preventing issues, and improving user experience. In this section, we will analyze useful strategies and patterns for effective memory management.

Garbage Collection on Android

Android uses a garbage collection (GC) mechanism to autonomously manage the memory, freeing objects no longer used. However, calling the GC frequently could lead to system pauses and a jerky UI.

Best practices:

- Reduce the number of temporary objects created inside cycles or frequently called methods.
- Avoid the massive use of data structures such as **ArrayList** or **HashMap** when they are not necessary.
- Use primitive types (**int**, **float**) instead of wrapper objects (**Integer**, **Float**) to save memory.

Memory Leaks Prevention

Memory leaks occur when an object is not allocated from the memory due to some pointers that unnecessarily reference it. This problem can drastically increase the memory consumption, causing crashes on devices with low resources.

Common causes and solutions:

- **Listeners and callbacks not removed**: Use **WeakReference** to prevent the listener from holding the object.

  Example:

  ```
  class Listener {
      fun onEvent() = println("Event received!")
  }

  class EventSource(listener: Listener) {
      private val weakListener = WeakReference(listener)

      fun triggerEvent() {
          weakListener.get()?.onEvent() // Calls the listener if
  it's still available
      }
  }

  fun main() {
      val listener = Listener()
      val source = EventSource(listener)

      source.triggerEvent() // Output: Event received!
  }
  ```

  WeakReference ensures that **EventListener** can be garbage collected if no strong references exist.

- **Mismanaged Activities or Fragments**: Avoid static references to these components.

- **Unoptimized Singletons**: The Singleton should not hold references to any context except for the **applicationContext**.

  Example:

```
class MySingleton private constructor(private val context:
Context) {
          companion object {
              private var instance: MySingleton? = null
        fun getInstance(context: Context): MySingleton {
            if (instance == null) {
                // Don't do
                // instance = MySingleton(context)
                // Do
                instance = MySingleton(context.application
Context)
            }
            return instance!!
        }
    }
}
```

Image Optimization

Images are one of the main memory consumption factors in Android applications, especially when they are loaded without optimizations.

Optimization techniques:

- **Resizing**: Load images using the resolution that is really needed in order to avoid large bitmaps.
- **Caching**: Use libraries such as Glide or Coil to memorize images inside the cache.
- **Bitmap Pooling**: Recycling bitmaps already used to reduce the memory allocation.

Memory Caching

This option consists in reducing the number of network requests and disk access. These operations are costly in terms of computation, and reducing them means to significantly improve the performance.

A way to implement memory caching is to use LRU Cache, that is a cache that maintains only the objects that are the most used recently, removing automatically those ones that are less used.

`WeakReference` and `SoftReference`

These classes implement two different logics to keep in memory the objects only as long as they are requested, avoiding memory leaks and overloads.

- **`WeakReference`**: Release the object if it is no longer referenced by any pointer.
- **`SoftReference`**: Maintain the object in memory as long and the overall memory usage is not critical.

```
val weakRef = WeakReference<Bitmap>(bitmap)
val softRef = SoftReference<Bitmap>(bitmap)
```

Memory management and optimization requires a combination of good practices and effective tools. Implementing techniques such as caching, image resizing, and using weakly referenced objects not only improves performance, but also avoids crashes and memory leaks. A well-managed memory is fundamental to ensure a seamless and reliable user experience.

Design Patterns to Reduce CPU Usage

High CPU usage is a common issue in Android development, as it can drain the battery faster, slow down the device, and negatively impact the user experience. Design patterns can address this problem by optimizing the CPU usage, delegating costly operations, reducing redundant computations, and leveraging asynchronous approaches. In this section, we will analyze some of the most useful patterns to reduce CPU usage and improve overall app performance.

Command Pattern

The Command pattern is ideal for delegating complex operations, and it is particularly useful in scenarios in which we need asynchronous operation or a customized management of queues of commands.

How it helps to reduce CPU usage:

- Allows us to execute complex operations in separate threads, freeing the main thread.
- Allow us to plan and enqueue tasks, avoiding unnecessary parallel operations.

Use case: An image manipulation app that applies heavy filters on loaded photos. The pattern Command sends each filter as a separate command to a worker thread.

Producer-Consumer Pattern

The Producer-Consumer pattern is useful to balance the workload between the producer (who generates data or tasks) and the consumer (who processes them). This pattern avoids CPU overload, thus balancing task distribution.

How it helps to reduce CPU usage:

- It prevents the CPU from being overloaded with simultaneous tasks.
- It uses buffers to enqueue data or operations, ensuring a tidy management.

Use case: A streaming video app that downloads packages of data (producer) and decodes them for playback (consumer).

Observer Pattern

The Observer pattern is particularly useful for reducing redundant calculations and updating only what is necessary on the UI.

How it helps to reduce CPU usage:

- It removes continuous polling to detect modifications on the data.
- It updates only the necessary components, saving calculation cycles.

Use case: A weather app that updates the UI only when forecasts change, instead of continuously checking data on the servers.

Repository + Caching

Combining the pattern Repository with a Caching mechanism helps to get rid of redundant requests to the network or the database, significantly reducing the CPU load.

How it helps to reduce CPU usage:

- Fetch the data from the local cache instead of requesting them again.
- Reduce complex calculations, thanks to preprocess or memorized data.

Use case: An e-commerce app that saves the data of the products in the cache to avoid requesting them to the server every time the user scrolls the list.

Builder Pattern

The Builder pattern optimizes the creation of complex subjects, avoiding repetitive or unnecessary computations during the building process.

How it helps to reduce CPU usage:

- It enables the creation of objects step by step, avoiding redundant and costly initialization phases.

- Reduce the number of instances that are created, using only the needed parameters.

Use case: The configuration of complex network requests, such as the ones for loading data based on custom parameters.

The adoption of well-choosing design patterns helps us to optimize the CPU usage, improving both performance and energy efficiency of the app. Patterns such as Command, Producer-Consumer, Repository, and Caching not only delegate and optimize complex operations, but also offer a clear and scalable architecture. Using these patterns allows us to create more reactive and performant Android apps.

Improve App Responsiveness

Responsiveness is a crucial feature if we want to provide a good user experience in Android applications. A reactive app responds immediately to user interactions and maintains a smooth and slowdown-free UI, even if there are complex processes running in background. In this section, we will explore tools and techniques to improve the responsiveness of the app, providing a focus on modern approaches such as Kotlin Coroutines, WorkManager, and Jetpack Compose.

Use of Kotlin Coroutines

Kotlin Coroutines offers a simple and efficient way to handle asynchronous operations, reducing the complexity of thread management.

How it improves responsiveness:

- Executes long operations, such as network requests or database access, while keeping the main thread free.
- Enables to write a more readable code, thanks to **suspend** functions.

  Example:

  ```
  fun fetchData(viewModelScope: CoroutineScope) {
      viewModelScope.launch(Dispatchers.IO) {
          val data = fetchFromNetwork()
          withContext(Dispatchers.Main) {
              updateUI(data)
          }
      }
  }
  ```

Worker Threads and WorkManager

Regarding complex and repetitive tasks, such as data synchronization and file compressions, it is essential to use worker threads or solutions like WorkManager.

Worker threads:

- Ideal for tasks that must be executed immediately or terminated rapidly.
- Tools such as **ExecutorService** or libraries such as **RxJava** can be used to handle these tasks.

  Example:

  ```
  val executor = Executors.newSingleThreadExecutor()

  fun runTask() {
      executor.execute {
          // Simulate a background task
          println("Running a quick background task")
      }
  }
  ```

WorkManager:

- It is perfect for persistence or scheduled tasks that must be survived to the start of the app.
- Offers a simple API to manage asynchronous operations, such as file uploading.

  Example:

  ```
  class UploadWorker(appContext: Context, workerParams: Worker
  Parameters) : Worker(appContext, workerParams) {
      override fun doWork(): Result {
          // Simulate file upload
          println("Uploading file...")
          return Result.success()
      }
  }

  // Enqueue WorkManager task
  fun scheduleUpload(context: Context) {
      val uploadRequest = OneTimeWorkRequestBuilder<UploadWorker>
  ().build()
      WorkManager.getInstance(context).enqueue(uploadRequest)
  }
  ```

Rendering Optimization with Jetpack Compose

Jetpack Compose, the modern toolkit to build UIs on Android, is designed to improve the responsiveness of the UI rendering.

How it improves responsiveness:

- Reduces useless redrawing of the components, thanks to its state-based composition.
- Updates only the UI components that are really changed, minimizing the workload on the main thread.

  Example:

```
@Composable
fun UserListScreen(users: List<User>) {
    LazyColumn {
        items(users) { user ->
            Text(text = user.name)
        }
    }
}
```

Smart Event Handling

Events such as click or scrolling should be handled in a smart way in order to avoid UI freezes.

- **Debounce**: Delays the processing of frequent events to execute only the last event in a given time window.
- **Throttle**: Limits the execution of events to regular time intervals.

  Example of Debounce:

```
val job = Job()
val coroutineScope = CoroutineScope(Dispatchers.Main + job)

fun onUserInput(input: String) {
    coroutineScope.launch {
        delay(300) // Debounce: delay the execution by 300ms
        performSearch(input)
    }
}
```

Asynchronous Resource Handling

Loading the resources asynchronously improves the UI responsiveness.

- **Lazy loading**: It avoids the early loading of all the resources, instead, they are loaded only when they become visible.
- **Caching**: It reduces loading times by accessing pre-downloaded or pre-processed data.

The responsiveness of an Android app is the result of an efficient management of background operations and UI rendering. Modern tools such as Kotlin Coroutines, WorkManager, and Jetpack Compose offer simple and powerful approaches to maintain a smooth and reactive app. Implementing these strategies not only improves the performance, but also provides optimal user experience, which is fundamental for successful apps.

Profiling and Measurement Tools

Measuring and optimizing the performance of an Android app is crucial if we want to provide the best user experience. Profiling and measurement tools allow developers to detect bottlenecks, analyze the resource usage, and monitor the app behavior at runtime. In this section, we will explore the main tools available and the techniques to leverage them.

Android Studio Profiler

Android Studio Profiler is the main tool used to analyze the performance of an application. It provides a suite of tools to monitor CPU, memory, network, and battery in real time.

Main characteristics:

- **CPU Profiler**: Analyze the CPU usage and detect methods and threads that use too many resources. It allows us to record execution traces to perform detailed analysis.
- **Memory profiler**: Displays the memory usage, highlighting possible memory leaks and unnecessary objects. It allows us to take snapshots to verify the presence of unreleased objects.
- **Network profiler**: Displays the network traffic, highlighting requests, responses, and latency.
- **Energy profiler**: Monitors the energy consumption of the app, which is useful to detect functionalities that use too much battery.

Example usage:

1. Run the app in debug mode on a physical device or emulator.
2. Open the Profiler tab in Android Studio.

3. Select the parameter you want to analyze (CPU, memory, network, or battery) and observe the charts and the details.

Systrace

Systrace is an advanced tool designed to analyze the performance at system level. it records low-level events such as UI rendering, kernel activities, and network access.

How to use it:

1. Start a trace using Android Studio or the common **`systrace`** on the terminal.
2. Analyze the result in a HTML report that highlights the main processes, execution times, and bottlenecks.

When to use it:

- To analyze UI rendering issues (such as janks or frame drops).
- To optimize complex operations that involve multiple threads or processes.

Firebase Performance Monitoring

Firebase Performance Monitoring is a cloud-based service that provides detailed statistics about app performance in real scenarios.

Main characteristics:

- Monitor screen loading times.
- Analysis of network requests, including latency and data size.
- Custom event tracing to measure specific execution times.

Advantages:

- Analysis based on real data, collected from user devices.
- Auto detection of issues without having to connect the app to debug tools.

Debug GPU Overdraw

The tool allows us to analyze UI rendering, highlighting situations in which graphical elements are redrawn unnecessarily.

How to enable it:

1. Enable Debug Option on the device.
2. Enable the option Debug GPU Overdraw.
3. Observe the colors on the UI that represent the amount of overdraw.

When to use it:

- To optimize the layout and reduce the rendering workload.
- To identify views or layouts that cause redundant renderings.

LeakCanary

LeakCanary is an open-source library that helps to detect memory leaks during development.

How it works:

- Monitors objects such as activities, fragments, and views to detect references that prevent them to be deallocated.
- Shows a detailed report on memory leaks, providing stacktraces.

Advantages:

- Easy project integration.
- Autodetection of issues which do not need manual actions.

Profiling and measurement tools are fundamental to improve the performance of an Android app. Android Studio Profiler, Firebase Performance Monitoring and Systrace offer detailed insights on the app behavior, allowing us to detect and solve bottlenecks. By combining these tools with libraries such as LeakCanary, developers can create more efficient, stable, and responsive apps. Measuring and optimizing regularly the performance is a crucial step towards offering an excellent user experience.

Conclusion

The performance is a fundamental aspect in the world of Android development, because they directly influence the user experience and the overall success of the app. This chapter has explored the main challenges linked to performance, highlighting how facing common problems, optimizing memory, and reducing CPU usage improve app responsiveness.

We have analyzed the most effective design patterns for optimizing performance, such as Command and Producer-Consumer, which delegate complex operations. We have also analyzed useful combinations such as Repository + Caching, which reduce the workload derived from network requests. Additionally, tools such as Android Studio Profiler, Systrace, and libraries such as LeakCanary offer precious support to identify and solve bottlenecks.

The heart of good optimization resides in balancing–avoid resource waste without sacrificing functionalities and complexity. The use of design patterns and appropriate tools not only improves performance, but also contributes to keeping a code clear and maintainable.

In conclusion, optimizing the performance is not only a technical matter but a fundamental step to offer the users a satisfying experience. With the knowledge acquired in this chapter, we can address the most critical challenges and ensure that our Android application is responsive, efficient, and ready to face the needs of the model market.

In the next chapter, we will learn how to test design patterns.

Points to Remember

- **Performance is crucial**: Poor performance in an Android app can lead to dissatisfaction on the part of the users, and high uninstall ratio and negative reviews, making optimization a priority.
- **Memory leaks**: Memory leaks, often caused by unnecessary references, can lead to crashes or an overuse of RAM. It is important to use tools such as LeakCanary to identify and solve them.
- **Garbage collection management**: The execution of too many operations that require the garbage collector can cause UI slowdowns. Reducing temporary objects and preferring primitive types help to limit slowdowns.
- **Data caching**: The caching, especially the one achieved by using combinations such as Repository + Caching, reduces the network load and access data time, improving the overall performance.
- **Reduction of CPU usage**: Patterns such as Command and Producer-Consumer delegate heavy operations to separate threads, reducing the impact on the main thread.
- **UI responsiveness**: Tools such as Kotlin Coroutines and modern libraries like Jetpack Compose optimize asynchronous processing and UI rendering, smoothness, and reactiveness.
- **Profiling tools**: Android Studio Profiler and Systrace are essential to analyze the behavior of the app and detect bottlenecks in CPU, memory network, and battery.
- **Image optimization**: Resizing images, using libraries such as Glide and Coil, and applying techniques to bitmaps avoid the overload of the graphic memory.
- **Debounce and Throttle**: These approaches help to handle repetitive events such as tap or scrolling, preventing useless elaborations, and improving reactivity.

- **Balance between performance and simplicity**: While it is important to optimize performance, we must avoid solutions that are too complex and which can complicate the code and reduce the maintainability of the app.

Multiple Choice Questions

1. Which is one of the main advantages of using Repository + Caching?
   a. Increase the complexity of the code.
   b. Reduce the number of network requests.
   c. Avoid garbage collection.
   d. Improve UI rendering.
2. Which tool is useful to identify memory leaks?
   a. Android Studio Profiler
   b. Systrace
   c. LeakCanary
   d. Firebase Performance Monitoring
3. Which design pattern is ideal to delegate operations to background threads?
   a. Singleton
   b. Adapter
   c. Decorator
   d. Command
4. Which is the main advantage of using Jetpack Compose instead of the traditional XML-based UI?
   a. It reduces the app startup times.
   b. It avoids memory leaks.
   c. It optimizes the rendering, updating only the necessary components.
   d. It ensures a faster image loading.

5. Which of the following tools allow us to monitor the battery consumption of an app?
    a. Memory Profiler
    b. Energy Profiler
    c. CPU Profiler
    d. Network Profiler

Answers

1. b
2. c
3. d
4. c
5. b

Questions

1. What are the main causes of memory leaks in an Android application? How can we solve them?
2. Explain how the Command pattern can be used to improve the performance of an app. Provide a practical example.
3. How does the data caching contribute to reducing the CPU usage, thus improving the performance?
4. Describe how Jetpack Compose improves the responsiveness of the UI with respect to traditional XML-based approach.
5. What are the profiling tools available in Android studio which we can use to analyze the performance of an app?

References

1. **Overview of measuring app performance | App quality | Android Developers** - https://developer.android.com/topic/performance/measuring-performance
2. **Android App Performance and Optimization | by Md Hanif | Simform Engineering | Medium** - https://medium.com/simform-engineering/android-app-performance-and-optimisation-26214d856fe4
3. **Overview of memory management | App quality | Android Developers** - https://developer.android.com/topic/performance/memory-overview
4. **Manage your app's memory | App quality | Android Developers** - https://developer.android.com/topic/performance/memory
5. **Record a system trace | Android Studio** - https://developer.android.com/studio/profile/cpu-profiler
6. **Power Profiler | Android Studio** - https://developer.android.com/studio/profile/power-profiler
7. **Capture a system trace on the command line | App quality | Android Developers** - https://developer.android.com/topic/performance/tracing/command-line
8. **Inspect GPU rendering speed and overdraw | App quality | Android Developers** - https://developer.android.com/topic/performance/rendering/inspect-gpu-rendering
9. **Find and Fix Memory Leaks with LeakCanary in Android** - https://www.youtube.com/watch?v=VvkRe9vP5Oc

Chapter 10
Testing with Design Patterns

Introduction

Testing is a crucial step if we want to provide quality and reliability to our Android applications. Inside a complex ecosystem such as mobile development, where there are many devices and configurations, verifying that every component works correctly is fundamental to offering an optimal user experience. However, testing is not only a matter of verifying the code, but a continuous process that improves the maintainability of the project and reduces the risks of critical bugs.

In this chapter, we will explore how design patterns improve the testing process, making the code more modular and testable. We will analyze how to write effective unit tests using **JUnit**, automate the testing of the user interface with **Espresso**, and simulate complex dependencies by using mocking tools such as **Mockito** and **MockK**. In the end, we will go through the best practices for writing tests.

This chapter will provide a practical guide for implementing effective tests and leveraging design patterns, helping us to build high-quality, robust, and maintainable Android applications.

Structure

In this chapter, we will cover the following topics:

- Testing in Android Development
- Unit Testing with JUnit
- UI Testing with Espresso
- Mocking with Mockito and MockK
- Best Practices for Testing

Testing in Android Development

Testing is a fundamental part of Android development. It ensures code quality, improves the maintainability of the project, and allows us to identify bugs and anomalies before they reach the final user. In a complex environment like Android, with different operating system versions, screen sizes, and hardware configurations, tests help to manage the variety and prevent unforeseen behaviors.

Types of Tests:

In Android, there are three main test categories, each with a specific role:

- **Unit tests**
    - Verify the behavior of single components and functions isolatedly.
    - Ideal to test business logic, such as math calculations or validation functions.
    - Use tools such as JUnit.
- **Integration tests**
    - Test the interaction between components, verifying that they correctly work together.
    - Might include calls to local databases or network APIs, often mimicking dependencies.
- **UI tests**
    - Concentrate on the user interface, verifying that the users can correctly interact with the application.
    - Simulate actions such as clicks, gestures, and text inputs.
    - Use tools such as Espresso.

Benefits of Testing:

Implementing a well-defined testing strategy offers numerous advantages:

- **Improved code quality**: Test reduces the chance of introducing bugs during the development or refactoring.
- **Greater maintainability**: It is easier to modify or extend the code without compromising other parts of the app if we have well-written tests.
- **Early issue detection**: Tests help to find errors or potential bugs before the code is delivered.
- **Facilitation in refactoring**: Automated tests give security during the improvement of existing code.

The Role of Design Patterns in Tests:

The use of well-designed design patterns can significantly simplify the testing process.

- **Modularity**: Patterns such as MVVM separate the business logic and the UI, making it easier to write unit tests for the ViewModel.
- **Isolation of responsibilities**: Patterns such as Factory or Singleton allow us to isolate the creation logic or instance management, thus facilitating tests.
- **Reduction of strict dependencies**: Patterns such as Dependency Injection allow us to replace real dependencies with mocks during tests, simplifying the simulation of complex behaviors.

Main Tools:

In Android, tests are written and managed using a combination of tools:

- **JUnit**
    - Standard for unit tests.
    - Allows us to verify a single function or class.
- **Espresso**
    - Used for UI tests.
    - Simulates the user interaction with the interface.
- **Mockito**
    - It is a mocking tool.
    - Allows us to simulate objects or behaviors to test single parts of the apps without involving the real dependencies.

A well-structured approach to testing is essential if we want to ensure the quality and reliability of our Android applications. Thanks to design patterns and modern tools, developers can write clear, modular, and maintainable tests, reducing the risk of bugs and improving the overall user experience.

Unit Testing with JUnit

Unit testing is the foundation of every effective testing strategy. It allows us to verify the behavior of single units of code, such as functions or classes, in isolation, ensuring that each component works correctly. In Android, the framework JUnit is the standard for writing unit tests, providing a powerful and flexible API to cover a wide range of use cases.

Why Use JUnit

What makes JUnit an essential tool for unit testing is its simplicity and compatibility. Here are some reasons to use it:

- Makes it easy to spot bugs inside single code units.
- Allows to write automated tests that can run with different inputs, including edge cases.
- It is directly integrated into Android Studio, making it simple to execute tests and analyze results.

Main Characteristics:

JUnit offers different useful functionalities to write effective unit tests:

- **Assertions**: Verify that a condition is true, otherwise they throw an exception that causes the failure of the test. For example, **`assertEquals`** verifies that two values are equal.
- **Annotations**: We can use **`@Test`**, **`@Before`**, **`@After`** and other keywords to handle the test execution and the configuration of the test.
- **Parameterized Tests**: This allows us to execute the same test with different values, thus reducing the redundancy of the code.

How Design Patterns Improve Testability

When well implemented, design patterns enhance testability by promoting modular, decoupled, and reusable code. This makes it easier to isolate components and write effective unit tests.

Writing Unit Tests for Design Patterns

Unit testing is essential to ensure that design patterns are correctly implemented and function as expected. In this section, we will revisit some of the unit tests we have written for design patterns in previous chapters.

1. **Testing Singleton**

Singleton ensures that one class has only one instance at a given time. In the unit tests, it is important to verify that:

- The instance is unique.
- The behavior of the class remains consistent.

Example from *Chapter 3, Creational Patterns*:

```
object NetworkClient {
    fun sendNetworkRequest(): Int {
        // Perform network request
        return 0
```

```
    }
}

class SingletonTest {
@Test
fun singletonTest() {
    val instance1 = NetworkClient
    val instance2 = NetworkClient
    assert(instance1 == instance2)
}


@Test
fun sendNetworkRequestTest() {
    val response = NetworkClient.sendNetworkRequest()
    assert(response == 0)
}
}
```

2. **Testing Factory**

Factory centralized the creation of the objects. Inside tests, we verify that:

- The factory creates the correct objects.
- Created objects have the expected behavior.

Example from *Chapter 3*, *Creational Patterns*:

```
class EntityFactory {
    companion object {
        fun createEntity(type: String): Entity {
            return when(type) {
                "concreteEntity1" -> ConcreteEntity1()
                "concreteEntityN" -> ConcreteEntityN()
                else -> throw IllegalArgumentException("Unknown
type")
            }
        }
    }
}

class FactoryTest {
      @Test
      fun createConcreteEntityTest() {
          val entity = EntityFactory.createEntity("concrete
Entity1")
          assert(entity is ConcreteEntity1)
```

```
            val entity = EntityFactory.createEntity("concrete
EntityN")
    assert(entity is ConcreteEntityN)
}

@Test(expected = IllegalArgumentException::class)
fun createUnknownEntityTest() {
    EntityFactory.createEntity("unknownEntity")
}
}
```

Parameterized tests with JUnit

In order to reduce redundant code, there is an annotation that allows us to tell the framework that we want to run a test more than once, each time with different input values.

Example:

```
@ParameterizedTest
@ValueSource(strings = ["concreteEntity1", "concreteEntity2",
"concreteEntityN"])
fun `test factory with multiple inputs`(input: String) {
    val entity = EntityFactory.createEntity(input)
    assertNotNull(entity) // Verifies that the factory always
create a valid object
}
```

Best Practices for Unit Tests:

- **Isolate code to test**: Avoid external dependencies such as databases or networks in unit tests.
- **Write modular tests**: Each test should verify only a single aspect of the code.
- **Keep tests updated**: When the code changes, we must update tests accordingly.

JUnit is a powerful tool to provide code quality in Android applications. By testing patterns such as Singleton and Factory, we can verify that the architectural foundations of the project are solid and functional. A well-defined unit testing strategy reduces bugs and makes it easy to maintain the code in the long term.

UI Testing with Espresso

Testing the user interface (UI) is very important to ensure that the users will be able to interact with the application without problems. Espresso, a framework provided by Google, is a powerful tool to write UI tests on Android. It allows us to simulate user interactions, verify UI states, and make sure that the app responds correctly in different scenarios.

Advantages of using Espresso:

Espresso is designed specifically to test user interactions in Android applications. Among its main advantages are:

- **Automation of user actions**: It simulates clicks, scrolling, text inputs, and more.
- **Automated synchronization**: It is automatically synchronized with the main thread, making tests more reliable.
- **Simple and readable API**: The code of the tests is intuitive and easy to write.

How Espresso Works

Espresso uses an architecture which is based on three main components:

- **ViewMatchers**: Detect the UI elements, for example, **`withId(R.id.button)`**.
- **ViewActions**: Execute actions on the UI elements, for example, **`click()`**.
- **ViewAssertions**: Verify the UI state, for example, **`matches(isDisplayed())`**.

Writing UI Tests with Espresso

Espresso is ideal for testing app activities built with architectural design patterns such as MVVM or MVI, which separate the business logic and the UI, making tests more modular and maintainable.

1. **Test basic interactions**

Suppose we have a button with the id **`myButton`**, and when the user clicks it, the textview with the id **`myTextView`** is updated, showing the word "**`Updated`**". This example shows how to test it.

```
@Test
fun `test button click updates text`() {
    // Launch the Activity
    val activityScenario = ActivityScenario.launch(MainActivity
::class.java)

    // Find the button and click it
    onView(withId(R.id.myButton)).perform(click())

    // Verify that the text has been updated
    onView(withId(R.id.myTextView)).check(matches(withText
("Updated")))
}
```

2. **Test Dynamic Lists (`RecyclerView` or `LazyColumn`)**

Dynamic lists are a fundamental part of Android applications. Espresso provides a way to test specific elements in a list. In the following example, an activity called

MainActivity is launched, and a list of items is displayed. The test verifies that when the user clicks on the item at position 2, a new activity containing the TextView with ID **detailTextView** is displayed.

```
@Test
fun `test recycler view item click`() {
    val activityScenario = ActivityScenario.launch(MainActivity
::class.java)

    // Scroll to the specific item in the RecyclerView and click
it
    onView(withId(R.id.recyclerView)).perform(
        RecyclerViewActions.actionOnItemAtPosition<MyAdapter.
ViewHolder>(2, click()))

    // Verify that the new Activity has been launched
    onView(withId(R.id.detailTextView)).check(matches
(isDisplayed()))
}
```

3. **Testing UI based on MVVM**

When we use MVVM, the UI strictly depends on the state of the ViewModel. Espresso can verify that the changes on the ViewModel correctly reflect on the UI.

```
@Test
fun `test live data updates UI`() {
    val activityScenario = ActivityScenario.launch(MainActivity
::class.java)

    // Simulate an action which updates the data
    onView(withId(R.id.loadDataButton)).perform(click())

    // Verify that the new state is visualized
    onView(withId(R.id.dataTextView)).check(matches(withText("New
Data")))
}
```

In the preceding example, the test performs a click on **loadDataButton**, which we assume is responsible for uploading the data on the ViewModel, and then it checks if the update on the ViewModel is reflected on **dataTextView**.

4. **Testing accessibility**

Espresso can also be used to verify that the app is compliant with accessibility guidelines, such as the addition of textual descriptions to visual content.

```
@Test
fun `test content description for accessibility`() {
```

```
    onView(withId(R.id.imageView)).check(matches(withContent
Description("Image Description")))
}
```

Best Practices for UI Testing:

- **Avoid dependency on external data**: Use mock or default data to provide consistency to tests.
- **Keep tests modular**: Do not verify multiple functionalities in a single test.
- **Use idling resources**: To synchronize asynchronous operation in order to prevent failures due to loading times.

Espresso is an essential tool to ensure that the UI of Android applications is functional, responsive, and accessible. Thanks to its support for design patterns such as MVVM and its ability to simulate complex user interactions, Espresso allows us to create reliable UI tests which improves the overall quality and the user experience.

Mocking with Mockito and MockK

Mocking is an important testing technique that allows us to simulate the behavior of complex objects or real components, simplifying the testing of complex units without unwanted dependencies. In Android, Mockito is one of the most used tools to create mocks and verify interaction between objects. In modern Android development, the framework MockK offers advanced functionalities that better integrate with the specific features of Kotlin.

Why Use Mocking

Mocking is useful for:

- **Isolate the code to test**: It avoids external dependencies such as databases, API, or filesystems that influence the test.
- **Simulate complex behaviors**: We can mock components such as repositories, API, or ViewModels.
- **Verify interactions**: We can check whether a method is called for and the parameters it uses.

Main features of Mockito

Mockito provides multiple tools for marking, such as:

- **Mocking of objects**: Simulate the behavior of objects or classes.
- **Verification of interactions**: Check if a method has been called for and how many times.
- **Stubbing**: Define the behavior of specific methods.

Example of a test with Mockito:

```
// Class to test
class DataFetcher(private val repository: Repository) {
    fun fetchData(): String {
        return repository.getData() ?: "Default Data"
    }
}

// Test with Mockito
class DataFetcherTest {

    @Test
    fun `test fetchData with mock repository`() {
        val repository = mock(Repository::class.java)
        `when`(repository.getData()).thenReturn("Mock Data")

        val dataFetcher = DataFetcher(repository)
        val result = dataFetcher.fetchData()

        // Verify the behavior
        assertEquals("Mock Data", result)
        // Verify that the method has been called
        verify(repository).getData()
    }
}
```

MockK: Mocking for Kotlin

Since Mockito is based on Java, there is an emerging framework that basically does the same things as Mockito, but it is optimized for Kotlin. This framework is called MockK, and it is designed to leverage the features of the language, such as final classes, extension functions, and coroutines.

Features of MockK:

- Mock of final classes and functions.
- Support for **suspend** methods and coroutines.
- Intuitive domain-specific language (DSL) to verify interactions and define behaviors.

In the preceding example, we can replace Mockito with MockK:

```
// Test with MockK
class DataProcessorTest {

    @Test
    fun `test processData with MockK`() {
```

```
            val repository = mockk<Repository>()
            every { repository.getData() } returns "MockK Data"

            val dataProcessor = DataProcessor(repository)
            val result = runBlocking { dataProcessor.processData() }

            // Verify the result
            assertEquals("MockK Data", result)
            // Verify the interaction
            verify { repository.getData() }
        }
    }
```

Best Practices for Mocking:

- **Mock only what is needed**: Avoid mocking all the dependencies, we must concentrate only on the necessary ones.
- **Verify critical interactions**: Check that the key methods are called for with the correct parameters.
- **Use mocking to isolate**: Simulate only the external dependencies, leaving unaltered the logic of the behavior that is tested.

Mocking is a powerful tool to isolate and test units of code, especially in modular applications that use design patterns such as Repository or MVVM. Both Mockito and MockK offer advanced features to create reliable and maintainable tests. Choosing the right framework depends on the specific needs of the project and the language used, but both represent essential tools for writing high-quality tests.

Best Practices for Testing

Writing effective tests is as important as writing quality code. A good testing strategy improves the maintainability of the project, reducing the risk of bugs and making the code more robust. Some of the best practices to optimize the testing process in Android development are as follows, with particular attention to the design patterns.

Plan the testing strategy

Before starting to write tests, we should define a strategy that covers:

- **Unit tests** to verify single units of code.
- **Integration tests** to verify the interaction between components.
- **UI tests** to simulate the user experience.

We should also concentrate on which parts of the code should be tested and define priorities based on the complexity and criticality of the components.

Leverage design patterns

Design patterns, if used correctly, help us simplify the testing process:

- **MVVM** isolates the presentation logic in the ViewModel, making it simpler to test state changes.
- **Repository** lets us easily mock data searches such as databases or network API.
- **Factory** makes it easy to create mock objects for specific tests.

Use modern tools

We should choose the right tools based on the specific needs of our projects:

- **JUnit** for unit tests, with features such as parameterize the tests and stubbing.
- **Espresso** for UI tests to simulate real user interactions.
- **Mockito and MockK** to create mock objects and verify interactions.
- **Android Studio Profiler** to analyze the performance of the test.

Isolate dependencies

- Use mocking to simulate external dependencies such as databases, APIs, or system resources.
- Implement the Dependency Injection pattern to easily pass real dependencies or mocks.
- Avoid tests that require physical resources, such as a real network connection or a specific physical device.

Keep tests modular

Each test should concentrate only on a single use case:

- Write small and comprehensive tests.
- Avoid a test to be dependent on other tests.
- Make tests reusable for similar components.

Automate tests

Integrate tests in the CI/CD pipeline to automatically execute:

- Unit test every time a new commit is pushed.
- Integration tests for every main build.
- UI test before each release.

Tools such as GitHub Actions, Jenkins, or Gitlab CI simplify the testing automation.

Write updatable and accessible tests

- Use clear names for tests, such as **`test_fetchData_returnsValidResult`**, that describe their purpose.
- Update the tests every time the code is changed to avoid outdated or invalid tests.
- Document complex tests to make it easy to understand them.

Test borderline cases

We should make sure to cover:

- Borderline or invalid inputs.
- Behaviors in the condition of limited resources, such as low memory or poor network connectivity.
- Unexpected states or errors, such as a network not available.

Prioritize critical tests

It is better to concentrate on the most important part of the app:

- Core features that are essential to the purpose of the app.
- Components that have a high impact on the user experience, such as the main UI.
- Parts of the code that interact with external dependencies, such as APIs or databases.

Monitor the results

- Analyze test reports to detect the tests that fail frequently.
- Optimize low and unreliable tests.
- Use code coverage to verify that the test covers the most important parts of the app.

Following best practices will help us to write more effective, modular, and maintainable tests, ensuring, at the same time, a high level of quality to our Android application. By combining design patterns and modern tools, the test process becomes smoother and more integrated, improving productivity and reducing the risk of bugs in the final phases of development.

Conclusion

Testing is an indispensable part of the development of high-quality Android applications, and the adoption of design patterns makes this process a lot easier. In this chapter, we have explored how tools such as JUnit, Espresso, Mockito, and MockK can be used to verify the behavior of the code, from the small unit to the complete UI.

Through practical examples, we have demonstrated how design patterns improve modularity and are able to isolate units of code, making tests more reliable and maintainable. We have also seen how patterns such as MVVM can improve the testing of the business logic, while patterns such as Repository or Factory allow us to easily create mockable dependencies.

This chapter has underlined the importance of a structured approach to testing, combining manual and automated tests to provide reliability. The introduction of best practices and advanced tools allows us to significantly reduce the risk of bugs, improving the overall quality of the application.

In conclusion, testing is not only a development phase but a continuous process that ensures stability, scalability, and a high quality user experience. By using the techniques explored in this chapter, we can integrate testing into our development flow and take full advantage of design patterns to build robust and reliable Android applications.

In the next chapter, we will explore how to refactor code with design patterns.

Points to Remember

- **Testing ensures quality and reliability**: Using automated tests to verify the code helps to detect the bugs earlier, reducing costs, and improving user experience.
- **Design patterns make testing easy**: Patterns such as MVVM and Repository isolate the business logic and the UI, making tests simpler and more modular.
- **JUnit is the standard for unit tests**: It allows us to verify single functions or components in isolation, improving maintainability and reducing bugs.
- **Espresso automates UI tests**: It simulates real user interactions, such as clicks and scrolling, ensuring that the UI responds correctly in various scenarios.
- **Mockito and MockK simplify mocking**: They allow us to simulate complex dependencies, like APIs or databases, isolating the code to test.
- **Modular tests improve readability**: Tests should concentrate only on a single use case, avoiding dependencies between tests.
- **Execute tests regularly during development**: We should plan and execute tests iteratively, ensuring that every new functionality or modification is verified before proceeding with the rest of the project.
- **Verify borderline cases and invalid inputs**: Tests should cover extreme situations or unexpected states to ensure robustness.

- **Keeping tests updated is essential**: When the code changes, tests must be reviewed to reflect the changes and avoid outdated results.
- **Modern tools make testing more efficient**: Using a combination of JUnit, Espresso, Mockito, and MockK to face every level of testing, from single components to the complete UI.

Multiple Choice Questions

1. Which design patterns simplify the testing of business logic?
   a. MVVM
   b. Singleton
   c. Decorator
   d. Adapter
2. Which tool is mainly used to test user interface?
   a. JUnit
   b. Espresso
   c. Mockito
   d. MockK
3. Which of the following options correctly describes an advantage of mocking?
   a. Allows to execute tests on real devices.
   b. Removes the need to write unit tests.
   c. Simulates external dependencies.
   d. Improves UI performance.
4. Which annotation is used by JUnit to define a test method?
   a. @Mock
   b. @RunWith
   c. @Test
   d. @Before

5. Which approach should be taken to test a dynamic list such as RecyclerView?
    a. Use JUnit to verify the data in the list.
    b. Write UI tests with Espresso to simulate the scrolling and the interaction with the elements.
    c. Mocking every single element of the list with Mockito.
    d. Test the list directly with the profiling tools.

Answers

1. a
2. b
3. c
4. c
5. b

Questions

1. How do design patterns such as MVVM and Repository simplify the testing process in an Android app?
2. What is the difference between unit tests, integration tests, and UI tests?
3. Explain how to use Mockito or MockK to simulate complex dependencies in a unit test.
4. What are the best practices to keep tests modular and maintainable in an Android Project?
5. How does Espresso allow us to verify that the UI responds correctly to user interactions?

References

1. **Test apps on Android** - https://developer.android.com/training/testing
2. **Fundamentals of testing Android apps** - https://developer.android.com/training/testing/fundamentals
3. **Testing an Android Application with Example - GeeksforGeeks** - https://www.geeksforgeeks.org/testing-an-android-application-with-example/

4. **Build local unit tests | Android Developers** - https://developer.android.com/training/testing/local-tests
5. **Build instrumented tests | Android Developers** - https://developer.android.com/training/testing/instrumented-tests
6. **Automate UI tests | Android Developers** - https://developer.android.com/training/testing/ui-tests
7. **Espresso | Android Developers** - https://developer.android.com/training/testing/espresso
8. **The Ultimate Guide to Android Testing (Unit Tests, UI Tests, End-to-End Tests) - Clean Architectur**e - https://www.youtube.com/watch?v=nDCCwyS0_MQ

Chapter 11
Refactoring with Design Patterns

Introduction

Over the life of a software project, the code could become complex, hard to read and maintain, mainly when it grows rapidly or it is modified by multiple developers. This issue can be solved through a process called **refactoring**.

We begin this chapter with an introduction about refactoring. We will then learn how to use design patterns during this process to remedy structural problems and improve readability, modularity, and scalability of the code. We will start learning how to identify **code smells**, the signals that help us to detect where the code needs to be refactored. Subsequently, we will see how established design patterns such as MVVM and Builder are able to transform the complex code into a robust and clean code base.

In addition to practical examples, we will also explore the best practices for refactoring, which will help us to execute the process in a safe and incremental way. This chapter will provide us the tools and techniques we need to improve our code, making it not only functional, but also valuable.

Structure

In this chapter, we will cover the following topics:

- Introduction to Refactoring
- Benefits of Refactoring with Design Patterns
- Identify Code Smells
- Refactoring Examples Using Common Patterns
- Best Practices for Refactoring

Introduction to Refactoring

Refactoring is a process of improving the internal structure of an existing code without modifying the external behavior. It is an essential practice in software development to ensure that the code remains readable, maintainable, and scalable over time, especially in projects which are in continuous evolution.

In Android projects, refactoring could help to handle common situations such as the duplicated code, strong coupling between components, or functions whose responsibilities are unclear. These issues not only make it hard to add new functionalities, but also increase the risk of introducing bugs during modifications.

Design patterns play a crucial role in refactoring. Introducing established patterns such as Singleton, Factory or Dependency Injection during refactoring can solve code smells (structural anomalies) and improve the overall quality of the code. These patterns provide standard solutions to common problems, making it easy to organize and extend the project.

Benefits of Refactoring with Design Patterns

Performing refactoring with design patterns is not only a practice to improve the code, but an investment that ensures a solid and maintainable structure for the future. Applying design patterns during refactoring helps to solve structural problems, improves the readability, and offers a clear model for the development of new functionalities.

Maintainability Improvement

Introducing design patterns during refactoring helps to separate responsibilities, reducing the coupling between components.

This makes it easier to:

- Modify the code without altering other parts of the app.
- Find and correct bugs, thanks to a more readable and clearer structure.

Example: Using the pattern MVVM in a complex screen allows us to separate the business logic and the UI, making future changes easier.

Scalability Increment

Over time, every project tends to grow in terms of functionalities and complexity.

Design patterns such as Factory or Facade make the code more scalable, allowing us to add new functionalities without having to rewrite existing parts.

Example: While developing an application that used the pattern Factory to handle the creation of objects, we can easily add new types of objects without modifying the existing code.

Greater Modularity

Refactoring with design patterns promotes the creation of independent modules that can be reused in other parts of the same project, or even in separate projects. Patterns such as Observer or Strategy favors a modular approach.

Example: A notification system implemented using Observer allows us to add new listeners incrementally, without modifying the code that already exists.

Easier Testing

Design patterns that are well implemented are able to simplify the testing. Patterns like Repository and Dependency Injection allow us to isolate the dependencies and easily mock the components during the tests.

Example: Mocking a Repository to test a Model, which is part of the pattern MVVM, allows us to verify the business logic without depending on a real database.

Performance Improvement

Some design patterns help to optimize the code in order to improve the overall performance of the app. Patterns such as Caching or Proxy are able to reduce the workload on the resources, such as networks or databases.

Example: A Proxy that implements data caching avoids to perform redundant requests to the server, improving the responsiveness of the app.

Recognizability and Standardization

Using established design patterns makes the code more recognizable and standardized. This fact makes the collaboration between developers easier, reducing the time spent to understand the project and contribute to it.

Example: A project that uses the pattern Singleton to manage shared resources (for example, network clients) follows a comprehensive standard for everyone who has familiarity with the pattern.

Carrying out refactoring with design patterns not only improves the existing code, but also contributes to creating a solid basis for future development. Maintainability, modularity, scalability, and testability are only some of the benefits that make refectoring with design patterns a mandatory strategy for every ambitious Android project. Implementing these techniques means to invest in the longevity and quality of the software.

Identify Code Smells

A code smell is an indication that the code can be improved to make it more readable, maintainable, and efficient. It is important to be cautious that code smells are not bugs. Sometimes, the code works currently, but it presents structural problems which can cause difficulties in the long term, such as the occurrence of bugs, challenges in testing, or complexity in adding new functionalities.

In this section, we will explore how to identify the main types of code smells and how to address them using refactoring with design patterns.

Code Duplication

Description: Similar or identical blocks of code which are repeated in different parts of the project. This problem makes it hard to bring modifications, because every occurrence of the duplicated code has to be updated manually.

Example:

In the following code, if we want to switch from the calculation of the price to the calculation of the weight, we need to replace all the occurrences of **calculateTotalPrice()** to **calculateTotalWeight()**. The number of these occurrences can be very high.

```
fun calculateTotalPrice(items: List<Item>): Double {
    return items.sumOf { it.price }
}

fun calculateTotalWeight(items: List<Item>): Double {
    return items.sumOf { it.weight }
}
```

Solution with design patterns:

Use the Strategy pattern to abstract the common behavior. The clients call the function **CalculationStrategy.calculate()**, which does not depend on the underlying implementation, meaning that we are able to change implementation without affecting the clients.

```
interface CalculationStrategy {
    fun calculate(items: List<Item>): Double
```

```
}
class PriceCalculation : CalculationStrategy {
    override fun calculate(items: List<Item>): Double = items.
sumOf { it.price }
}

class WeightCalculation : CalculationStrategy {
    override fun calculate(items: List<Item>): Double = items.
sumOf { it.weight }
}
```

Function/Classes With Too Many Responsibilities

Description: A class or a function which manages more responsibilities than it should, violating the Single Responsibility Principle (SRP). This makes the code hard to read, test, and maintain.

Example:

```
class OrderManager {
    fun placeOrder(order: Order) {
        // Logic to save the order
        // Logic to send a notification
        // Logic to generate the invoice
    }
}
```

Solution with design patterns:

Use the Facade pattern to centralize the access to the different responsibilities, delegating each step to a separate class.

```
class OrderManager(
    private val orderRepository: OrderRepository,
    private val notificationService: NotificationService,
    private val invoiceService: InvoiceService
) {
    fun placeOrder(order: Order) {
        orderRepository.save(order)
        notificationService.notify(order)
        invoiceService.generate(order)
    }
}
```

Strong Coupling

Description: Class of functions that strictly depend on each other, making the code rigid and hard to modify.

Example:

```
class ReportGenerator {
    private val database = DatabaseConnection()

    fun generateReport() {
        database.query("SELECT * FROM reports")
    }
}
```

Solution with design patterns:

Use the Dependency Injection pattern to make the code more flexible.

```
class ReportGenerator(private val database: DatabaseConnection) {
    fun generateReport() {
        database.query("SELECT * FROM reports")
    }
}
```

Large Methods or Classes

Description: Functions or classes that contain too much logic in a single block, making the code hard to read and test.

Example:

```
fun processOrder(order: Order) {
    validateOrder(order)
    calculateTotal(order)
    applyDiscount(order)
    saveOrder(order)
    sendNotification(order)
}
```

Solution with design patterns:

Use the Chain of Responsibility pattern to divide the logic in modular steps.

```
interface OrderProcessor {
    fun process(order: Order)
}

class ValidationProcessor : OrderProcessor {
    override fun process(order: Order) {
```

```
            // Logic for validation
        }
    }


    class DiscountProcessor : OrderProcessor {
        override fun process(order: Order) {
            // Logic to apply discounts
        }
    }
```

Lack of Abstraction

Description: A code that directly uses concrete implementations, making it hard to replace or modify the behavior.

Example:

```
    fun sendReport(report: PDFReport) {
        report.generatePDF()
    }
```

Solution with design patterns:

Use the Factory pattern to abstract the creation of objects:

```
    interface Report {
        fun generate()
    }

    class PDFReport : Report {
        override fun generate() {
            // Logic to generate PDF
        }
    }

    class ReportFactory {
        fun createReport(type: String): Report {
            return when (type) {
                "PDF" -> PDFReport()
                else -> throw IllegalArgumentException("Unsupported
    type")
            }
        }
    }
```

Recognizing code smells is the first step towards an improvement of the quality of the code. Issues such as code duplication, strong coupling, and unclear responsibilities can be addressed or prevented by using design patterns. Implementing these solutions during refactoring allows us to build a more readable, modular, and maintainable code, ready to face future needs.

Refactoring Examples Using Common Patterns

In this section, we will explore concrete examples on how to apply design patterns to refactoring code affected by too much complexity and poor readability. Each example takes into examination a real scenario and shows how the use of patterns such as MVVM, Builder, Command, and Decorator are able to transform an existing code base into a structure which is more modular, scalable, and easy to test.

Refactoring of an User Interface with MVVM

The pattern MVVM (Model-View-ViewModel) separates the business logic, the presentation logic, and the UI implementation, promoting modularity, easy testing, and maintainability of the code. In this example, we will perform a refactoring of the screen that directly handles the business logic inside the composable. We will apply MVVM to move the business logic into the Model and the presentation logic inside the ViewModel, leaving only the composable as responsible for implementing the View.

Before Refactoring

In the initial version, the logic for loading and manipulating the data is located inside the composable. This creates a strong coupling between the UI and the business logic, making the code hard to maintain and test.

```
@Composable
fun UserScreen() {
    var users by remember { mutableStateOf(emptyList<User>()) }
    var isLoading by remember { mutableStateOf(true) }

    LaunchedEffect(Unit) {
        isLoading = true
        try {
            // Business logic inside UI
            users = fetchUsersFromNetwork()
        } catch (e: Exception) {
            // Error handling
        } finally {
            isLoading = false
        }
    }
```

```
        if (isLoading) {
            CircularProgressIndicator()
        } else {
            LazyColumn {
                items(users) { user ->
                    Text(text = user.name)
                }
            }
        }
    }

    data class User(val name: String)

    suspend fun fetchUsersFromNetwork(): List<User> {
        // Business logic: simulation of a network request
        return listOf(User("Alice"), User("Bob"))
    }
```

Identified problems:

- **Strong coupling**: Network logic, which is part of the business logic, is implemented inside the UI (View).
- **Testing difficulty**: It is not possible to test the logic for loading the data in isolation.
- **Lack of reusability**: The composable cannot be reused without replicating the logic.

After Refactoring

With MVVM, we create the Model to hold the business logic and the ViewModel to manage the presentation logic. With these changes, the composable will be only responsible for displaying the data retrieved from the observable states provided by the ViewModel, improving the principle of loose coupling.

Model: The model deals with data management, which is the business logic. In this case, it simulates an access to a network data source.

```
data class User(val name: String)

class UserRepository {
    suspend fun fetchUsers(): List<User> {
        // Simulation of a network request
        return listOf(User("Alice"), User("Bob"))
    }
}
```

ViewModel: The ViewModel coordinates the retrieving of the data from the model (**UserRepository**) and exposes them to the UI in an observable state.

```
class UserViewModel(private val repository: UserRepository) :
ViewModel() {
    private val _users = MutableStateFlow<List<User>>(emptyL-
ist())
    val users: StateFlow<List<User>> = _users

    private val _isLoading = MutableStateFlow(true)
    val isLoading: StateFlow<Boolean> = _isLoading

    init {
        repository.fetchUsers()
    }

    private fun fetchUsers() {
        viewModelScope.launch {
            _isLoading.value = true
            try {
                _users.value = repository.fetchUsers()
            } catch (e: Exception) {
                // Error handling
                _users.value = emptyList()
            } finally {
                _isLoading.value = false
            }
        }
    }
}
```

View: The composable is now leaner because it was freed from the code that is not strictly responsible for rendering the UI.

```
@Composable
fun UserScreen(viewModel: UserViewModel = viewModel()) {
    val users by viewModel.users.collectAsState()
    val isLoading by viewModel.isLoading.collectAsState()

    if (isLoading) {
        CircularProgressIndicator()
    } else {
        LazyColumn {
            items(users) { user ->
                Text(text = user.name)
            }
        }
```

```
    }
}
```

Benefits gained:

- **Separation of concerns**: The business logic resides in the Model, the ViewModel coordinates the data and transforms them in a state suitable for the View, and the View deals only with the presentation.
- **Improved testability**: ViewModel can be tested mocking the Model, and the Model can be tested isolatedly.
- **Maintainability and reusability**: The Model can be reused in other parts of the app or been modified without impacting the View, and the View is completely decoupled from the business logic.

This refactoring shows how MVVM, combined with Jetpack Compose, is able to significantly improve the quality and maintainability of the code in a modern Android application.

Simplify a Complex Class with Builder

When a class requires a lot of parameters, the use of traditional constructors can make the code cumbersome and hard to manage, especially if some parameters are optional or have default values. The Builder pattern is an effective solution to separate the building logic from the object representation, improving the readability, flexibility, and maintainability of the code. In this example, we will perform a refactoring on a class that uses an overloaded and barely readable constructor, providing to it a clearer and modular structure.

Before Refactoring

As shown in the following code, we have a class that requires a lot of input parameters.

```
class UserProfile(
    val name: String,
    val age: Int,
    val email: String,
    val phone: String?,
    val address: String?
)

// Usage
fun createUser(): UserProfile {
    return UserProfile(
        name = "Lorenzo",
        age = 30,
        email = "lorenzo@example.com",
```

```
            phone = null,
            address = "123 Main St"
        )
    }
```

Identified problems:

- **Bulky constructor**: Passing all the parameters, even the optional ones, makes the code harder to read.
- **Hard to modify**: Adding or removing parameters requires modifications to the constructors and to every piece of code that uses it.
- **Low flexibility**: It is not possible to build the object incrementally.

After Refactoring

We can introduce a class **`Builder`** inside our class **`UserProfile`** to address the identified problems.

```
class UserProfile private constructor(
    val name: String,
    val age: Int,
    val email: String,
    val phone: String?,
    val address: String?
) {
    data class Builder(
        var name: String = "",
        var age: Int = 0,
        var email: String = "",
        var phone: String? = null,
        var address: String? = null
    ) {
        fun setName(name: String) = apply { this.name = name }
        fun setAge(age: Int) = apply { this.age = age }
        fun setEmail(email: String) = apply { this.email = email
}
        fun setPhone(phone: String?) = apply { this.phone = phone
}
        fun setAddress(address: String?) = apply { this.address =
address }

        fun build() = UserProfile(name, age, email, phone, ad-
dress)
    }
}
```

```
// Usage
fun createUser(): UserProfile {
    return UserProfile.Builder()
        .setName("Lorenzo")
        .setAge(30)
        .setEmail("lorenzo@example.com")
        .setAddress("123 Main St")
        .build()
}
```

Benefits gained:

- **Improved readability**: The code is more readable, thanks to the descriptive methods of the Builder.
- **Flexibility**: It is possible to build the object incrementally, passing only the necessary parameters.
- **Maintainability**: Adding or removing parameters become easier, as the Builder interface is more modular than the original constructor.

This example has shown how the Builder pattern can be used to improve the readability and the flexibility of the code, making it less error prone and easier to manage.

Introduction of Command for Asynchronous Operations

Complex asynchronous operations, such as batch data processing or the execution of scheduled tasks, could become difficult to manage and test when they are written in a sequential way or encapsulated in a single method. The Command pattern offers an elegant solution to represent each operation as an independent object, encapsulating the execution logic and allowing us to enqueue, reorder, and execute tasks in a dynamic way.

In this example, we will see how to refactor a system that manages asynchronous operations into a more modular and scalable structure using the Command pattern.

Before Refactoring

A single function manages the processing of multiple tasks sequentially or in parallel. The logic is written in a monolithic way, making it difficult to add new types of tasks or modify the sequence of the operations.

```
suspend fun processTasks() {
    val data = fetchDataFromNetwork()
    saveDataToDatabase(data)
    sendNotification("Processing complete")
}
```

```
fun fetchDataFromNetwork(): List<String> {
    // Simulate a network request
    return listOf("item1", "item2")
}

fun saveDataToDatabase(data: List<String>) {
    // Logic to save to database
}

fun sendNotification(message: String) {
    // Logic to send a notification
}
```

Identified problems:

- **Strong coupling**: All the operations are located inside a single method, making it hard to separate and reorder tasks.
- **Testing difficulty**: It is not possible to test each operation individually without executing the entire process.
- **Poor extensibility**: Adding new tasks requires us to perform modifications directly to the method, increasing the risk of introducing bugs.

After Refactoring

With the Command pattern, operations are represented as individual objects that share a common interface. This allows us to enqueue, execute, and reorder the tasks without modifying the main logic.

```
// Command pattern interface
interface Command {
    suspend fun execute()
}

// Class to share data between commands
class CommandContext {
    var data: List<String>? = null
}

// Implementation of the commands
class FetchDataCommand(private val context: CommandContext) :
Command {

    override suspend fun execute() {
        context.data = fetchDataFromNetwork()
        println("Data loaded: ${context.data}")
    }
```

```
    private suspend fun fetchDataFromNetwork(): List<String> {
        // Simulate a network request
        delay(2000)
        return listOf("item1", "item2")
    }
}

class SaveDataCommand(private val context: CommandContext) :
Command {

    override suspend fun execute() {
        val data = context.data ?: throw IllegalStateException
("No data available")
        saveDataToDatabase(data)
        println("Data saved on database")
    }

    private suspend fun saveDataToDatabase(data: List<String>) {
        // Simulate logic to save to database
        delay(1000)
    }
}

class SendNotificationCommand(private val message: String) :
Command {

    override suspend fun execute() {
        sendNotification(message)
        println("Notification sent: $message")
    }

    private suspend fun sendNotification(message: String) {
        // Simulate logic to send a notification
        delay(500)
    }

}

// Command Manager
class CommandExecutor(context1: CommandContext) {
    private val commands = mutableListOf<Command>()

    fun addCommand(command: Command) {
        commands.add(command)
    }
```

```
    suspend fun executeAll() {
        for (command in commands) {
            command.execute()
        }
    }
}

// Usage
fun main() = runBlocking {
    val context = CommandContext()
    val executor = CommandExecutor(context)

    executor.addCommand(FetchDataCommand(context))
    executor.addCommand(SaveDataCommand(context))
    executor.addCommand(SendNotificationCommand("Processing
complete"))

    executor.executeAll()
}
```

Benefits gained:

- **Modularity**: Each task is isolated in a dedicated class, making the code more readable and maintainable.
- **Reusability**: The commands can be used in other parts of the app or enqueued dynamically.
- **Improved Testability**: Each command can be tested individually, simplifying the debugging.
- **Extensibility**: New tasks can be added without modifying the existing logic, instead, we only need to create new commands.

Thanks to the introduction of the Command pattern, the code has become more robust and flexible, allowing us to handle asynchronous operations in a structured and scalable way. This approach is particularly useful in applications which perform complex and repetitive tasks.

Functionality Extension with Decorator

When we need to dynamically extend the functionalities of an object without modifying the original class or creating complex hierarchies, the Decorator pattern represents a flexible and elegant solution. It allows us to decorate an object, assigning to it new responsibilities and encapsulating the original object inside one or more decorators.

In this example, we will see how to refactor a system which uses methods added dynamically to a main class, introducing Decorator to separate the functionalities and make the code more modular.

Before Refactoring

A main class contains multiple methods that implement additional functionalities. As the functionalities grow, the class becomes cumbersome and hard to maintain.

```
class DataProcessor {
    fun processData(data: String): String {
        return data.uppercase()
    }

    fun processDataWithLogging(data: String): String {
        println("Processing data: $data")
        return data.uppercase()
    }

    fun processDataWithEncryption(data: String): String {
        // Naive encryption for demonstration purpose
        val encryptedData = StringBuilder()
        for (char in data) {
            encryptedData.append(char + 1)
        }

        return encryptedData
    }
}
```

Identified problems:

- **Monolithic class**: All the functionalities are centralized in a single class, making the code hard to maintain.
- **Low flexibility**: Adding new functionalities requires a direct modification of the class, which implies the risk of introducing bugs.
- **Reuse difficulty**: Functionalities cannot be dynamically combined together (for example, combining logging with encryption).

After Refactoring

With the Decorator pattern, each functionality is encapsulated in a standalone decorator which can be dynamically combined with others.

```
interface DataProcessor {
    fun process(data: String): String
}
```

```
class BasicDataProcessor : DataProcessor {
    override fun process(data: String): String {
        return data.uppercase()
    }
}

// Decorators
// Each decorator adds a new functionality, delegating the rest
to the wrapped object.

class LoggingDecorator(private val processor: DataProcessor) :
DataProcessor {
    override fun process(data: String): String {
        println("Logging data: $data")
        return processor.process(data)
    }
}

class EncryptionDecorator(private val processor: DataProcessor) :
DataProcessor {
    override fun process(data: String): String {
        val processedData = processor.process(data)
        // Naive encryption for demonstration purpose
        val encryptedData = StringBuilder()
        for (char in processedData) {
            encryptedData.append(char + 1)
        }
        return encryptedData
    }
}

// Usage
fun main() {
    val basicProcessor = BasicDataProcessor()

    val loggingProcessor = LoggingDecorator(basicProcessor)
    val encryptedProcessor = EncryptionDecorator(loggingProcessor)

    val data = "Hello, World"
    val result = encryptedProcessor.process(data)
}
```

Benefits gained:

- **Modularity**: Each functionality is encapsulated in a separated class, making the code more readable and maintainable.

- **Flexibility**: The functionalities can be combined dynamically without modifying the original classes.
- **Reusability**: The decorators can be applied to different objects that implement the same interface, increasing the reusability of the code.
- **Maintainability**: Adding new functionalities requires only to create new decorators, without having to modify the existing classes.

This refactoring demonstrates how the Decorator pattern can be used to improve the modularity and the flexibility of the code, allowing us to add functionalities in a dynamic way, without compromising the simplicity of the base class.

Best Practices for Refactoring

Refactoring is an essential practice to keep the code readable, modular, and maintainable over time. However, performing refactoring without a clear strategy can introduce new issues or slow down the development. Following the best practice helps to ensure that the process is effective, safe, and contributes to the improvement of the quality of the project. Let us now see the best practices to perform refactoring.

Identify and Prioritize the Critical Areas

- We should start refactoring from the parts of the code that show clear problems, such as code smells or strong couplings.
- We should prioritize the parts that are frequently modified or which have a high impact on the main functionalities.
- There are tools to perform a static analysis of the code to rapidly identify problematic areas.

Keep the Behavior of the Code

- Refactoring should not modify the external behavior of the code. Before starting, we should write or update tests to ensure that the logic remains the same.
- We should execute the test frequently during refactoring to verify that no bugs are introduced.

Apply Refactoring in Small Steps

- It is better to divide the whole refactoring in incremental tasks, rather than modify huge portions of the code at once.
- This approach reduces the risk of errors and simplifies the detection of issues.

Example

- Begin separating responsibilities using the patterns such as Facade.

- Then, introduce more advanced patterns, such as Strategy or Command, to optimize the code.

Use Design Patterns to Improve the Structure

- We can leverage the same patterns to solve specific architectural problems, such as:
    - MVVM to separate the business logic and the UI.
    - Repository to centralize the access to the data.
    - Decorator to extend functionalities without modifying the original code.
- Design patterns are able to standardize the structure of the code, thus improving readability and fostering team collaboration.

Incremental Refactoring Supported by Automated Tests

- We should integrate automated tests (unit tests, integration tests, and UI tests) to continuously verify the proper functioning of the refactored code.
- Tools such as JUnit, Espresso, and Mockito allow us to test in isolation each component that has been modified.

Avoid Over-Engineering

- Refactoring should solve actual issues but not anticipate future needs. We should avoid introducing patterns that might be too complex for the requirements of our project.
- We should always choose pragmatic solutions and keep the code as simple as possible.

Document the Modifications

- It is better to keep track of the changes applied during refactoring. We should add clear comments and update the project documentation.
- If we work in a team, we should share the reason behind the changes, especially if we have introduced new patterns or restructured existing components.

Use Refactoring as a Chance to Improve Tests

- We can take advantage of refactoring to add or improve automated tests. Each component modified should have sufficient test coverage.
- For example, if we introduce a Repository, we have to ensure to mock the data sources in the unit tests.

Engage the Team

- Discuss the plans with the team to ensure that all the developers understand the changes and are able to contribute.
- Use code reviews to identify potential issues or room for improvement.

Continuous Refactoring

- Refactoring is not a one-shot operation. We should include it in the continuous development cycle to maintain the high quality of the code.
- We can plan specific moments during the development to perform code review aimed at improving the code.

Following these best practices ensures an effective refactoring, reducing the risk of bugs, and improving the quality of the code. Introducing appropriate design patterns, using automated tests and collaborating with the team are key elements to transform refactoring in a smooth and productive process. With a structured approach, refactoring is not only a matter of correcting the code, but an investment on the maintainability and the scalability of the project.

Conclusion

Refactoring is more than an operation of code cleaning–it is an essential strategy to keep the high quality of the project and ensure its growth over time. In this chapter, we have explored how refactoring, combined with design patterns, is able to transform complex or badly structured code into a solid, modular, and maintainable code base.

We have seen how to detect code smells, those signals which indicate the need of structural improvements, and how to apply design patterns to solve them. From simpler patterns such as Singleton and Factory to more advanced ones such as MVVM, Command, and Decorator, each example has demonstrated how introducing established logics can improve modularity, readability, and scalability.

The adoption of best practices for refactoring offers a practical guide to ensure that the process is safe and effective, reducing risks and improving the cohesion of the code. Moreover, refactoring is an opportunity to implement automated tests and improve the comprehension of the project by the team.

In conclusion, refactoring is not only a phase or the development cycle, but a continuous process that enhances the developers' work and prepares the code for the future. If we integrate design patterns into refactoring, we not only address actual issues, but we create a solid basis to successfully face future development challenges. Using the tools and the techniques learned in this chapter, we are able to transform the code into a valuable asset that is ready to grow alongside the project.

This is the end of the theoretical part of this book. From the next chapter onwards, we start to build. There are three projects that are waiting for us to put into practice what we have learned so far.

Points to Remember

- **Refactoring improves the code quality**: It is the process of restructuring the code to make it more readable, modular, and maintainable without changing the external behavior.
- **Code smells indicate structural problems**: Signals such as duplication of the code, strong coupling, and classes with too many responsibilities highlight areas that require improvements.
- **Design patterns simplify refactoring**: Patterns such as MVVM, Factory, and Builder offer standard solutions to common problems, and are able to improve the structure and the flexibility of the code.
- **Separate the logic with MVVM**: Using MVVM to move the business logic outside the implementation of the UI makes the code more testable and reusable.
- **Centralize the access to the data with Repository**: The Repository pattern improves modularity, centralizing the management of data sources and making the data caching easier.
- **Simplify complex interactions with Facade**: This design pattern centralizes the access to modules or complex subsystems, making the code more readable, easy to maintain, and reducing the coupling between components.
- **Dynamically extend functionalities with Decorator**: The Decorator pattern allows us to add new responsibilities to objects in a flexible way, without modifying the original classes.
- **Incremental refactoring**: Dividing refactoring in small steps reduces the risk of introducing bugs and simplifies the analysis of the modification.
- **Testing as an ally of refactoring**: Automated tests ensure that the changes to the code do not alter the expected behavior, thus helping us to keep the stability of the project.
- **Refactoring is a continuous process**: Regularly including it in the development cycle helps us to deliver high quality code prepared to face new functionalities.

Multiple Choice Questions

1. What is the main purpose of refactoring?
   a. Add new functionalities to the app.
   b. Improving the internal structure of the code without changing its external behavior.

   c. Completely remove the dependencies in the code.

   d. Convert the code in another programming language.

2. Which design pattern is particularly useful to separate the business logic from the UI?

   a. Singleton

   b. Decorator

   c. Builder

   d. MVVM

3. When should we use the pattern Decorator?

   a. When we want to centralize the access to the data.

   b. When we want to dynamically add new functionalities to an object without modifying the original class.

   c. When we have to manage complex states in a system.

   d. When we want to create a unique instance for a class.

4. Which is one of the main benefits of using Repository during refactoring?

   a. Centralize the network logic and reduce the code duplication.

   b. Manage the access to main threads.

   c. Add dynamic functionalities to objects.

   d. Allow us to handle the UI logic.

5. Which of the following is the best strategy to perform a refactoring in a project?

   a. Modify big portions of the code all at once.

   b. Refactor the code only when the project is complete.

   c. Apply the refactoring in small steps, with frequently verifying the behavior using tests.

   d. Ignoring the tests during refactoring to speed up the process.

Answers

1. b
2. d
3. b
4. a
5. c

Questions

1. What are code smells and how can they help us to identify the areas of the code that need refactoring? Provide an example.
2. Explain how the pattern MVVM improves the maintainability and the testability of the code in an Android project.
3. What are the advantages of the Decorator pattern in the context of refactoring and what are the scenarios in which we should use it?
4. Explain how the Repository pattern is able to centralize the access to the data and simplify the logic of the project during refactoring.
5. What best practices do you suggest to perform a safe refactoring in a complex project?

CHAPTER 12
Building an E-Commerce App

Introduction

Creating an e-commerce app is a challenge that requires a structured approach and the use of the latest technologies to meet user and market demands. This chapter will guide the reader through the entire development cycle of an e-commerce app, from the initial design to the testing phase, offering a practical and concrete example.

***Figure 12.1**: Icon of the E-Commerce App*

Starting with the requirements analysis, we will identify the app's main features and usage flows, providing a solid foundation for the design. Next, in the modular design phase, we will define the main modules, outlining their responsibilities and interactions to ensure modularity and reusability.

During the implementation phase, we will apply best practices in modern Android development, leveraging tools like Jetpack Compose, Hilt, and StateFlow to build a scalable and maintainable application. Finally, in the testing phase, we will demonstrate how to verify the reliability and correctness of the app's main components.

This chapter is not just a guide to developing an e-commerce app but also an example of a structured approach that leverages design patterns and can be applied to projects of various kinds. Let us now explore the details of each phase to understand how to create high-quality applications by following Android development best practices.

Structure

In this chapter, we will cover the following topics:

- Requirement Analysis
- Design
- Implementation
- Testing

Requirement Analysis

The development of an e-commerce app requires a curated planning to ensure that the app satisfies user expectations and market requirements. The requirements analysis phase is fundamental to identify the main functionalities, the technical requirements, and the project constraints. This analysis allows us to have a clear vision of the goals, helping the team build a scalable, safe, and intuitive application.

In this section, we will examine the main requirements of our e-commerce app, focusing on:

- The key use cases which will guide us to find the right features to develop for this project.
- The essential features for the users, such as the catalog navigation, cart management, and order submission.
- The technologies and the tools we need to satisfy the expectation of the users while ensuring a solid technical base.

Through this analysis, we will establish the foundations for the whole process of design, implementation, and testing. Let us begin defining the main goals and the essential requirements for our e-commerce app.

Target Users

To develop a successful e-commerce app, it is mandatory to understand the different types of users who will use it. Each category of users has specific needs and expectations, which must be considered during the design. In this section, we will identify the profiles of the target users and analyze their characteristics and needs, providing a base to define the key functionalities of the app.

The app targets three main categories of users, each with specific needs:

Casual users:

- **Characteristics:**
  - They use the app to look for a specific product.
  - They evaluate the available options based on price, reviews, and availability.
- **Key needs:**
  - An intuitive user interface that allows them to rapidly search the products.
  - Clear information about products, such as description, price, and availability.

Regular users:

- **Characteristics:**
  - They place orders frequently and use advanced functionalities, such as wishlists and order history.
  - They tend to search for similar products or order the same items multiple times.
- **Key needs:**
  - Fast access to personal area and order history.
  - Synchronization between devices to maintain the cart and preferences.

Professional users:

- **Characteristics:**
  - They order large quantities of products or use the app for commercial purposes.
  - They might require bills or prefer specific payment methods.
- **Key needs:**
  - Simplified management for complex orders.
  - Support for multiple shipping addresses and custom payment methods.

Identifying the target user and their needs allow us to design a customized and intuitive user experience. By fitting the app to the different user profiles, we are able to ensure that it satisfies the expectations of both, the casual users and the regular or professional ones, thereby creating a successful and versatile product.

Use Cases

Use cases represent the main scenarios of interaction between the users and the application. Defining these flows helps immensely because every use case drives the design of the functionalities and their technical implementation. We will now explore the main use cases for an e-commerce app and see how design patterns can be applied to support each scenario.

- **Product exploration and search**: The users open the app to visualize the catalog of the available products. They can navigate through specific categories (for example, electronics or clothing), apply filters to restrict results (for example, price, ratings, availability), and use a search bar to rapidly find specific articles.
- **Visualization of product details**: When the users select a product from the catalog, they access a screen containing detailed information about that product. This includes a complete description, multiple images, customer reviews, and customization options (for example, colors). The users can add the product to the cart directly from this screen or add it to a wish list.
- **Cart management**: A dedicated screen allows the users to visualize the product added to the cart, modify quantities, and remove items. The cart automatically calculates the total of the prices of the articles, applying taxes, shipping costs, or discounts. The state of the cart is linked to the user account.
- **Checkout and payment**: After completing the choice of the products, the users proceed to the checkout. This flow guides the users through the necessary steps: insertion of shipping address, selection of the payment method (for example, credit card, PayPal), and order confirmation. The app shows a summary of the costs, giving the possibility to modify the information before the final confirmation. Once completed, users receive a confirmation of the order.
- **Registration and login:** The users create a new account to save their data or log in to an existing account. During registration, the users insert information such as name, email, and password. Login unlocks custom functionalities, such as saving the state of the cart, or accessing history and favorite shipping addresses. A password recovery feature is also available.
- **Order management**: The users visualize order history in a dedicated screen. For each order, the following information is displayed: order number, date of the order, amount and status of the order (in process, shipped, delivered).

These use cases represent the main scenarios of our e-commerce app and define the functionalities that the app must provide to the users. As we notice, this is not an exhaustive list, because we can mention additional use cases, such as wish list management and custom notification. However, they are enough to let us put into practice what we have learned about design patterns in the e-commerce field. Each scenario outlines the key interaction between the user and the system, providing a solid base to derive functional requirements, which we will examine in the sections that follow.

Main Requirements

Now that we have defined the use cases, we need to identify the main requirements of our product. These requirements focus on satisfying user needs, and providing an intuitive and seamless experience. At the same time, they guarantee an efficient management of the resources and functionalities. In the next section, we identify the main requirements that can be classified into functional and non-functional requirements.

Functional Requirements

Functional requirements describe what the app should do to satisfy user needs. In the scope of an e-commerce app, these include:

- **Product exploration and search**
    - Visualize products in a list with filtering and sorting options (for example, category, price, reviews).
    - Provide an intuitive search bar to rapidly find the desired products.
- **Visualization of product details**
    - A product page is available for each item. The page contains relevant information such as name, description, price, images, ratings, reviews, and availability.
    - The product page gives the users the possibility to add the product to the card in the desired quantity.
- **Cart management**
    - Allow the users to add, remove, or modify the quantities of the product in the cart.
    - Automatically calculate the card total and apply taxes or discounts.
- **Checkout and payment**
    - Guide the users during the checkout in a clear and safe way.
    - Provide payment options, such as credit card or PayPal, and shipping options.
- **Registration and login**
    - Provide the registration and login forms, and option for password recovery.
    - Allow the users to visualize and manage their own profile, accessing the history of orders and shipping addresses.

- **Order management**
  - Create order based on the content of the cart.
  - Send the order to a separate API for the processing and provide feedback about the result of the operation (for example, order confirmation).

Non-Functional Requirements

Non-functional requirements define the technical and qualitative characteristics of the app, ensuring performance and reliability.

- **High performance**
  - Fast data loading, even on low powered devices.
  - Optimization for slow mobile networks, minimizing the quantity of data to transfer.
- **Security**
  - Protection of users' personal data and payment credentials.
  - Safe communication through HTTPS and encrypted storage of sensitive data.
- **Accessibility**
  - Support for users with visual disabilities.
  - Compatibility with screen reader and interfaces optimized for mobile devices.
- **Scalability**
  - Design the app to manage an increasing number of users and products without compromising the performance.
  - Modular structure to facilitate the addition of new functionalities.
- **Intuitive design**
  - Simple and easy to navigate user interface.
  - Visual and interaction consistency in all of the screens of the app.

Technical Requirements

The technical requirements set the technological foundations for the development and maintainability of the app.

- **Modern architecture**
  - Adopt the most widely used architectural pattern in Android development, MVVM, to separate the business logic, the presentation logic, and the UI.
  - Use the Repository pattern to centralize the access to the data.

- **Up-to-date technologies**
  - Use Jetpack Compose to create a modern and responsive user interface.
  - Handle the network communication with Retrofit.
  - Implement the local database with Room.
- **Leverage design patterns**
  - Apply the Singleton pattern to manage single instances, such as the network client or the local database, ensuring an efficient usage of the resources.
  - Implement the Factory pattern to centralize and simplify the creation of complex objects, such as product instances or configuration objects.
- **Testing**
  - Implement unit tests, integration tests, and UI tests to ensure the correctness of the code.
  - Use tools like Espresso and Mockito to simulate real scenarios and specific behaviors.

Clearly defining the main requirements help us to keep the project focused on user needs and technical constraints. The combination of functional and non-functional requirements ensure that the application offers an excellent user experience, which is supported by a reliable and scalable technical base.

Design

Now that we have established the requirements of our e-commerce app, we can rely on them to begin design.

General Architecture

To build a robust and scalable e-commerce app, it is important for us to adopt a modern and well-structured architecture. This section describes how to use the pattern MVVM (Model-View-ViewModel) in combination with technologies such as Repository, Room and Retrofit to build a solid base to separate the responsibilities and ensure modularity, testability, and maintainability. Additionally, the use of the Dependency Injection pattern will make it easy to develop and extend the application.

Architectural Pattern: MVVM

The structure of the app will follow the MVVM pattern, which divides the application on three main levels:

- **Model**
  - Contains the data and the business logic.
  - Includes the implementation of Repository to ensure a structured access to the data from multiple sources.

  Example: `ProductRepository` to access data about products.
- **ViewModel**
  - Coordinates the presentation logic and acts as an intermediary between the View and the Model.
  - Exposes observable states to the view through StateFlow.

  Example: `ProductListViewModel` to manage the product retrieval and the filtering logic.
- **View**
  - Is made up of user interface elements built with Jetpack Compose.
  - Observes the state of the ViewModel and reacts to its changes.

  Example: Composables such as `ProductListScreen` or `CartScreen`.

Structure of the Project

The project will be organized into feature-based modules. In this type of code organization, each feature is self-contained into its package, promoting separation of concerns, parallel development, and testability. Each module can be reused in multiple projects independently.

Main modules:

- **Product catalog**: For product visualization and search.
- **Cart**: To manage articles ready for the purchase.
- **Checkout**: To complete the purchase with the shipping and payment data.
- **Authentication**: For login, registration, and user profile management.
- **Order management**: To visualize and track past orders.

Package Structure:

Each module is divided into packages to separate the components:

- `model`: Contains the data classes (for example, `Product`, `Order`).
  - `repository`: Contains the logic to access the data.
- `viewmodel`: Contains the ViewModels for each screen.
- `view`: Contains the Composable for the UI.

Dependency Management

In order to avoid strong coupling and improve modularity, we will use Hilt for the Dependency Injection.

Advantages:

- To make it easy to insert dependencies in the ViewModel and in the Repository.
- Reduces the boilerplate code for the creation and initialization of dependencies.
- Improve us the testability, allowing us to easily replace the dependencies with mocks inside the tests.

Communication and Asynchronism

To handle the communication between components and keep the user interface responsive, we will use:

- Kotlin Coroutines to execute network or database operations in the background without blocking the main thread.
- StateFlow to expose observable data from the ViewModel to the View in a responsive way and without boilerplates.
- Retrofit to manage the API calls and fetch the data from the server.
- Room to archive the data locally and improve the offline functionalities.

The general architecture of the app, based on MVVM, well-defined modules, and modern technologies, offers a solid base for implementation. This structure provides separation of concerns and makes it easy to test the features, letting us have a project that is simple to maintain and extend. In the next step, we will design the details of each module for implementing the key use cases.

Design of Individual Modules

Since we have already defined what will be the modules of our app, we can now approach the design one module at a time. breaking down our original problem of designing a whole e-commerce application into five small problems: product catalog, cart, checkout, authentication, and order management. For each module:

- We define the main functionalities.
- We show how it is structured, using UML diagrams that represent its classes and relationships.

This approach ensures that each module is self-contained and transferable.

Product Catalog

This module is the heart of the e-commerce app and allows the users to explore, search and filter the available products. Additionally, it includes the possibility to visualize the details of a specific product with all the information about it.

Main Functionalities:

- Visualize a list of products based on categories.
- Allow the user to search and sort results.
- Provide complete details for each product, including images, description, and customization options.
- Alarm for the interaction with other models, such as the cart, to add to it the selected products.

UML Diagram:

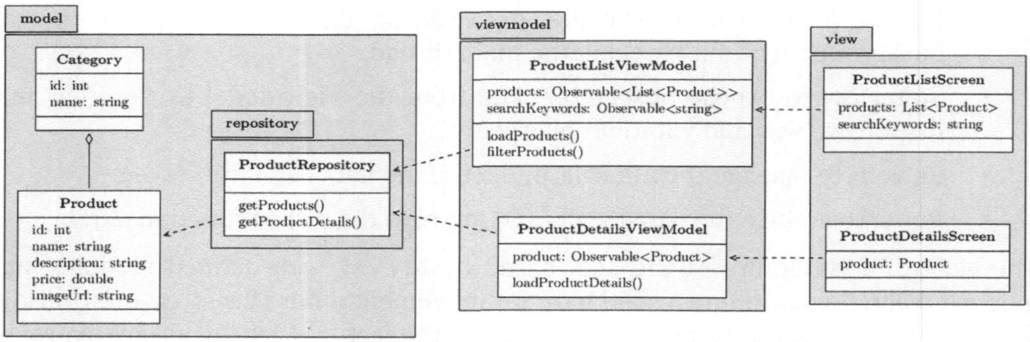

***Figure 12.2**: UML diagram of the module Product Catalog*

Package `model`

- **Category**: Model that represents product category, with attributes such as name and ID.
- **Product**: Model that represents a product, with attributes search as Ed name, description, price, image.
- **ProductRepository**: Provides access to data, centralizing the API or database calls.

Package `viewmodel`

- **ProductListViewModel**: Coordinates the logic to load and filter the products. It exposes an observable state to the UI.
- **ProductDetailsViewModel**: Coordinates the logic to visualize the details of a product. It exposes these details to the UI through an observable state.

Package `view`

- **ProductListScreen**: Represents the screen of the list of products.
- **ProductDetailsScreen**: Represents the screen of the details of a product.

Relationships

- **ProductListScreen** depends on **ProductListViewModel**: It observes the state containing the list of products and performs actions such as filtering or searching for products.
- **ProductDetailsScreen** depends on **ProductDetailsViewModel**: It observes the state containing the details of the selected product and notify about users' actions (such as adding the product to the cart).
- **ProductListViewModel** and **ProductDetailsViewModel** depend on **ProductRepository**: They fetch the data from the repository and update their state with this data.
- **ProductRepository**: Retrieves the data from remote APIs or local databases and transforms them into objects of type **Product** or **Category**.

Interactions with Other Modules

- **ProductDetailsScreen** interacts with the module **Cart** to add a product to the cart.

This design clearly defines the key components of the module Product Catalog, providing a detailed vision about the structure of the module and its classes, which is able to guide the implementation.

Cart

The model Cart allows the users to add, remove, and modify the product they selected for the purchase, providing a clear summary of the costs and the quantities. It is a crucial component of every e-commerce app, which links the product catalog to the checkout process.

Main Functionalities:

- Add and remove products from the cart.
- Modify the quantity of a product added to the cart.
- Visualize a summary of the costs, including taxes and shipping charges.
- Synchronize cart contents over sessions (local persistence).

UML Diagram

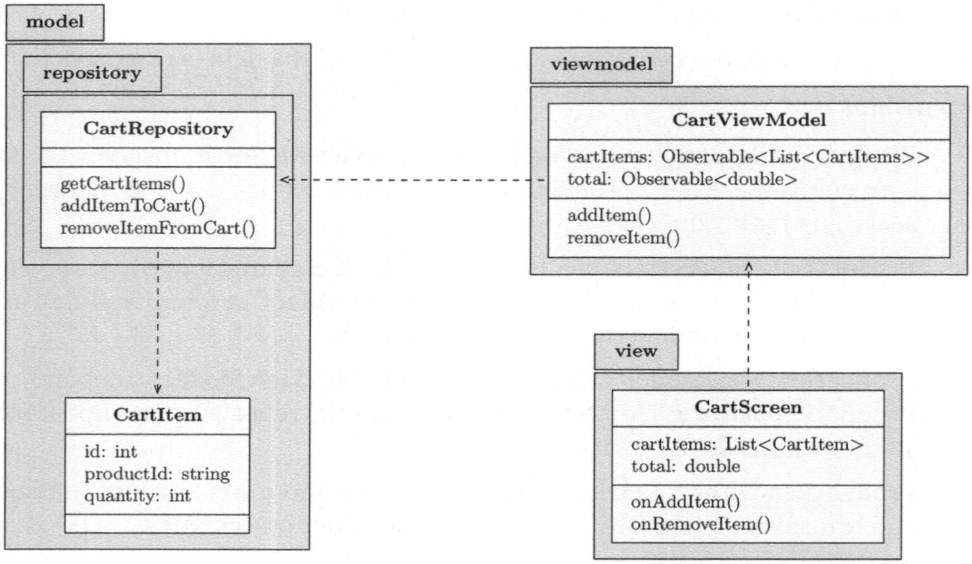

Figure 12.3: *UML diagram of the module Cart*

Package `model`

- **CartItem**: Module that represents a single item into the cart.
- **CartRepository**: Manages the persistence of the data on the cart, both locally and remotely.

Package `viewmodel`

- **CartViewModel**: Coordinates the logic to add, remove, and modify the products on the cart.

Package `view`

- **CartScreen**: Represents the user interface to visualize and interact with the content of the cart.

Relationships

- **CartScreen** depends on **CartViewModel**: It observes the state of the cart and the totals. It also notifies the ViewModel about user actions such as addition or removal of products from the cart.
- **CartViewModel** depends on **CartRepository**: It fetches the content of the cart from the repository and calls the repository to update data according to user actions.
- **CartRepository**: Manages the persistence of local and remote data using **CartItem**.

Interactions with Other Modules

- **CartRepository** interacts with the module **Checkout** to send the list of the products the user wants to purchase, and with the module **Authentication** to know if the data of the cart must be synchronized remotely.

The module Cart is designed to be modular and self-sufficient, making it easy to implement dynamic product management.

Checkout

The module Checkout guides the user to the process of order submission. It includes gathering of information about shipment and payment, summary of the order and the final confirmation. This module is fundamental to ensure an easy and safe shopping experience.

Main Functionalities:

- Collect shipping data (name, address, phone number).
- Manage payment methods (such as credit card, PayPal).
- Visualize the order summary, including products, costs, and taxes.
- Send the order to the server and provide a confirmation to the user.

UML Diagram

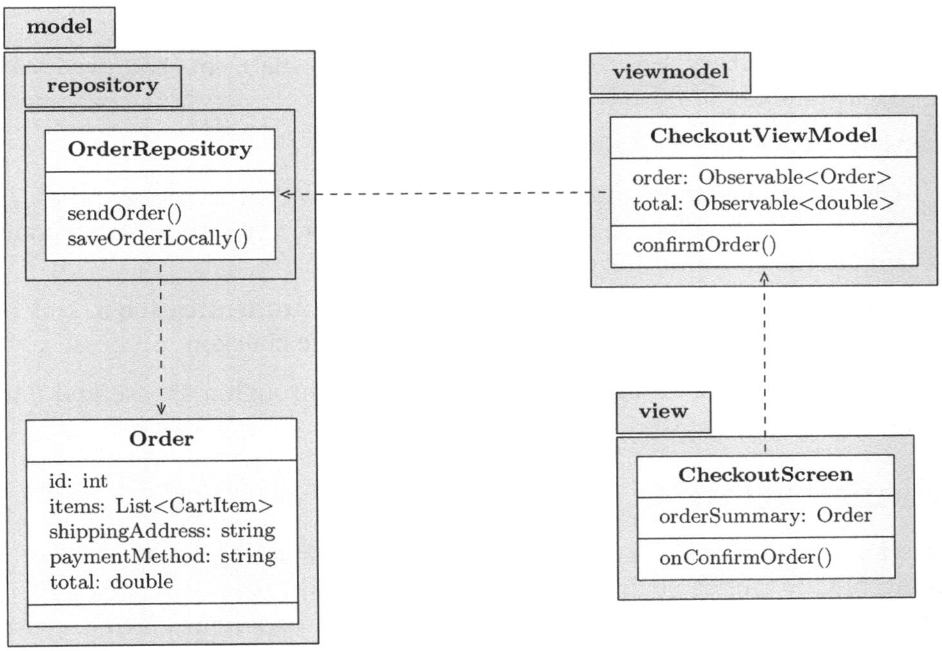

Figure 12.4: *UML diagram of the module Checkout*

Package `model`

- **Order**: Model that represents an order, with details such as list of products, shipping address, and payment method.
- **OrderRepository**: Manages the logic of creating and sending the orders to the server. It also provides feedback about the success or the failure of the operation.

Package `viewmodel`

- **CheckoutViewModel**: Coordinates the logic of the checkout, such as data validation and the computation of total costs.

Package `view`

- **CheckoutScreen:** Represents the user interface to collect the shipping and payment data. It visualizes the summary of the order and button to confirm it.

Relationships

- **CheckoutScreen** interacts with **CheckoutViewModel**: It receives the actual state of the checkout and notifies about user interactions (for example, order confirmation). Additionally, it displays possible validation errors and success messages.
- **CheckoutViewModel** depends on **OrderRepository**: It creates an order depending on the data inserted by the user and stores it locally or sends it to the server, providing handling for network errors.
- **OrderRepository** uses the class **Order** to encapsulate data retrieved from the local database or from the remote server.

Interactions with Other Modules

- **CheckoutViewModel** interacts with the module **Cart** to retrieve the content of the cart and build the summary of the order, and notifies that module to empty the cart after the order confirmation.
- **CheckoutViewModel** interacts with the module **Authentication** to know if the user is authenticated before proceeding with the checkout process.

The Checkout module is designed to guide the user through a secure and intuitive shopping experience.

Authentication

The model Authentication is responsible for the management of user accounts, providing functionalities such as login, registration, and password recovery. It is a fundamental module to ensure a customized and secure experience, allowing users to access their data and synchronize information over different devices.

Main Functionalities:

- Provide registration for new accounts.
- Provide login functionality with credentials.
- Password recovery through email.
- Handling to keep the user logged.

UML Diagram

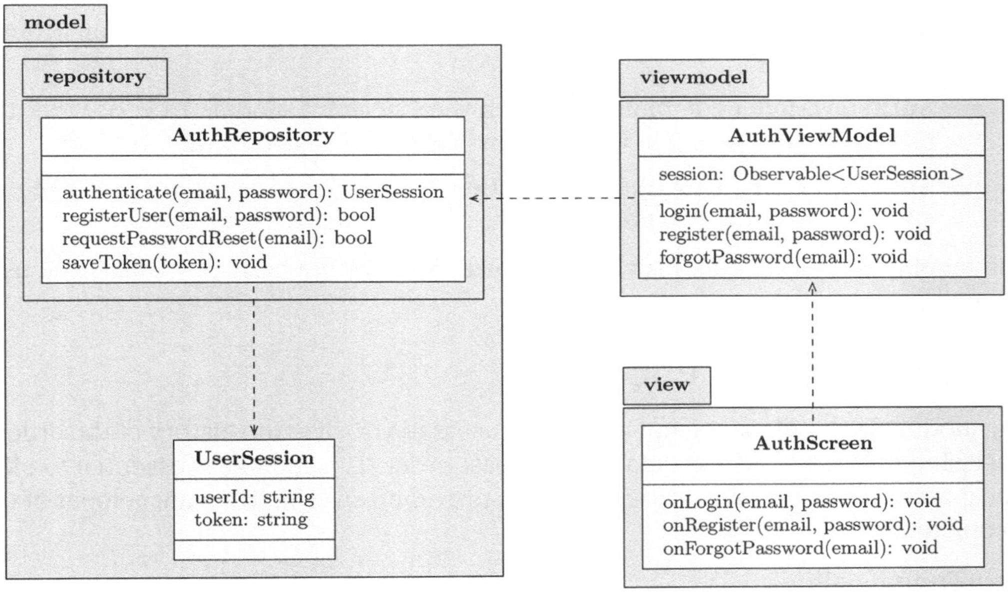

***Figure 12.5**: UML diagram of the module Authentication*

Package `model`

- **UserSession**: Model that represents the session of the user, including IDs and tokens.
- **AuthRepository**: Manages the operations about authentication, such as credential check and registration of new users.

Package `viewmodel`

- **AuthViewModel**: Coordinates the logic to authenticate the user and manage the sessions. It exposes the state of the session to the UI.

Package `view`

- **AuthScreen**: User interface for login, registration, and password recovery. It is designed to show error or confirmation messages based on user actions.

Relationships

- **AuthScreen** interacts with **AuthViewModel**: Notifies about user actions, such as login or registration. It also receives updates about the session and errors.
- **AuthViewModel** depends on **AuthRepository**: It verifies the credentials, obtains the access tokens, and saves the status of the session.

Interactions with Other Modules

- **AuthViewModel** interacts with the module **Cart** to synchronize the content of the local cart with the user account after logging, providing consistency across devices.
- **AuthViewModel** communicates with the **Checkout** module to verify that the user is already logged in before allowing him to proceed with the order.
- **AuthRepository** uses the module **Core** to save the access tokens using an encryption method to protect the user's credentials.

The module Authentication provides a secure and scalable basis to manage the user account and sessions.

Order Management

The module Order Management allows the users to visualize the history of the orders, track shipments, and access data of every past order. This module is essential to offer transparency and improve user experience, providing an effective management of the completed purchases.

Main Functionalities:

- Visualize a list of the orders placed with basic information (order number, date, status).
- Access the details of each order, including purchased products, costs, and information about shipment.
- Track an order.

UML Diagram

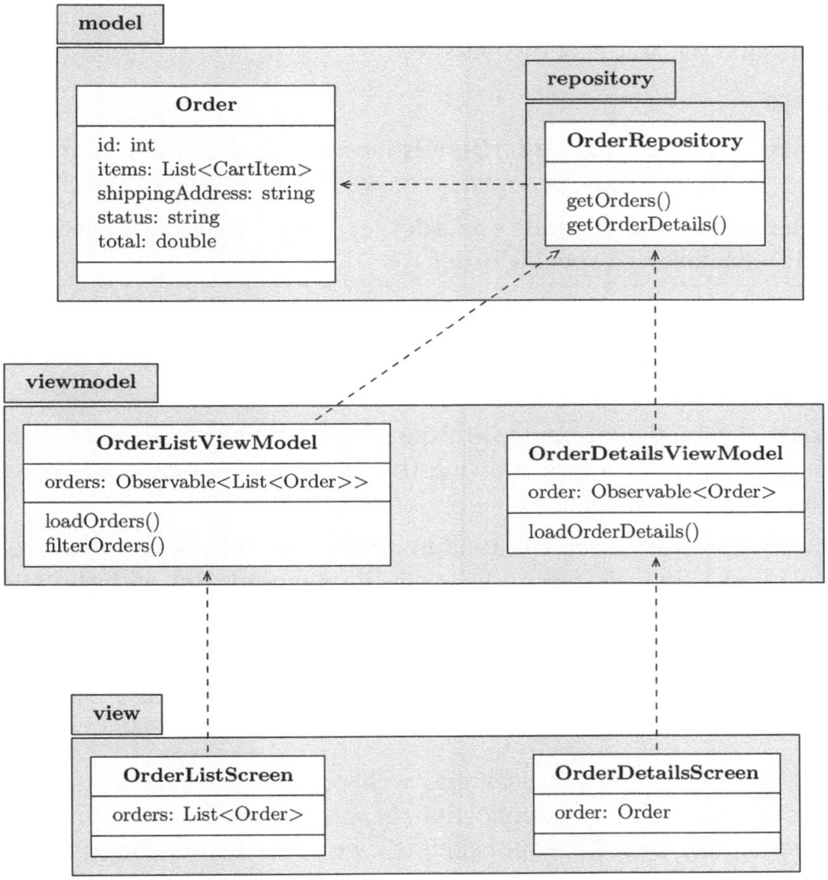

***Figure 12.6**: UML diagram of the module Order Management*

Package `model`

- **Order**: Model which represents an order, holding information about products, shipping address, and status.
- **OrderRepository**: Manages the fetching of the order from the server or the local database, and provides features to track shipments.

Package `viewmodel`

- **OrderViewModel**: Coordinates the logic to retrieve and update the state of the orders and exposes the orders to the UI using an observable state.

Package `view`

- **OrderListScreen**: Displays a list of orders with details, such as number of order, date, and status. It also allows the user to select an order and visualize its details.

- **OrderDetailsScreen**: Shows the details of a specific order, including products, costs, and the status of the shipment.

Relationships

- **OrderListScreen** and **OrderDetailsScreen** interact with **OrderViewModel** to observe the list of the orders or retrieve the details about specific order.
- **OrderViewModel** depends on OrderRepository to fetch the list of the orders and the details of a specific order.

Interactions with Other Modules

- **OrderViewModel** might interact with the module **Cart** to allow the user reorder items already bought.
- **OrderViewModel** interacts with the module **Authentication** to verify that the user is logged in before showing the list of past orders, and to synchronize data with the user account.
- **OrderRepository** uses the module **Shared** to save and retrieve the orders, providing offline access. Additionally, it communicates with the API to obtain updates on the status of the orders and shipments.

The module Order Management is designed to provide to the users a clear understanding of their purchases and expeditions, improving the transparency and the reliability of the service.

Module-based design offers a clear and well-organized structure to implement a complex e-commerce Android application. Leveraging the division into independent modules, each having specific responsibilities, we provide modularity, maintainability, testability, and reusability of the code.

In this section we have:

- Explored the main modules of the app: Product Catalog, Cart, Checkout, Authentication, and Order Management.
- Defined the key functionalities of each module, highlighting how they interact with each other.
- Represented the logic structure of modules using uml diagrams, clearly separating UI, presentation logic, and business logic.
- Outlined the interaction with the package Shared, which acts as a base for common components such as database models and network tools.

Key Points:

- Each module is the sign to be self-contained and standalone, facilitating parallel development and scalability.

- Interactions between modules are clearly defined to ensure consistency and seamless integration.
- The feature-based structure supports the future expansion of the app, allowing us to add new functionalities without influencing the existing components.

This design provides us a solid base to step into the next phase, the implementation, where we turn the class diagrams into code. The next phase will represent the translation of our design into concrete application, and we will make sure that each module works correctly and integrates with other modules to offer a valuable user experience.

Implementation

The development phase represents the practical translation of modular design into a functional Android application. After clearly defining the responsibilities of each module and their interactions, we now proceed to implement the classes, screens, and logic that form the core of the e-commerce app.

Objectives of the Implementation Phase

- Implement the Modules:
    - Translate into Kotlin code the classes designed for the main modules: Product Catalog, Cart, Checkout, Authentication, and Order Management.
    - Ensure consistency across modules by leveraging modern technologies and consolidating interactions.
- Integrate Android Technologies:
    - Use Jetpack Compose to create a modern and responsive user interface.
    - Manage presentation logic with ViewModel and observable states via StateFlow.
    - Centralize data access with the Repository pattern, integrating Room for local persistence and Retrofit for API calls.
    - Simplify dependency management with Hilt.
- Support User Flows:
    - Implement key flows such as product navigation, adding items to the cart, and order completion, ensuring a smooth and consistent user experience.

Technologies and Tools Used

- Jetpack Compose:
    - Modern framework for building declarative user interfaces.
    - Enables efficient creation of dynamic and responsive screens.

- ViewModel and StateFlow:
  - Manages screen states and separates business logic from presentation.
  - Observable state allows real-time UI updates.
- Repository Pattern:
  - Centralizes data access to reduce coupling and improve maintainability.
- Room and Retrofit:
  - Room: Stores data locally and ensures offline functionality.
  - Retrofit: Facilitates secure and efficient server API communication.
- Hilt:
  - Simplifies Dependency Injection, making it easier to inject components such as Repositories or ViewModels.

Structure of the Implementation Phase

The development phase will be organized by modules, each implemented following the defined design:

- Product Catalog:
  - Creation of product lists and details.
  - Management of search and filters.
- Cart:
  - Implementation of dynamic item management and total calculations.
  - Data persistence between sessions.
- Checkout:
  - Development of the order confirmation flow and integration of the payment system via Factory.
- Authentication:
  - Implementation of login, registration, and credential recovery.
  - User session management.
- Order Management:
  - Display of order history and shipment tracking.

This phase focuses on applying best practices in modern Android development, ensuring a modular and maintainable implementation. We will proceed with the implementation of the first module: Product Catalog, which represents the functional foundation of the e-commerce app.

Before starting, it is important to point out that the following section will not contain the full code of the implementation of the application, since it will require too much space. What we are going to see are the parts of the implementation that are worth discussing, and we invite the reader to explore the source code available on the repository of this project to have a deep understanding of the implementation.

Product Catalog

The implementation of the Product Catalog module translates the design into a working system, leveraging modern Android technologies such as Jetpack Compose, ViewModel, Repository, and Hilt. In this section, we focus on the most significant parts of the code, demonstrating how responsibilities are distributed and interactions are managed.

1. **Retrieving Products via the Repository**

The **`ProductRepository`** uses the Repository pattern to centralize data access. The logic for fetching products from the server is separated from the UI, ensuring modularity and testability.

```
class ProductRepository @Inject constructor(
    private val apiService: ApiService
) {
    suspend fun fetchProducts(): List<Product> {
        val apiProducts = apiService.getProducts()
        return apiProducts.map { it.toDomainModel() }
    }
}
```

- The **`fetchProducts`** method converts the API data (**`apiProducts`**) into domain models using the **`toDomainModel()`** extension, keeping the data and business layers separated.

***Figure 12.7:** Screen of the application showing the list of products*

2. **Managing State with StateFlow**

The **`ProductViewModel`** uses StateFlow to expose the state of the product list to the UI, enabling reactive and unidirectional updates.

```
@HiltViewModel
class ProductViewModel @Inject constructor(
    private val repository: ProductRepository
) : ViewModel() {

    private val _products = MutableStateFlow<List<Product>>(emp-
tyList())
    val products: StateFlow<List<Product>> = _products

    init {
        fetchProducts()
    }
```

```
        private fun fetchProducts() {
            viewModelScope.launch {
                _products.value = repository.fetchProducts()
            }
        }
    }
```

- The product state is managed through **_products** (internal) and **products** (external, observable by the UI).
- The use of **viewModelScope.launch** ensures that operations are performed asynchronously without blocking the main thread.

3. **Screen Navigation**

The navigation system uses **NavGraphBuilder** to define the flow between the product list and the details of the selected product.

```
fun NavGraphBuilder.productNavGraph(navController: NavController)
{
    composable("product_list") {
        ProductListScreen(
            onProductClick = { productId ->
                navController.navigate("product_details/$
productId")
            }
        )
    }
    composable("product_details/{productId}") { backStackEntry ->
        val productId = backStackEntry.arguments?.getString
("productId")
        ProductDetailsScreen(productId = productId)
    }
}
```

- The **ProductDetailsScreen** uses the **productId** argument to retrieve and display information about the selected product.

4. **Interaction Between Modules**

In the **ProductDetailsScreen**, the "**Add to Cart**" button communicates with the Cart module using a shared instance of the **CartRepository**.

```
Button(onClick = { cartRepository.addToCart(product) }) {
    Text("Add to Cart")
}
```

This interaction demonstrates how the modules collaborate to create a seamless user flow.

The implementation of the Product Catalog module shows how to organize responsibilities among Repository, ViewModel, and UI in a modular and maintainable way. Particularly noteworthy are the use of StateFlow for state management, the Repository pattern for data access, and navigation with Jetpack Compose. These elements make the module flexible and easily integrable with others.

Cart

The Cart module is designed to dynamically manage the content selected by users, provide a cost summary, and enable the transition to the Checkout module. We will now examine the most significant parts of the code, highlighting the use of modern technologies such as Jetpack Compose, Room, and Hilt.

1. **Managing Local Database with Room**

The module uses Room for cart data persistence, with a clear and scalable configuration.

```
@Dao
interface CartDao {
    @Query("SELECT * FROM cart_items")
    suspend fun getAllCartItems(): List<CartItem>

    @Insert(onConflict = OnConflictStrategy.REPLACE)
    suspend fun insertCartItem(cartItem: CartItem)

    @Delete
    suspend fun deleteCartItem(cartItem: CartItem)

    @Query("DELETE FROM cart_items")
    suspend fun clearCart()
}
```

- The DAO provides methods to retrieve, add, remove, and clear the cart.
- Persistence through Room ensures offline access to cart data.

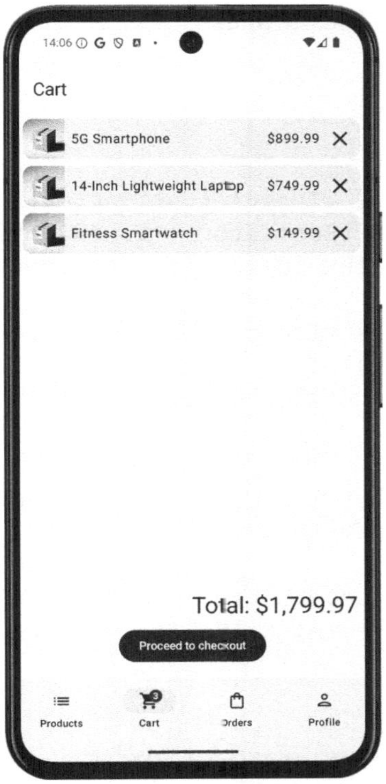

Figure 12.8: Screen of the application showing the cart

2. **Centralized Repository**

The **`CartRepository`** acts as an intermediary between the **DAO** and the **ViewModel**, encapsulating data access logic.

```
class CartRepository @Inject constructor(
    private val cartDao: CartDao
) {
    suspend fun fetchCartItems(): List<CartItem>
= cartDao.getAllCartItems()

    suspend fun addItemToCart(cartItem: CartItem) {
        cartDao.insertCartItem(cartItem)
    }

    suspend fun removeItemFromCart(cartItem: CartItem) {
        cartDao.deleteCartItem(cartItem)
    }
}
```

- **`fetchCartItems`** centralizes the retrieval of cart items.
- **`addItemToCart`** and **`removeItemFromCart`** handle database modifications.

3. **State Management in the ViewModel**

The **CartViewModel** uses **StateFlow** to expose the cart state reactively, enabling smooth UI updates.

```
@HiltViewModel
class CartViewModel @Inject constructor(
    private val cartRepository: CartRepository,
    private val authRepository: AuthRepository
) : ViewModel() {
    private val _cartItems = MutableStateFlow<List<Car-
tItem>>(emptyList())
    val cartItems: StateFlow<List<CartItem>> = _cartItems.
asStateFlow()

    private val _total = MutableStateFlow(0.0)
    val total: StateFlow<Double> = _total.asStateFlow()

    private val _isUserLoggedIn = MutableStateFlow(false)
    val isUserLoggedIn: StateFlow<Boolean> = _isUserLoggedIn.
asStateFlow()

    init {
        getCartItemsList()
        viewModelScope.launch {
            _isUserLoggedIn.value = authRepository.isUserLoggedIn()
        }
    }

    fun getCartItemsList() {
        viewModelScope.launch {
            _cartItems.value = cartRepository.fetchCartItems()
            _total.value = cartItems.value.sumOf { it.price }
        }
    }

    fun removeFromCart(cartItem: CartItem) {
        viewModelScope.launch {
            cartRepository.removeItemFromCart(cartItem)
            _cartItems.value = cartRepository.fetchCartItems()
            _total.value = cartItems.value.sumOf { it.price }
        }
    }
}
```

- The cart state, total amount, and authentication status are exposed to the UI.
- Operations such as item removal immediately update the state.

4. **User Interface with Jetpack Compose**

The cart screen uses **Jetpack Compose** to create a dynamic and reactive UI.

```
@Composable
fun CartScreen(
    modifier: Modifier = Modifier,
    navgateToCheckout: () -> Unit = {}
) {
    val viewModel: CartViewModel = hiltViewModel()
    val cartItems = viewModel.cartItems.collectAsStateWith
Lifecycle()
    val total = viewModel.total.collectAsStateWithLifecycle()
    val isUserLoggedIn = viewModel.isUserLoggedIn.collectAsState-
WithLifecycle()

    Column(modifier = modifier.fillMaxWidth()) {
        cartItems.value.forEach { cartItem ->
            CartListItem(cartItem = cartItem) {
                viewModel.removeFromCart(cartItem)
            }
        }
        Text(
            text = "Total: ${total.value}",
            modifier = Modifier.padding(8.dp).align(Alignment.End),
            style = MaterialTheme.typography.headlineMedium,
        )
        Button(
            onClick = navgateToCheckout,
            enabled = isUserLoggedIn.value,
            modifier = Modifier.align(Alignment.CenterHorizontally)
        ) {
            Text(text = "Proceed to checkout")
        }
        if (!isUserLoggedIn.value) {
            Text(
                text = "You need to be logged in to proceed to
checkout.",
                modifier = Modifier.align(Alignment.CenterHorizon-
tally)
            )
        }
    }
}
```

- Cart items are displayed in a dynamic list.

- The UI adapts to the user's state (logged in or not) and provides appropriate feedback.

5. **Integration with the Authentication Module**

The **CartViewModel** checks the authentication status through the **AuthRepository**, affecting the UI and access to advanced features.

```
viewModelScope.launch {
    _isUserLoggedIn.value = authRepository.isUserLoggedIn()
}
```

The Cart module is an excellent example of modular and reactive design. With Room for persistence, StateFlow for state management, and Jetpack Compose for the UI, the module is scalable, maintainable, and easily integrable.

Checkout

The Checkout module guides the user through the order completion process, including entering shipping details, selecting a payment method, and final confirmation. This implementation leverages Jetpack Compose for the UI, Hilt for Dependency Injection, and a Factory pattern for managing payment methods.

1. **Managing Payment Methods with the Factory Pattern**

The Factory pattern is used to create specific instances of **PaymentMethod**, ensuring flexibility and scalability in managing new payment methods.

```
class PaymentFactory {
    fun createPaymentMethod(
        paymentMethod: PaymentMethodEnum,
        cardNumber: String? = null,
        expirationDate: String? = null,
        cvv: String? = null
    ): PaymentMethod {
        return when (paymentMethod) {
            PaymentMethodEnum.CREDIT_CARD -> if (cardNumber !=
null && expirationDate != null && cvv != null) {
                CreditCardPayment(cardNumber, expirationDate,
cvv)
            } else {
                throw IllegalArgumentException("Missing credit
card details")
            }
            PaymentMethodEnum.CASH_ON_DELIVERY -> CashOnDelivery-
Payment()
            else -> throw IllegalArgumentException("Invalid
payment method: $paymentMethod")
```

```
            }
        }
    }
```

The Factory pattern allows the creation of payment methods such as **CreditCardPayment** and **CashOnDeliveryPayment**, separating the specific logic for each method.

2. **Validation and State Managed in the ViewModel**

The **CheckoutViewModel** manages the state of checkout data and real-time validation using StateFlow.

```
fun validateCardNumber(cardNumber: String): Boolean {
    val cardNumberNoSpaces = cardNumber.replace(" ", "")
    return cardNumberNoSpaces.length == 16 && cardNumberNoSpaces.
matches(Regex("\\d{16}"))
}

fun updateCardNumber(cardNumber: String) {
    val cardNumberNoSpaces = cardNumber.replace(" ", "")
    if (cardNumberNoSpaces.length > 16) return
    val newCardNumber = StringBuilder()
    repeat(cardNumberNoSpaces.length) { index ->
        val char = cardNumberNoSpaces[index]
        newCardNumber.append(char)
        if (index % 4 == 3 && index < cardNumberNoSpaces.length -
1) newCardNumber.append(" ")
    }
    _cardNumber.value = newCardNumber.toString()
}
```

The validation of fields such as the card number, expiration date, and CVV ensures the integrity of payment data.

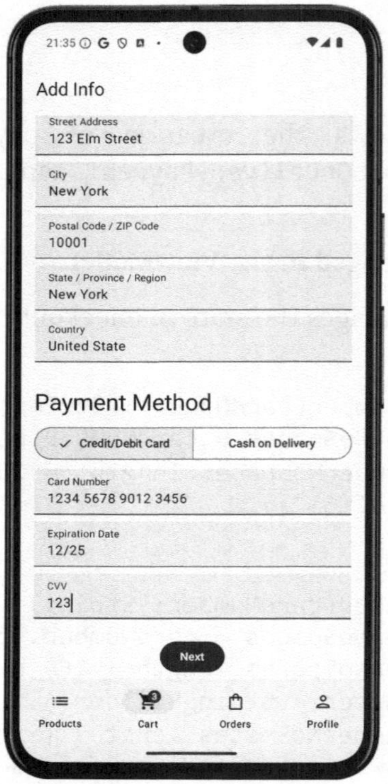

***Figure 12.9**: Screen of the application for adding checkout information*

3. **Multi-Screen Navigation**

The navigation between checkout screens (information, summary, confirmation) is managed through a specific NavGraph.

```
fun NavGraphBuilder.includeCheckoutGraph(navController:
NavHostController, route: String) {
    navigation(
        route = route,
        startDestination = CheckoutScreen.CheckoutAddInfoScreen.
route
    ) {
        composable(CheckoutScreen.CheckoutAddInfoScreen.route) {
            CheckoutAddInfoScreen(
                navigateNext = { navController.navigate(Check-
outScreen.CheckoutSummaryScreen.route) }
            )
        }
        composable(CheckoutScreen.CheckoutSummaryScreen.route) {
            CheckoutSummaryScreen(
                navigateNext = { navController.navigate
```

```
(CheckoutScreen.OrderConfirmationScreen.route) }
                )
            }
            composable(CheckoutScreen.OrderConfirmationScreen.route) {
                OrderConfirmationScreen()
            }
        }
    }
```

The navigation is smooth, allowing the user to transition from one screen to the next in sequence.

4. **UI Management with Compose**

The **CheckoutAddInfoScreen** collects user data and dynamically displays the required fields based on the selected payment method.

```
@Composable
fun CheckoutAddInfoScreen(viewModel: CheckoutViewModel, navgate
Next: () -> Unit) {
    val fullName = viewModel.fullName.collectAsStateWithLifecycle()
    val paymentMethod = viewModel.paymentMethod.collectAsState-
WithLifecycle()

    Column {
        TextField(
            value = fullName.value,
            onValueChange = { viewModel.updateFullName(it) },
            label = { Text("Full Name") }
        )
        SingleChoiceSegmentedButtonRow {
            PaymentMethodEnum.entries.forEach { method ->
                SegmentedButton(
                    onClick = { viewModel.updatePaymentMethod
(method.value) },
                    selected = paymentMethod.value == method.
value,
                    label = { Text(method.value) }
                )
            }
        }
        Button(onClick = navgateNext, enabled = fullName.value.
isNotEmpty()) {
            Text("Next")
        }
    }
}
```

The UI uses StateFlow to dynamically update fields and provide real-time feedback.

5. **Interaction with Other Modules**

The **CheckoutViewModel** interacts with:

- **CartRepository** to retrieve cart items and calculate the total.
- **OrderRepository** to create and send an order to the server.

```
fun createOrder() {
    viewModelScope.launch {
        val result = orderRepository.createAndSendOrder(
            fullName = fullName.value,
            paymentMethod = paymentMethod.value,
            items = cartItems.value.toOrderItems()
        )
        if (result) {
            cartRepository.clearCart()
        }
    }
}
```

The Checkout module is an advanced example of modular and reactive design, combining the use of patterns such as Factory for payment method management, StateFlow for state management, and Jetpack Compose for a dynamic UI. The multi-screen navigation and integration with the **Cart** and **Order** modules ensure a smooth and effective user flow.

Authentication

The Authentication module handles registration, login, session management, and logout. It is implemented using Hilt for Dependency Injection, DataStore for secure credential persistence, and Jetpack Compose for a modern and dynamic UI. This section examines the most significant aspects of the implementation.

1. **Secure Persistence with DataStore**

The module uses DataStore to securely store the authentication token and username.

```
class AuthDataStore @Inject constructor(
    @ApplicationContext private val context: Context
) {
    private val USERNAME = stringPreferencesKey("username")
    private val TOKEN_KEY = stringPreferencesKey("auth_token")

    val authToken: Flow<String?> = context.dataStore.data
        .catch { exception ->
            if (exception is IOException) emit(emptyPreferences())
else throw exception
```

```
        }
        .map { preferences -> preferences[TOKEN_KEY] }

    suspend fun saveAuthToken(token: String) {
        context.dataStore.edit { preferences ->
            preferences[TOKEN_KEY] = token
        }
    }
}
```

- Uses **preferencesDataStore** to read and write data securely.
- The **saveAuthToken** function allows saving the authentication token, used to maintain the session state.

2. **Repository for Authentication**

The **AuthRepositoryImpl** centralizes interaction with the API and credential management through DataStore.

```
class AuthRepositoryImpl @Inject constructor(
    private val apiService: ApiService,
    private val authDataStore: AuthDataStore
) : AuthRepository {

    override suspend fun loginUser(username: String, password:
String): ApiUser {
        val request = ApiUserLoginRequest(username, password)
        val result = apiService.login(request)
        authDataStore.saveAuthToken(result.token)
        authDataStore.saveUsername(result.username)
        return result
    }

    override suspend fun isUserLoggedIn(): Boolean {
        return authDataStore.authToken.firstOrNull() != null
    }
}
```

- The **loginUser** method authenticates the user via the API, saving the token and username through DataStore.
- **isUserLoggedIn** checks the authentication status.

Figure 12.10: *Screen of the application showing the status of user authentication*

3. **State Management with AuthViewModel**

The **`AuthViewModel`** coordinates the authentication state, exposing data via StateFlow.

```
@HiltViewModel
class AuthViewModel @Inject constructor(
    private val authRepository: AuthRepository
) : ViewModel() {

    private val _authToken = MutableStateFlow<String?>(null)
    val authToken: StateFlow<String?> = _authToken

    private val _username = MutableStateFlow<String?>(null)
    val username: StateFlow<String?> = _username

    fun login(username: String, password: String) {
        viewModelScope.launch {
            try {
                val user = authRepository.loginUser(username, 
password)
                _authToken.value = user.token
                _username.value = user.username
            } catch (e: Exception) {
                Log.e("AuthViewModel", "Login failed", e)
```

```
            }
        }
    }

    fun logout() {
        viewModelScope.launch {
            authRepository.logout(_username.value ?: "")
            _authToken.value = null
            _username.value = null
        }
    }
}
```

- **login** authenticates the user, updating the observable state to synchronize the UI.
- **logout** handles session termination, clearing stored data.

4. **Composable UI for Login and Logout**

The main **AuthScreen** is a dynamic UI that adapts to the user's state (logged in or not).

```
@Composable
fun AuthScreen() {
    val viewModel: AuthViewModel = hiltViewModel()
    val authToken by viewModel.authToken.collectAsStateWith
Lifecycle()
    val username by viewModel.username.collectAsStateWithLife
cycle()

    if (authToken != null && username != null) {
        Text("Welcome, ${username!!}!")
        Button(onClick = { viewModel.logout() }) {
            Text("Logout")
        }
    } else {
        var inputUsername by remember { mutableStateOf("") }
        var inputPassword by remember { mutableStateOf("") }

        TextField(value = inputUsername, onValueChange =
{ inputUsername = it }, label = { Text("Username") })
        TextField(value = inputPassword, onValueChange =
{ inputPassword = it }, label = { Text("Password") })
        Button(onClick = { viewModel.login(inputUsername,
inputPassword) }) {
            Text("Login")
        }
    }
}
```

- The UI automatically reacts to changes in the authentication state.
- It displays fields for username and password when the user is not logged in.

5. **Dependency Injection with Hilt**

The dependencies for the Authentication module are managed in **`AuthModule`**.

```
@Module
@InstallIn(SingletonComponent::class)
class AuthModule {
    @Provides
    @Singleton
    fun provideAuthRepository(apiService: ApiService, authData-
Store: AuthDataStore): AuthRepository {
        return AuthRepositoryImpl(apiService, authDataStore)
    }

    @Provides
    @Singleton
    fun provideAuthDataStore(@ApplicationContext context:
Context): AuthDataStore {
        return AuthDataStore(context)
    }
}
```

The Authentication module is designed to provide a secure and reactive experience, combining state management with StateFlow, persistence with DataStore, and a flexible UI with Jetpack Compose. Integration with Hilt ensures modularity and maintainability.

The implementation phase has brought the design to life, resulting in the implementation of the modules of the e-commerce app. Each module was developed using modern technologies such as Jetpack Compose for the UI, Hilt for dependency management, and StateFlow for reactive state handling, ensuring modularity, maintainability, and scalability.

We explored the main modules in detail:

- **Product Catalog**, featuring smooth navigation between the product list and details.
- **Cart**, designed to dynamically manage items with local persistence.
- **Checkout**, incorporating a multi-screen system and a Factory pattern for managing payment methods.
- **Authentication**, leveraging DataStore for secure persistence and providing a reactive user experience.

Each module was developed with a strong focus on modularity and integration, ensuring seamless flows between functionalities. With this solid foundation, the app is now ready for the testing phase, which will ensure the stability and reliability of each component.

Testing

The testing phase ensures that the implemented modules meet the defined requirements, guaranteeing stability, reliability, and correct integration between components. In this section, we focus on unit, integration, and UI tests for the app's main modules, writing meaningful tests that cover practical use cases and common scenarios.

Product Catalog

Here are the tests that we will cover for this module:

Unit Tests:

- For **`ProductRepository`**, verifying correct mapping and retrieval of products.

Integration Tests:

- For **`ProductViewModel`**, ensuring communication between the repository and state.

UI Tests:

- For **`ProductListScreen`**, validating UI behavior.

1. **Unit Tests for `ProductRepository`**

The repository is the core of data access, so it is crucial to test product retrieval and mapping accurately.

```
@OptIn(ExperimentalCoroutinesApi::class)
class ProductRepositoryTest {

    private val mockApiService = mockk<ApiService>()
    private lateinit var productRepository: ProductRepository

    @Before
    fun setUp() {
        productRepository = ProductRepository(mockApiService)
    }

    @Test
    fun `fetchProducts should return mapped products`() = runTest
{
```

```
        val mockApiProducts = listOf(
            ApiProduct(1, "Product 1", "Description 1", 10.0, 0),
            ApiProduct(2, "Product 2", "Description 2", 20.0, 0)
        )
        coEvery { mockApiService.getProducts() } returns
mockApiProducts

        val result = productRepository.fetchProducts()

        assertEquals(2, result.size)
        assertEquals("Product 1", result[0].name)
        assertEquals(10.0, result[0].price, 0.01)
    }
}
```

2. **Integration Tests for `ProductViewModel`**

We ensure that the ViewModel correctly updates the state based on data from the repository.

```
@OptIn(ExperimentalCoroutinesApi::class)
class ProductRepositoryTest {

    @Test
    fun `fetchCategories should update categories state`() =
runTest {
        val mockCategories = listOf(
            Category(1, "Electronics"),
            Category(2, "Clothing")
        )
        coEvery { mockRepository.fetchCategories() } returns
mockCategories

        viewModel.getCategoryList()
        advanceUntilIdle()

        val state = viewModel.categories.value
        assertEquals(2, state.size)
        assertEquals("Electronics", state[0].name)

        println("Mock repository: $mockRepository")
        println("Categories in ViewModel: ${viewModel.categories.
value}")

        coVerify { mockRepository.fetchCategories() }
    }
}
```

3. UI Tests for `ProductListScreen`

We validate that the product list screen displays data correctly.

```
class ProductListScreenTest {

    @get:Rule
    val composeTestRule = createComposeRule()

    @Test
    fun productListScreen_displaysProductsCorrectly() {
        val mockProducts = listOf(
            Product(1, "Product 1", "Description 1", 10.0, 0),
            Product(2, "Product 2", "Description 2", 20.0, 0)
        )

        composeTestRule.setContent {
            ProductListScreen(
                products = mockProducts
            )
        }

        composeTestRule.onNodeWithText("Product 1").assert
Exists()
        composeTestRule.onNodeWithText("Product 2").assert
Exists()
    }

}
```

The tests for the Product Catalog module cover the main components and flows, ensuring that the repository, ViewModel, and UI work correctly and cohesively.

Conclusion

This chapter guided the reader through the entire development process of an e-commerce app, from design to implementation and finally to the testing phase. Each step was designed to ensure modularity, scalability, and maintainability, leveraging modern technologies such as Jetpack Compose, Hilt, StateFlow, and testing tools such as JUnit, MockK, and Espresso.

During the design phase, we clearly defined the app's main modules—Product Catalog, Cart, Checkout, Authentication, and Order Management—identifying the responsibilities of each module and their interactions. This approach provided a clear structure to confidently tackle the implementation.

During the development phase, we translated the design into code, focusing on key modules to build a functional and easily expandable application. Each module was developed with particular attention to the separation of responsibilities, ensuring robust integration between the UI, business logic, and data management.

Finally, during the testing phase, we ensured that the app's main components were stable and functional, with targeted tests on repositories, ViewModels, and UI. Although space did not allow us to cover all modules, the approach taken is consistently applicable to every part of the app.

Through this chapter, the reader has gained a comprehensive understanding of how to design, develop, and test an e-commerce app using Android best practices. This serves as a solid foundation for tackling future projects with confidence and expertise.

In the next chapter, we will use the approach presented in this chapter to build a social media app.

Points to Remember

- **Modular Design**: Dividing the app into independent modules—Product Catalog, Cart, Checkout, Authentication, and Order Management—ensures modularity and ease of maintenance.
- **Architectural Patterns**: Using MVVM to separate business logic from the UI improves code maintainability and testability.
- **State Management**: StateFlow is a powerful tool for managing state reactively and unidirectionally, enabling seamless updates between the ViewModel and UI.
- **Persistence and Data**: Room is essential for managing local data persistence, such as cart items, ensuring offline functionality.
- **Server Communication**: Retrofit simplifies API calls, making it easy to integrate server data with the app.
- **Dependency Injection with Hilt**: Centralizing dependency management with Hilt reduces boilerplate code and enhances project modularity.
- **Factory Pattern for Payment Methods**: Using a Factory Pattern to handle scalable payment methods, such as credit cards and cash-on-delivery, increases system flexibility.
- **Comprehensive Testing**: Covering each module with unit, integration, and UI tests ensures application stability and minimizes bugs.
- **UI with Jetpack Compose**: Creating reactive and modern interfaces with Jetpack Compose enhances the user experience and simplifies development.
- **User Focus**: Ensuring consistent flows between modules and intuitive navigation is key to delivering a quality user experience.

Multiple Choice Questions

1. What is the main purpose of modular design?
    a. To separate business logic from data.
    b. To divide the app into independent units for easier maintenance and scalability.
    c. To reduce the number of classes in the application.
    d. To ensure that all data is saved locally.
2. Which tool is used to handle local persistence for structured data?
    a. Retrofit
    b. DataStore
    c. Room
    d. Hilt
3. What is the purpose of the Factory Pattern in the Checkout module?
    a. To create and manage scalable and flexible payment methods.
    b. To map data received from the API into domain models.
    c. To expose observable state to the UI.
    d. To test interaction between ViewModel and Repository.
4. Which technology is used to create a declarative and reactive user interface?
    a. XML Layouts
    b. Jetpack Compose
    c. ViewPager
    d. RecyclerView
5. What is the main advantage of using Hilt in the project?
    a. Improving thread management.
    b. Making the code more compatible with older Android versions.
    c. Facilitating database access.
    d. Reducing boilerplate for dependency management.

Answers

1. b
2. c
3. a
4. b
5 d

Questions

1. What are the main advantages of modular design in the context of an e-commerce app? Provide a practical example.
2. Describe how the Factory Pattern was used in the Checkout module to manage payment methods. What benefits does this implementation provide?
3. Explain how StateFlow is used in ViewModels to handle state reactively. What are the advantages compared to alternatives like LiveData?
4. How does the Cart module ensure data persistence? Why is it important to guarantee that items are accessible offline?
5. What testing strategies would you use to ensure the stability of the Authentication module? Focus on unit and integration tests.

CHAPTER 13
Building a Social Media App

Introduction

In this chapter, as the second project of this book, we will develop a social media app, following a structured approach similar to the previous chapter–from requirements analysis to design, implementation, and testing. This process will allow us to practically apply the concepts covered in previous chapters, building a modular, scalable, and well-organized application. As expected, design patterns will also play a key role in this project.

Figure 13.1: *Icon of the social media app*

The app will consist of four main modules: **User Profile, Feed, Notifications, and Post Creation**. Each module will be designed and developed separately, ensuring a clear separation of responsibilities and smooth integration between components. We will use Jetpack Compose for the UI, StateFlow for state management, and Retrofit for communication with a mock backend.

By following the steps listed earlier, we will apply design patterns and best practices in Android development, creating a fully functional and tested social media app.

Structure

In this chapter, we will cover the following topics:

- Requirement Analysis
- Design
- Implementation
- Testing

Requirement Analysis

The analysis of requirements is the first step in developing a functional and well-structured social media app. This phase focuses on identifying the needs of the target users and defining what the app must do (functional requirements), how it must do it (non-functional requirements), and which technologies and tools will be necessary (technical requirements).

As discussed in the previous chapter, a thorough requirements analysis helps establish a clear direction for design and implementation, reducing the risk of errors or functional gaps.

In the context of this social media app, the requirements will be organized to support three main user segments–general users, content creators, and businesses. Starting with a detailed analysis of each segment's needs, we will define the key features that will guide all subsequent stages of development.

Target Users

A social media app must be designed taking into consideration the different categories of users who will use it. Each user segment has specific needs and goals, which guide the design of the core features. In the context of this project, we will focus on three main categories: generic users, content creators, and businesses.

Generic Users:

- **Characteristics:**
    - People who use the app for leisure, to explore interesting content, and interact with other users.
- **Key needs:**
    - An updated and intuitive feed for browsing content.
    - Simple functionalities to "like" and comment on posts.
    - Quick access to notifications to stay updated on their interactions.

Content Creators:

- **Features:**
    - Users who want to post personal or creative content, build an audience, and receive meaningful interactions.
- **Key needs:**
    - Simple and flexible tools to create and publish posts.
    - Immediate and detailed visualization of received interactions (for example, likes and comments).
    - Access to a customizable profile that represents their online identity.

Businesses:

- **Features:**
    - Profiles representing brands or businesses, using the app to promote products, services, or campaigns.
- **Key needs:**
    - Publishing content that highlights promotions, products, or business initiatives.
    - Monitoring engagement with posts, such as the number of likes, comments, and notifications.
    - A simple interface to update business information and customize the profile.

General needs:

Regardless of the segment, all users expect:

- **Accessibility**: A user-friendly and inclusive interface suitable for everyone.
- **Responsiveness**: Immediate feedback on actions, such as liking or posting content.
- **Privacy and Security**: User data must be handled securely.

Dividing target users into these three main categories allows us to design an app that meets the needs of both, those seeking leisure and those aiming to create or promote content. This structure will guide the design of the modules of the app, ensuring a balanced experience for all segments.

Use Cases

As discussed in the previous chapter about the e-commerce app, use cases help define the primary flows that guide the design and implementation of modules. In this section, we will focus on specific use cases for a social media app, tailoring them to the needs of the three identified user segments.

- **Feed Navigation:** The user opens the app and views a feed of posts generated by other users or businesses. They can scroll through the feed, like posts, and leave comments.

  Goals: (a) Provide an intuitive interface to explore interesting content; (b) enable quick interactions with posts (likes and comments); (c) dynamically update the feed with new content.

- **Post Creation**: The user creates a new post by adding a title, description, and optional image. The post is added to the feed and made visible to other users. **Goals**: (a) Provide a simple interface for creating content; (b) allow users to immediately see their post in the feed; (c) simulate positive feedback from the backend (for example, receiving likes or comments).

- **Profile Viewing and Editing:** The user accesses their profile page to view and update personal information, such as their name, profile picture, and description. **Goals**: (a) Provide a personalized view of the user's information; (b) enable simple and intuitive editing of personal data; (c) synchronize changes with the dummy backend.

- **Notification Management:** The user receives notifications about interactions on their posts (for example, "Mario liked your post"). Notifications are displayed on a dedicated screen.

  Goals: (a) Simulate notifications generated by interactions; (b) provide an interface to view and manage notifications; (c) allow triggering notifications manually via a button for demo purposes.

These use cases define the main flows of the social media app, providing a clear foundation for designing the modules and their interactions.

Main Requirements

Defining the main requirements is essential to ensure that the social media app meets user needs and delivers a high-quality experience. In this section, we divided the requirements into three main categories–functional, to describe what the app must do; non-functional, to define quality attributes; and technical, to establish the technologies and tools needed for development.

Functional Requirements

Functional requirements define the key features that the social media app must offer to its users. These requirements are directly tied to the described use cases and reflect the needs of the three identified user segments–generic users, content creators, and businesses.

- **User Profile**
  - Users must be able to view their profile with personal information such as name, picture, and bio.
  - It must be possible to edit profile details and save them in real time.
  - Users can access a summary of received interactions, such as likes and comments.
- **Feed**
  - Display a feed of posts sorted chronologically or by other predefined criteria.
  - Allow users to like and add comments to posts.
  - Support dynamic updates of the feed with new content fetched from the backend.
- **Post Creation**
  - Users must be able to create a new post by entering a title, description, and an optional image.
  - The post must be immediately visible in the user's feed.
  - Businesses can publish promotional posts and monitor the interactions they receive.
- **Notifications**
  - Display notifications about interactions on posts, such as received likes or comments.
  - Allow users to receive notifications when someone interacts with their posts.
  - Store notifications in a dedicated screen for later reference.
- **Post Interactions**
  - Allow users to like posts with a single click.
  - Enable the creation and display of comments on each post.
  - Updates to interactions must be immediately visible in the feed and post details.

These functional requirements represent the core features that the social media app must provide, ensuring a solid foundation to meet the needs of the target users.

Non-functional Requirements

Non-functional requirements describe the quality attributes of the social media app, ensuring that the user experience is smooth, secure, and scalable. These requirements support the proper functioning of the features defined in the functional requirements.

- **Performance**
  - The feed must load quickly, with response times under 2 seconds for fetching posts.
  - Interactions with posts (likes and comments) must update in real-time without blocking the interface.
- **Scalability**
  - The system must handle an increasing number of users and posts without significant performance degradation.
  - The app's structure should allow for the future addition of new features (for example, messaging or advanced analytics).
- **Accessibility**
  - The user interface must be designed following Android accessibility guidelines (for example, support for screen readers and keyboard navigation).
  - Colors and contrasts must be optimized for users with visual impairments.
- **Usability**
  - The app must be intuitive and easy to use for all user segments, with clear flows for navigation, post creation, and interactions.
  - Screens must be consistent with each other, maintaining a unified design.
- **Security**
  - Personal data, such as profile information and published content, must be handled securely, even in the context of a mock backend.
  - Any action that modifies sensitive data (for example, profile updates) must require visual confirmation.
- **Responsiveness**
  - The app must adapt seamlessly to different devices and orientations, including smartphones and tablets.
  - All content must remain visible without loss of information on screens of varying sizes.

- **Maintainability**
  - The code must be modular and readable, following best practices such as the MVVM pattern and separation of concerns.
  - Dependencies must be managed centrally with tools like Hilt to minimize the risk of errors.

Non-functional requirements ensure that the social media app provides not only useful features but also a superior user experience.

Technical Requirements

Technical requirements define the technologies, tools, and practices needed for the development and operation of the social media app. These requirements ensure a robust and scalable implementation, leveraging modern tools for Android development.

- **Architecture**
  - **MVVM Pattern**: Separate presentation logic (ViewModel) from business logic and UI, and expose observable states via StateFlow to ensure reactive updates.
  - **Modular Design**: Divide the app into separate modules (Profile, Feed, Notifications, Post Creation) to ensure maintainability and reusability.
- **Technologies**
  - **Jetpack Compose**: To create a declarative and reactive user interface, simplifying state management and the construction of dynamic layouts.
  - **Hilt**: For dependency management, reducing boilerplate and improving testability.
  - **StateFlow**: To manage screen state in a reactive and unidirectional manner.
  - **Retrofit**: To communicate with the mock backend and fetch/update data.
  - **Room**: For local data persistence, such as notifications or profile settings.
- **Testing Tools**
  - **JUnit and MockK**: For unit testing and verifying logic in ViewModels and Repositories.
  - **Espresso**: For user interface tests that simulate real interactions with the app.

This analysis of the main requirements provides a comprehensive overview of the functionalities and technical characteristics that will guide the design and implementation of the social media app. With clear and well-defined requirements, we can now move on to modular design.

Design

The design phase is essential for translating the main requirements of the social media app into a clear and modular structure. Following the approach already adopted in the previous chapter for the e-commerce app, this phase defines the general architecture and the specifics of individual modules, ensuring that each component is autonomous yet well-integrated.

In this section, we will focus on four main modules—**User Profile**, **Feed**, **Notifications**, and **Post Creation**. Each module will be designed to meet functional requirements and provide a smooth and scalable user experience, utilizing the MVVM architecture to maintain a clear separation between UI, presentation logic, and data access.

With particular attention to modularity and integration among components, this design will provide a solid foundation for the implementation phase, enabling a seamless transition from concept to code. Let us now proceed with the analysis of the app's general architecture.

General Architecture

As described in *Chapter 12, Building an E-Commerce App*, designing a well-structured application requires a modular architecture that separates responsibilities and promotes code reusability. Here too, we will use the MVVM (Model-View-ViewModel) pattern as a foundation to ensure clear state management and seamless interactions between the UI, presentation logic, and data access.

Modules

The social media app will be organized into four main modules:

- **User Profile**: Manages the display and editing of personal information.
- **Feed**: Allows users to view and interact with published posts.
- **Notifications**: Displays recent activities related to the users' posts.
- **Post Creation**: Enables users to create new content.

These modules will be integrated into a single application, each with well-defined responsibilities and minimal interactions between them, ensuring a modular and scalable design.

Interaction with the Mock Backend

While real social media applications rely on an actual server, to stay within the scope of this project, we will simulate a backend using mock APIs that return static or dynamic data for the feed, notifications, and user profile. Communication with the backend will be managed via Retrofit, with the following approach:

- The feed and notifications fetch simulated data.
- Post creation sends data to the mock backend and dynamically updates the feed.
- User profile updates are saved locally, simulating server-side persistence.

Technologies

- **Jetpack Compose**: To create a modern and declarative user interface.
- **Hilt**: For centralized dependency management.
- **StateFlow**: For reactive and observable state management.
- **Room**: For local data persistence (notifications and user settings).
- **Retrofit**: To simulate backend APIs.

With this general architecture, the social media app follows a modular and scalable structure, similar to the approach adopted in the previous chapter. Each module will be designed to function independently, ensuring flexibility and ease of maintenance.

Design of Individual Modules

After defining the general architecture of the social media app, we now move on to the detailed design of the individual modules.

In this section, we will focus on the four main modules—**User Profile**, **Feed**, **Notifications**, and **Post Creation**.

For each module, we will define the main functionalities, provide a UML diagram of the involved classes, and outline the interactions with the rest of the app, establishing a clear foundation for the subsequent implementation.

User Profile

The **User Profile** module allows users to view and edit their personal information, including their name, profile picture, and bio. This module is essential for personalizing the user experience and representing one's identity within the app.

Main Features

- **Profile Viewing:**
  - Display personal information, such as name, profile picture, and bio.
  - Show the total number of published posts and received interactions (likes and comments).

- **Profile Editing:**
    - Allow users to update their name, profile picture, and bio.
    - Save changes locally and simulate synchronization with the backend.
- **Activity History:**
    - Provide a summary of interactions received on posts, updated dynamically.

UML Diagram

Figure 13.2 shows the UML diagram of this module.

Package model

- **UserProfile:** Model representing user information, such as name, bio, and profile picture.
- **ProfileRepository:** Fetches and saves user profile data.

Package viewmodel

- **ProfileViewModel:** Coordinates the retrieval and updating of profile data and exposes the observable state of user information.

Package view

- **ProfileScreen:** The main screen for viewing and editing personal information.

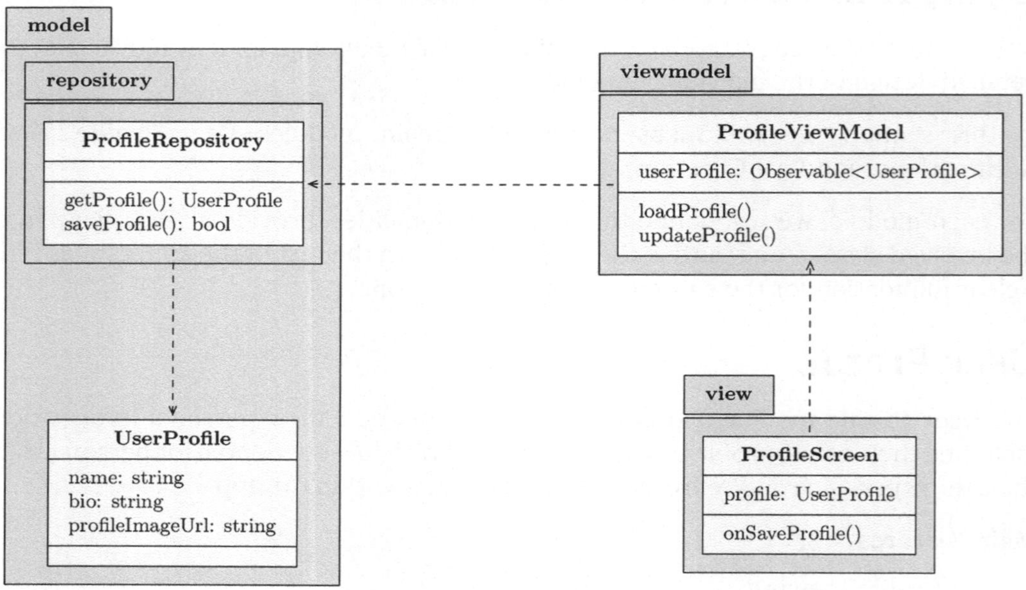

***Figure 13.2**: UML diagram of the module User Profile*

Relationships

- **ProfileScreen** interacts with **ProfileViewModel** to display the user's personal information and notify actions such as editing or saving the profile.
- **ProfileViewModel** interacts with **ProfileRepository** to fetch user profile data and save it when modifications are made.

Interactions with Other Modules

- **ProfileRepository** interacts with the module **Core** to manage profile data persistence and simulate retrieval and updates via APIs.

Feed

The **Feed** module allows users to explore posts published by other users or businesses, interact with them through likes and comments, and view post details. This module represents the core of the social media app, providing a smooth and dynamic browsing experience.

Main Features:

- **Feed Viewing**:
  - Display a list of posts fetched from the backend.
  - Allow users to scroll through the feed and refresh the content.
- **Post Interactions**:
  - Enable users to "Like" or comment on posts directly from the feed.
  - Show interaction updates.
- **Post Details**:
  - Provide a dedicated screen to view the full content of a post.
  - Display associated comments and allow users to add new ones.

UML Diagram:

Figure 13.3 shows the UML diagram of this module.

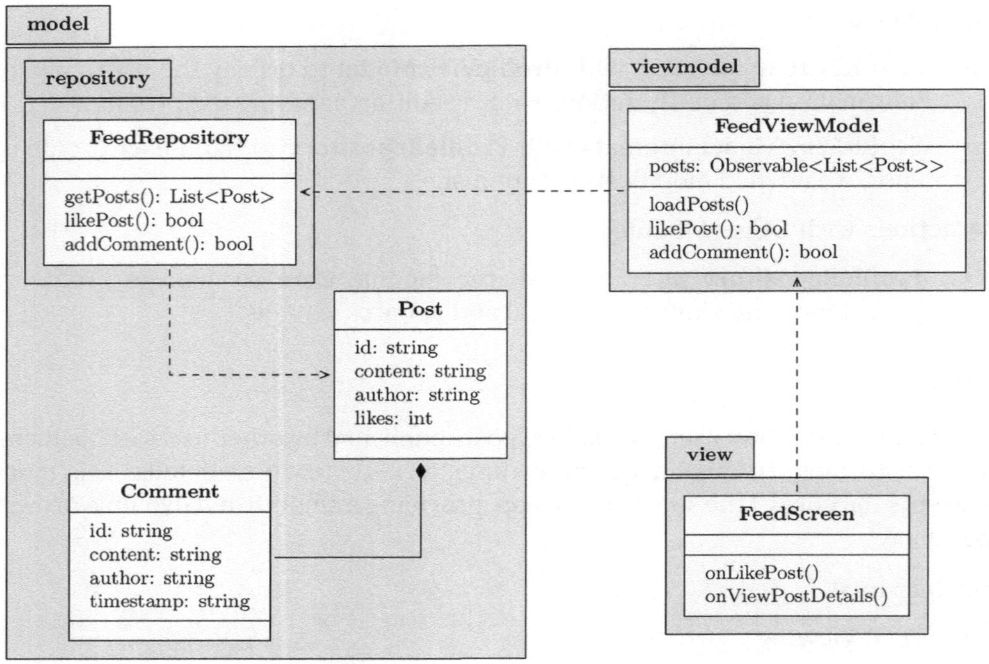

***Figure 13.3**: UML diagram of the module Feed*

Package model

- **FeedRepository:** Fetches posts, manages interactions with the content and interacts with the backend for data retrieval and interaction updates.
- **Post:** Model representing a post, with attributes such as title, content, author, and interaction count.
- **Comment:** Model representing a comment associated with a post.

Package viewmodel

- **FeedViewModel:** Coordinates the retrieval of feed data and the state of interactions. Exposes the feed as a StateFlow.

Package view

- **FeedScreen:** Main screen for displaying the list of posts and enabling interactions.
- **PostDetailsScreen:** Screen for viewing the details of a single post and its associated comments.

Relationships

- **FeedScreen** interacts with **FeedViewModel** to display the list of posts, notify actions such as likes and navigate to the post details screen.

- **PostDetailsScreen** interacts with **FeedViewModel** to display the details of a selected post and its associated comments, as well as to enable adding new comments.
- **FeedViewModel** interacts with **FeedRepository** to fetch feed data, update interactions, and save new comments associated with posts.

Interactions with Other Modules

- **FeedScreen** interacts with the module **User Profile** to display posts published by the user and provide quick access to the profile of a post's author.
- **FeedViewModel** interacts with **Notifications** to update the feed with notifications about interactions received on posts (for example, new likes or comments).
- **FeedRepository** interacts with the module **Core** to simulate the retrieval and updating of data related to posts and interactions.

The **Feed** module serves as a central platform for exploring and interacting with the app's content. With a modular and well-structured design, this module provides a seamless and interactive experience for all users.

Notifications

The **Notifications** module allows users to view and manage notifications related to interactions received on their posts. In this demo, the notification system is simulated through a mock backend, with an option to trigger manual notifications for demonstration purposes.

Main Features

- **Notification Viewing**:
    - Display a list of notifications related to likes and comments received on the user's posts.
    - Highlight unread notifications.
- **Notification Simulation**:
    - Allow users to manually generate notifications via a dedicated button.
- **Notification Management**:
    - Mark notifications as read.
    - Delete obsolete notifications.

UML Diagram

Figure 13.4 shows the UML diagram of this module.

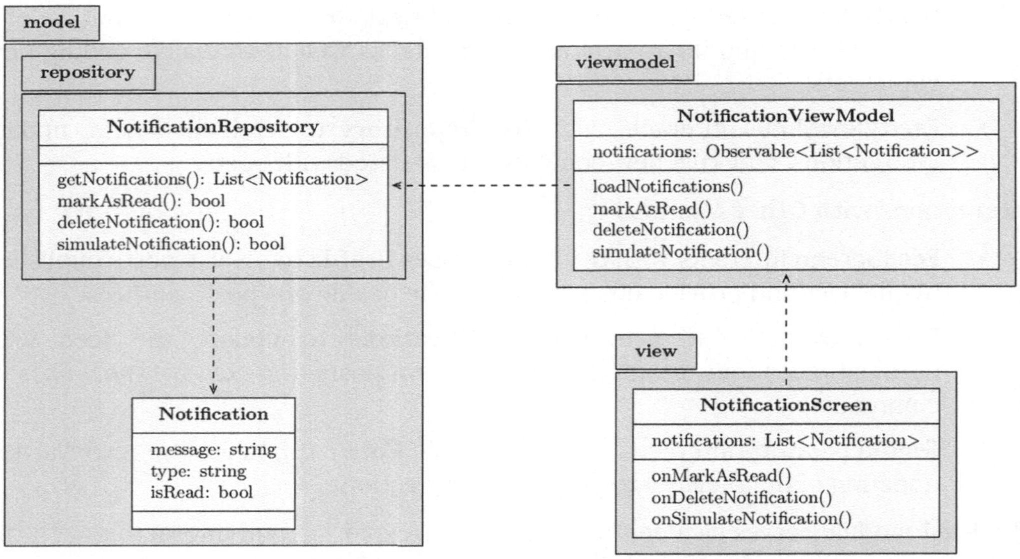

***Figure 13.4**: UML diagram of the module Notifications*

Package `model`

- **Notification:** Model representing a notification, with attributes such as type, message, and status.
- **NotificationRepository:** Fetches and updates notifications from the backend. It also simulates manual notification generation.

Package `viewmodel`

- **NotificationViewModel:** Coordinates the logic for retrieving, simulating, and updating the state of notifications. Exposes the notification state via StateFlow.

Package `view`

- **NotificationScreen:** Screen for viewing and managing the list of notifications.

Relationships

- **NotificationScreen** interacts with **NotificationViewModel** to display the list of notifications, notify actions such as marking a notification as read or deleting it, and simulate new notifications.
- **NotificationViewModel** interacts with **NotificationRepository** to fetch and update notifications, as well as to simulate adding new notifications.

Interactions with Other Modules

- **NotificationViewModel** interacts with the module **Feed** to notify updates related to post interactions, synchronizing notifications with the feed.
- **NotificationViewModel** interacts with the module **User Profile** to update the

summary of interactions in the user's profile, including the count of new likes and comments.

- **NotificationRepository** interacts with the module **Core** to simulate the persistence and retrieval of notifications.

The **Notifications** module provides an efficient way to manage interactions received on content, keeping the user informed in real time. With a simple yet functional simulation, the notification system enhances the user experience.

Post Creation

The **Post Creation** module allows users to create and share content in the form of posts. This module is essential for supporting social interactions within the app, enabling users to contribute new content to the feed. Each created post is simulated as being sent to the mock backend and dynamically added to the feed.

Main Features

- **Post Creation:**
  - Allow users to enter textual content and upload an image (optional).
  - Validate mandatory fields before publishing.
- **Saving and Synchronization**:
  - Simulate saving the post to the mock backend.
  - Dynamically add the new post to the user's feed.
- **Publishing Feedback**:
  - Display a success or error message after publishing.
  - Provide a preview of the post before confirmation.

UML Diagram

Figure 13.5 shows the UML diagram of this module.

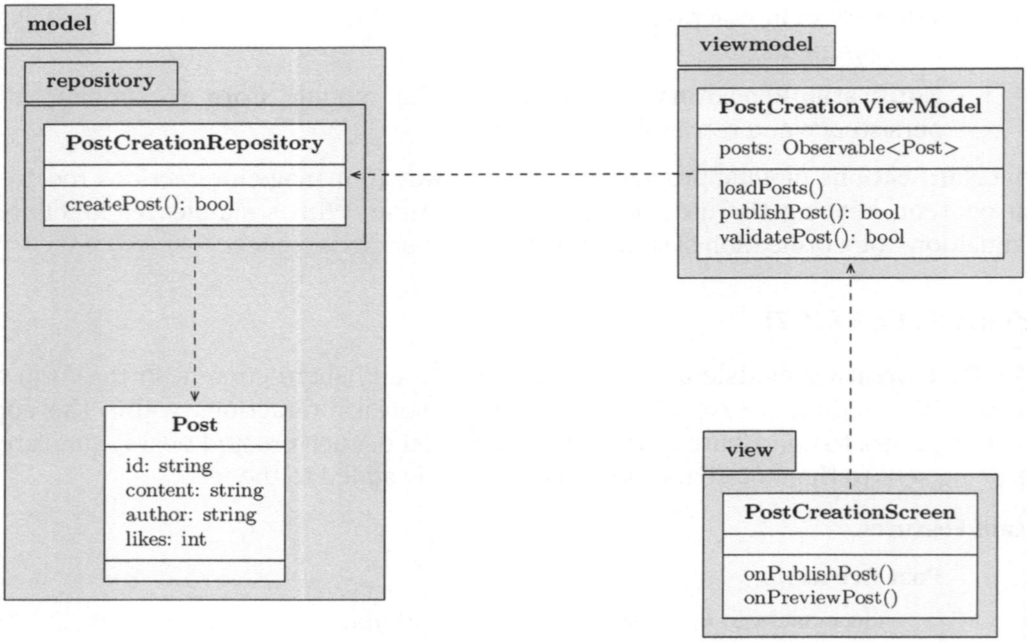

***Figure 13.5**: UML diagram of the module Post Creation*

Package `model`

- **Post:** Model representing the created post, shared with the Feed module.
- **PostCreationRepository:** Handles sending the post to the backend and returns a result indicating whether the publishing was successful or failed.

Package `viewmodel`

- **PostCreationViewModel:** Coordinates the logic for validating and publishing posts. Exposes the publishing state via StateFlow.

Package `view`

- **PostCreationScreen (UI Component):** Main screen for creating a new post and managing user input.

Relationships

- **PostCreationScreen** interacts with **PostCreationViewModel** to send post details, manage the preview, and notify the publishing action.
- **PostCreationViewModel** interacts with **PostCreationRepository** to validate and save the post, updating the feed state with the new content.

Interactions with Other Modules

- **PostCreationViewModel** interacts with the module **Feed** to dynamically update the feed with the newly published post.
- **PostCreationRepository** interacts with the module **Notification** to generate automatic notifications related to the new post (for example, "Your post has been successfully published").
- **PostCreationRepository** interacts with the module **Core** to simulate saving the post and return feedback on the result.

The **Post Creation** module enhances the social media app by allowing users to create content easily and instantly. With integration into the feed and notifications, this module ensures a seamless and consistent user experience.

The design of the modules for the social media app has established a clear and modular structure, with well-distributed responsibilities and well-defined interactions among the different components. Following an MVVM-based approach and principles of modularity, each module has been designed to be self-sufficient and scalable while ensuring seamless integration with others.

The four main modules, **User Profile**, **Feed**, **Notifications**, and **Post Creation**, have been crafted to meet the functional requirements and the needs of the target users. Here is a summary:

- The **User Profile** module enables full personalization and provides a summary of personal activities.
- The **Feed** is the core of the app, supporting content exploration and interactions.
- The **Notifications** module keeps users updated on real-time interactions they receive.
- The **Post Creation** module completes the usage cycle, enabling users to actively contribute to the feed.

With this modular design, the app is ready to move to the next phase, where the concepts defined here will take shape through code and modern technologies. Let us proceed with the implementation phase.

Implementation

After defining the architecture and design of the social media app, we now move on to the implementation phase. In this section, we will turn the design specifications into actual code, using the technologies and patterns established in the technical requirements. Following a modular approach, we will develop the four main modules—User Profile, Feed, Notifications, and Post Publishing.

As in the previous chapter, we will use Jetpack Compose to create a declarative and reactive user interface, Hilt for dependency injection, and StateFlow for efficient state management. Communication with the mock backend will be handled via Retrofit, while local persistence will leverage Room and DataStore, depending on the needs of each module.

The goal of this phase is to build a fully functional app while maintaining clean, scalable, and easily maintainable code.

General Structure

The implementation of the social media app follows a modular architecture to ensure a clear separation of concerns and facilitate both maintenance and code extensibility. In addition to the four main modules defined during the design phase (User Profile, Feed, Notifications, and Post Publishing), the app includes other supporting modules essential for overall functionality. The complete source code is available in this project's repository.

Main Modules

- **User Profile:** Manages the display and editing of the user's personal information.
- **Feed:** Displays user posts and allows interactions (likes, comments).
- **Notifications:** Simulates notifications for interactions received on posts.
- **Post Publishing:** Enables users to create and share new posts.

Supporting Modules

- **Core:** Contains shared components such as classes which use Retrofit for handling API calls to the mock server.
- **Fake Server**
  - Simulates a backend by providing a database for posts and users.
  - Handles API requests to retrieve or update data.
- **Authentication** (reused from the e-commerce app)
  - Manages user login and session handling.
  - Maintains the authentication token and verifies user status.

This modular structure ensures an organized, scalable, and easily testable implementation. With a clear separation between the user interface, state management, and backend simulation, we can now proceed with the analysis of the key aspects of the implementation of the first module, User Profile.

User Profile

The User Profile module allows users to view and edit their personal information, providing a smooth and interactive experience through the use of Jetpack Compose and StateFlow. Profile data is persistently managed via DataStore, ensuring fast loading and real-time updates. Additionally, the module is tightly integrated with the Authentication system to retrieve and manage user information.

***Figure 13.6**: Screen showing user profile with edit mode disabled (left) and edit mode enabled (right)*

1. **Profile Management with DataStore**

User profile data is retrieved and updated through AuthDataStore, simulating synchronization with the backend.

```
class ProfileRepositoryImpl @Inject constructor(
    private val authDataStore: AuthDataStore
): ProfileRepository {
    override suspend fun getUserProfile(): UserProfile {
        return UserProfile(
            username = authDataStore.getValue(KEY_USERNAME).
firstOrNull() ?: "",
            displayName = authDataStore.getValue(KEY_DISPLAY_
NAME).firstOrNull() ?: "",
```

```
                email = authDataStore.getValue(KEY_EMAIL).firstOr-
Null() ?: "",
                bio = authDataStore.getValue(KEY_BIO).firstOrNull() ?:
"",
                profileImageUrl = authDataStore.getValue(KEY_PROFILE_
IMAGE_URL).firstOrNull() ?: ""
            )
        }
    }
```

This repository provides an abstraction for retrieving and updating user data persistently.

2. **State Management with ViewModel and StateFlow**

The ProfileViewModel uses StateFlow to update the UI state reactively, ensuring that profile changes are immediately visible.

```
@HiltViewModel
class ProfileViewModel @Inject constructor(
    val profileRepository: ProfileRepository
) : ProfileContract, ViewModel() {

    private val _uiState = MutableStateFlow<ProfileUiState>
(ProfileUiState())
    val uiState: StateFlow<ProfileUiState> = _uiState.as-
StateFlow()

    init {
        fetchUserInfo()
    }

    override fun fetchUserInfo() {
        viewModelScope.launch {
            _uiState.update { currentState ->
                currentState.copy(userProfile = profileRepository.
getUserProfile())
            }
        }
    }
}
```

The **fetchUserInfo()** method retrieves profile information and automatically updates the state.

3. **UI Composable with Data Editing Support**

The profile screen is built with Jetpack Compose, allowing direct modification of elements such as the display name and bio.

```
@Composable
fun ProfileScreen(
    uiState: ProfileUiState,
    authContract: AuthContract? = null,
    profileContract: ProfileContract? = null
) {
    val editMode = remember { mutableStateOf(false) }
    LaunchedEffect(Unit) {
        profileContract?.fetchUserInfo()
    }

    Column(
        modifier = Modifier.fillMaxSize(),
        verticalArrangement = Arrangement.Center
    ) {
        Text(text = "@${uiState.userProfile.username}")
        EditableText(
            text = uiState.userProfile.displayName,
            editMode = editMode.value,
            onValueChange = { profileContract?.updateDisplay-
Name(it) }
        )
        EditableText(
            text = uiState.userProfile.bio,
            editMode = editMode.value,
            onValueChange = { profileContract?.updateBio(it) }
        )
        Button(onClick = { authContract?.logout(uiState.user
Profile.username) }) {
            Text("Logout")
        }
    }
}
```

The user can edit the display name and bio, and these changes are immediately reflected in the profile state.

4. **Logout Management and Authentication**

The Profile module is integrated with the Authentication system, allowing users to log out directly from the profile screen.

```
@HiltViewModel
class ProfileViewModel @Inject constructor(
    private val profileRepository: ProfileRepository,
    private val authRepository: AuthRepository
) : ViewModel() {
```

```
    private val _uiState = MutableStateFlow<ProfileUiState>(Pro-
fileUiState())
    val uiState: StateFlow<ProfileUiState> = _uiState.as-
StateFlow()

    fun logout() {
        viewModelScope.launch {
            authRepository.logout()
            _uiState.update { ProfileUiState(userProfile = UserPro-
file()) }
        }
    }
}
```

Logging out clears profile data and updates the app state to return to the login screen.

5. **Data Persistence and Background Loading**

The application retrieves the user profile in the background upon login, preventing delays in displaying personal information.

Using **`viewModelScope.launch`** ensures that read and write operations are executed asynchronously.

The implementation of the Profile module follows a modular and reactive approach, ensuring a seamless experience for viewing and editing personal information. Thanks to the integration with DataStore, data is persistently stored and retrieved, while Jetpack Compose provides a modern and interactive user interface.

Feed

The Feed module is the core of the social media app, allowing users to view, interact with, and manage published posts. The implementation leverages Jetpack Compose for the UI, StateFlow for state management, and Retrofit to retrieve simulated data from the mock backend. Additionally, it supports actions such as liking, commenting, and deleting user-owned posts.

Figure 13.7*: Screen showing the feed (left) and the list of posts of the logged user (right)*

1. **Fetching and Managing Posts from the Mock Backend**

The repository (**FeedRepositoryImpl**) communicates with **ApiRepository** to retrieve posts and update interactions.

```
class FeedRepositoryImpl @Inject constructor(
    private val apiRepository: ApiRepository
) : FeedRepository {

    override suspend fun fetchPosts(): List<Post> {
        return apiRepository.getPosts()
    }

    override suspend fun deletePost(postId: String) {
        apiRepository.deletePost(postId)
    }
}
```

The **fetchPosts()** method returns the list of available posts, while **deletePost()** allows the removal of posts.

2. **State Management with ViewModel and StateFlow**

The **`FeedViewModel`** uses StateFlow to update the UI and synchronize feed data.

```
@HiltViewModel
class FeedViewModel @Inject constructor(
    val feedRepository: FeedRepository,
    val profileRepository: ProfileRepository
) : FeedContract, ViewModel() {

    private val _uiState = MutableStateFlow<FeedUiState>
(FeedUiState())
    val uiState: StateFlow<FeedUiState> = _uiState.asStateFlow()

    init {
        viewModelScope.launch {
            _uiState.update { currentState ->
                currentState.copy(
                    loggedUser = profileRepository.getUserProfile(),
                    posts = feedRepository.fetchPosts()
                )
            }
        }
    }
}
```

The **`init`** function loads the user profile and posts when the module starts.

3. **Composable UI for Displaying the Feed and Posts**

The **`FeedScreen`** displays a list of posts and allows direct interaction with them.

```
@Composable
fun FeedScreen(
    uiState: FeedUiState,
    contract: FeedContract? = null
){
    var selectedTabIndex by remember { mutableIntStateOf(0) }
    val tabs = listOf("Feed", "Your Posts")

    LaunchedEffect(Unit) {
        contract?.fetchPosts()
    }

    Column {
        TabRow(selectedTabIndex = selectedTabIndex) {
            tabs.forEachIndexed { index, title ->
                Tab(
                    selected = selectedTabIndex == index,
```

```
                    onClick = { selectedTabIndex = index },
                    content = {
                        Text(modifier = Modifier.padding(12.dp),
text = title, fontSize = 22.sp)
                    }
                )
            }
        }
        LazyColumn {
            items(uiState.posts) { post ->
                PostOnFeed(postUiState = PostUiState(post =
post), contract = contract)
            }
        }
    }
}
```

The feed displays available posts and allows filtering between all posts and those published by the user.

4. **Managing Interactions: Likes**

Users can like posts directly from the feed.

```
override fun likeOrUnlikePost(postId: String) {
    if (isPostLiked(postId)) {
        unlikePost(postId)
    } else {
        likePost(postId)
    }
}

fun likePost(postId: String) {
    _uiState.update { currentState ->
        currentState.copy(
            posts = currentState.posts.map {
                if (it.id.toString() == postId) {
                    it.copy(likes = mutableListOf<UserProfile>().
apply {
                        addAll(it.likes)
                        add(uiState.value.loggedUser)
                    })
                } else it
            }
        )
    }
}
```

likeOrUnlikePost() handles adding or removing a like, updating the interaction count.

5. **Managing Post Deletion**

A user can delete their own posts, and the UI updates automatically.

```
override fun deletePost(postId: String) {
    viewModelScope.launch {
        feedRepository.deletePost(postId)
        _uiState.update { currentState ->
            currentState.copy(
                posts = currentState.posts.filter {
                    it.id.toString() != postId
                }
            )
        }
    }
}
```

deletePost() filters the feed to remove the deleted post, preventing unnecessary backend calls.

The Feed module has been implemented in a reactive and scalable way, allowing users to view, interact with, and manage posts in real time. With a smooth Jetpack Compose-based UI and optimized state management using StateFlow, this module ensures an intuitive and high-performance experience.

Notifications

The Notifications module has been designed to manage and display notifications related to user post interactions, but its implementation is still incomplete. This presents a great opportunity to apply the concepts learned in previous chapters by completing the missing functionalities.

In this section, we will provide a guide on how to implement the key notification management methods, including their display, state saving (read/unread), simulation, and potential persistence. By following these guidelines, readers can directly test concepts such as StateFlow, UI state modification in Jetpack Compose, and data management using repositories and ViewModel.

1. **Managing Notifications in the Repository**

The **NotificationRepositoryImpl** currently returns an empty list and contains unimplemented methods (TODO).

Hints:

- Add an internal mutable list to manage notifications in memory.
- *Implement* ***getNotifications()*** *to return simulated notifications.*

```
class NotificationRepositoryImpl : NotificationRepository {
    private val notifications = mutableListOf<Notification>()

    override fun getNotifications(): List<Notification> {
        return notifications
    }

    override fun simulateNotification(notification: Notification) {
        notifications.add(notification)
    }
}
```

2. **Displaying Notifications in the UI**

The **NotificationScreen.kt** file contains a basic screen implementation but does not display a real list of notifications.

Hints:

- *Integrate* ***LazyColumn*** *to display the list of notifications.*
- Show an icon next to unread notifications.

```
@Composable
fun NotificationScreen(
    uiState: NotificationUiState,
    contract: NotificationContract? = null
) {
    LazyColumn {
        items(uiState.notifications) { notification ->
            NotificationItem(notification = notification, onClick =
{
                contract?.markAsRead(notification.id)
            })
        }
    }
}
```

3. **Managing Notification State with ViewModel**

The **NotificationViewModel** uses StateFlow, but the methods **markAsRead()**, **deleteNotification()**, and **simulateNotification()** are not yet implemented.

Hints:

- *Implement **markAsRead()** to update the state of read notifications.*
- Add a method to remove a notification from the list.

```
override fun markAsRead(notificationId: String) {
    _uiState.update { currentState ->
        currentState.copy(
            notifications = currentState.notifications.map {
                if (it.id == notificationId) it.copy(isRead =
true) else it
            }
        )
    }
}
```

4. **Simulating Notifications**

The module supports manual notification generation for demonstration purposes.

Hints:

- Create a button in the UI to generate test notifications.
- *Implement the **simulateNotification()** method in **NotificationViewModel**.*

```
override fun simulateNotification(notification: Notification) {
    _uiState.update { currentState ->
        currentState.copy(
            notifications = currentState.notifications +
notification
        )
    }
}
```

5. **Notification Persistence (Optional)**

Currently, notifications are stored only in memory and are lost when the app restarts.

Hints:

- Integrate Room or DataStore for local persistence.
- Load saved notifications when the app starts.

```
class NotificationRepositoryImpl @Inject constructor(
    private val dataStore: NotificationDataStore
) : NotificationRepository {

    override suspend fun getNotifications(): List<Notification> {
        return dataStore.getNotifications()
    }
```

```
    override suspend fun saveNotification(notification: Notifica-
tion) {
        dataStore.saveNotification(notification)
    }
}
```

The **Notifications** module is a crucial part of the social media app, enhancing the user experience by providing updates on received interactions. While its structure is already defined, completing its implementation will allow the reader to strengthen their understanding of state management and reactive UI updates.

We encourage you to complete the missing functionalities, such as retrieving notifications, marking them as read, manual simulation, and, if you wish to go deeper, integrating Room or DataStore for local persistence. Once finished, you can test your implementation and observe how notifications integrate with the feed and user profile.

Post Creation

The Post Creation module allows users to create and share new content. Its implementation leverages Jetpack Compose for the UI, StateFlow for state management, and Retrofit for sending data to the mock backend. The flow includes writing the post, validating input, and publishing it to the feed.

1. **Managing Post Creation State**

The **`PostCreationViewModel`** uses StateFlow to update the UI based on user actions, such as text input or post publishing.

```
@HiltViewModel
class PostCreationViewModel @Inject constructor(
    val postCreationRepository: PostCreationRepository
) : PostCreationContract, ViewModel() {

    private val _uiState = MutableStateFlow(PostCreationUi-
State())
    val uiState: StateFlow<PostCreationUiState> = _uiState.as-
StateFlow()

    override fun updatePostContent(content: String) {
        _uiState.update { it.copy(post = it.post.copy(content =
content)) }
    }
}
```

The **`updatePostContent()`** method updates the post content reactively.

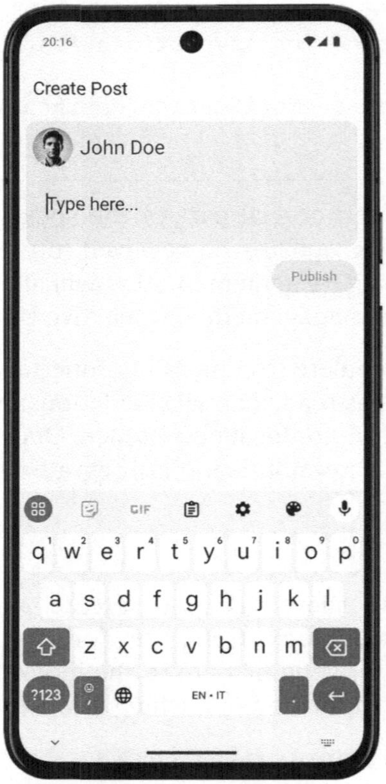

***Figure 13.8**: Screen for creating a new post*

2. **Sending the Post to the Mock Backend**

The **PostCreationRepositoryImpl** handles communication with the simulated backend.

```
class PostCreationRepositoryImpl @Inject constructor(
    private val apiRepository: ApiRepository
) : PostCreationRepository {

    override suspend fun createPost(post: Post): Boolean {
        val apiRequest = ApiPublishPostRequest(
            username = post.author.username,
            postContent = post.content
        )
        return apiRepository.publishPost(apiRequest).result
    }
}
```

The **createPost()** method converts the post into an API object and sends it to the mock backend.

3. **Composable UI for Post Creation**

The user interface dynamically updates its state based on user input.

```
@Composable
fun PostCreationScreen(
    uiState: PostCreationUiState,
    contract: PostCreationContract? = null
) {
    Column {
        TextField(
            value = uiState.post.content,
            onValueChange = { contract?.updatePostContent(it) },
            label = { Text("Type here...") }
        )
        Button(
            onClick = { contract?.publishPost(uiState.post) }
        ) {
            Text("Publish")
        }
    }
}
```

The text field and publish button are connected to **`PostCreationViewModel`**.

4. **Handling Publishing Errors**

If the post publishing fails, an error message is displayed, providing the option to retry.

```
override fun publishPost(post: Post) {
    viewModelScope.launch {
        _uiState.update { it.copy(isLoading = true) }
        val result = postCreationRepository.createPost(post)
        _uiState.update { it.copy(isLoading = false, isError =
!result) }
    }
}
```

The **`publishPost()`** method updates the state based on the operation's outcome.

5. **Refreshing the Feed After Publishing**

After publishing, the feed is updated to display the new post.

```
override fun publishPost(post: Post) {
    viewModelScope.launch {
        val result = postCreationRepository.createPost(post)
        if (result) {
            feedRepository.fetchPosts()
```

```
            }
        }
    }
```

The call to `fetchPosts()` ensures that the post is displayed immediately.

The implementation of the **Post Creation** module provides an intuitive interface for creating and sharing content, and seamless integration with the backend and feed. By leveraging StateFlow, Jetpack Compose, and Retrofit, the module is both reactive and scalable.

The implementation phase has transformed the design of the social media app into functional code, ensuring modularity, scalability, and a seamless user experience. Each module has been developed following modern Android development best practices, utilizing Jetpack Compose for the user interface, StateFlow for state management, and Retrofit for communication with the mock backend.

We have implemented the following modules:

- **User Profile**, which allows users to view and update personal information with persistence using DataStore.
- **Feed**, which displays published posts and enables users to interact with them through likes and comments.
- **Notifications**, which manages updates on received interactions and allows simulating notifications to test the app's behavior.
- **Post Creation**, which provides an intuitive interface for writing and sharing new content, automatically updating the feed.

The implementation followed a modular approach, ensuring that each component is independent yet well-integrated with the others. This separation of responsibilities makes the app easily extensible and maintainable.

Now that the app is fully implemented, we can move on to the testing phase, where we will verify the stability and proper functionality of the modules through unit, integration, and UI tests.

Testing

After completing the implementation of the social media app, the testing phase ensures that each module functions correctly and meets the defined requirements. Following the approach used in the previous chapter, we will use JUnit for unit tests, MockK for dependency mocking, and Espresso for UI tests.

The goal of testing is to identify and fix potential bugs, ensuring that key features (profile management, feed, notifications, and post creation) operate reliably. For this reason, tests will be categorized into three main types:

- **Repository Test:** Verifies data retrieval and updates, ensuring that the repository correctly interacts with the data source.
- **ViewModel Test:** Checks state management and repository calls, validating how the ViewModel processes and exposes data.
- **UI Test:** Simulates interactions with the profile screen, ensuring correct data display and modifications.

For space reasons, we will focus only on the tests for the first two modules: User Profile and Feed.

User Profile

The User Profile module allows users to view and edit their personal information. Testing for this module will focus on verifying state management in **`ProfileViewModel`**, checking interactions with **`ProfileRepository`** to ensure correct data retrieval and updates, and validating proper UI rendering in **`ProfileScreen`** to confirm that user information is displayed and modified correctly.

1. **Test for `ProfileRepository`**

Goal: Ensure that the repository correctly retrieves profile data.

```
@Test
fun `getUserProfile should return correct user profile`() = runTest
{
    val keys = listOf(KEY_USERNAME, KEY_DISPLAY_NAME, KEY_BIO,
KEY_PROFILE_IMAGE_URL, KEY_EMAIL)
    val values = listOf("testUser", "Test User", "Test Bio",
"testUrl", "testEmail")

    keys.forEachIndexed { index, key ->
        every { mockAuthDataStore.getValue(key) } returns
flowOf(values[index])
    }

    val result = profileRepository.getUserProfile()

    val resultKeys = listOf(result.username, result.displayName,
result.bio, result.profileImageUrl, result.email)

    resultKeys.forEachIndexed { index, key ->
        assertEquals(values[index], key)
    }
}
```

2. **Test for `ProfileViewModel`**

Goal: Verify that the ViewModel correctly manages profile state and interacts properly with the repository.

```
@Test
fun `fetchUserInfo should update state with user profile`() =
runTest {
    val mockProfile = UserProfile(username = "testUser", display-
Name = "Test User")
    coEvery { mockProfileRepository.getUserProfile() } returns
mockProfile

    viewModel.fetchUserInfo()
    advanceUntilIdle() // Wait for coroutine to complete

    val state = viewModel.uiState.value
    assertEquals("testUser", state.userProfile.username)
    assertEquals("Test User", state.userProfile.displayName)
}
```

3. **Test for `ProfileScreen`**

Goal: Ensure that the UI correctly displays profile information.

```
@Test
fun profileScreen_displaysUserProfileCorrectly() {
    val testProfile = UserProfile(username = "testUser", display-
Name = "Test User")

    composeTestRule.setContent {
        ProfileScreen(uiState = ProfileUiState(userProfile = test-
Profile))
    }

    with(composeTestRule) {
        onNodeWithText("@testUser").assertExists()
        onNodeWithText("Test User").assertExists()
    }
}
```

Testing for the User Profile module covered data retrieval and updates through **`ProfileRepository`**, state management with **`ProfileViewModel`**, and the proper display of information in **`ProfileScreen`**. These tests ensure that profile modifications are handled reliably and that the user interface responds correctly to interactions.

Feed

The Feed module is the core of the social media app, allowing users to view and interact with posts. Testing for this module will focus on verifying data management in **FeedRepository**, state handling in **FeedViewModel**, and proper display and interaction in **FeedScreen**.

1. **Test for FeedRepository**

Goal: Ensure that the repository correctly retrieves and updates posts and interactions.

```
@Test
fun `fetchPosts should return list of posts`() = runTest {
    val mockPosts = listOf(
        Post(id = 1, content = "Test Post 1", author
= UserProfile(username = "user1")),
        Post(id = 2, content = "Test Post 2", author
= UserProfile(username = "user2"))
    )
    coEvery { mockApiRepository.getPosts() } returns mockPosts

    val result = feedRepository.fetchPosts()

    assertEquals(2, result.size)
    assertEquals("Test Post 1", result[0].content)
}

@Test
fun `deletePost should remove post from backend`() = runTest {
    coEvery { mockApiRepository.deletePost("1") } just Runs

    feedRepository.deletePost("1")

    coVerify { mockApiRepository.deletePost("1") }
}
```

2. **Test for FeedViewModel**

Goal: Verify that the ViewModel correctly updates the state and manages interactions with the repository.

```
@Test
fun `fetchPosts should update state with post list`() = runTest {
    val mockPosts = listOf(
        Post(id = 1, content = "Test Post 1", author
= UserProfile(username = "user1"))
    )
```

```
        coEvery { mockFeedRepository.fetchPosts() } returns mockPosts

        viewModel.fetchPosts()
        advanceUntilIdle() // Wait for coroutine to complete

        val state = viewModel.uiState.value
        assertEquals(1, state.posts.size)
        assertEquals("Test Post 1", state.posts[0].content)
    }

    @Test
    fun `likeOrUnlikePost should toggle like status`() = runTest {
        val mockPost = Post(id = 1, content = "Test Post", likes =
    mutableListOf())
        val mockUser = UserProfile(username = "testUser")

        val initialState = FeedUiState(posts = listOf(mockPost),
    loggedUser = mockUser)
        viewModel.setState(initialState)

        viewModel.likeOrUnlikePost("1")

        val updatedPost = viewModel.uiState.value.posts.first()
        assertEquals(1, updatedPost.likes.size)
        assertEquals("testUser", updatedPost.likes.first().username)

        viewModel.likeOrUnlikePost("1")

        val revertedPost = viewModel.uiState.value.posts.first()
        assertEquals(0, revertedPost.likes.size)
    }
```

3. **Test for `FeedScreen`**

Goal: Ensure that the UI correctly displays posts and allows interactions, such as likes.

```
    @Test
    fun feedScreen_displaysPostsCorrectly() {
        val testPosts = listOf(
            Post(id = 1, content = "Test Post 1", author
    = UserProfile(username = "user1")),
            Post(id = 2, content = "Test Post 2", author
    = UserProfile(username = "user2"))
        )

        composeTestRule.setContent {
            FeedScreen(uiState = FeedUiState(posts = testPosts))
```

```
        }

        composeTestRule.onNodeWithText("Test Post 1").assertExists()
        composeTestRule.onNodeWithText("Test Post 2").assertExists()
    }

    @Test
    fun feedScreen_likeButtonUpdatesState() {
       val testPost = Post(id = 1, content = "Test Post", author =
    UserProfile(username = "user1"))
       val testUiState = FeedUiState(posts = listOf(testPost))
       var liked = false

       composeTestRule.setContent {
           FeedScreen(uiState = testUiState, contract = object :
    FeedContract {
                override fun fetchPosts() { }

                override fun deletePost(postId: String) { }

                override fun likeOrUnlikePost(postId: String) {
                    liked = !liked
                }

                override fun addComment(postId: String, comment:
    Comment) { }

                override fun isPostLiked(postId: String): Boolean =
    liked

                override fun isPostCommented(postId: String): Boolean
    = false
            })
        }

        composeTestRule.onNodeWithText("Test Post").assertExists()
        composeTestRule.onNodeWithContentDescription("Like Button").
    performClick()
        assertTrue(liked)
    }
```

Testing for the Feed module covered post retrieval and management through **FeedRepository**, state handling with **FeedViewModel**, and the proper display and interaction with content in **FeedScreen**. These tests ensure that posts load correctly, interactions such as "Like" are handled reliably, and the user interface responds properly to state updates.

The testing phase validated the proper functioning of each module in the social media app by dividing tests into three distinct levels—Repository, ViewModel, and UI. This approach ensured comprehensive coverage of functionalities, guaranteeing stability, reliability, and correct state management within the application.

Up till now we have tested:

- **User Profile**, verifying data retrieval and updates, state management with StateFlow, and an interactive UI with Jetpack Compose.
- **Feed**, ensuring that posts loaded and updated correctly, interactions were handled reliably, and the UI responded in real time.

With these tests, the social media app is now fully verified and we are ready to step into the project conclusion. This phase marks the completion of the development cycle, ensuring that the app meets the defined requirements and provides a smooth and consistent user experience.

Conclusion

In this chapter, we developed a complete social media app, starting from requirements analysis, moving through design and implementation, and concluding with testing. Before development, designers created UI/UX prototypes using industry-standard tools, ensuring a user-friendly and visually appealing experience. We applied design patterns, modern architectures, and best practices in Android development. Each step was approached modularly, ensuring that the app is well-structured, scalable, and easy to maintain.

We built four main modules—**User Profile**, for managing personal information; **Feed**, for viewing and interacting with posts; **Notifications**, to update users on received interactions; **Post Creation**, allowing users to create and share content.

The app was implemented using Jetpack Compose for the UI, StateFlow for state management, and Retrofit for communication with the mock backend. Finally, the testing phase ensured the proper functioning of each module, guaranteeing stability and reliability.

In the next chapter, we will build a third project focusing on the emerging architectural pattern in Android development, Model-View-Intent (MVI).

Points to Remember

- **Modular Design:** The social media app was divided into four main modules—User Profile, Feed, Notifications, and Post Creation, ensuring a scalable and maintainable architecture.

- **MVVM Architectural Pattern:** Each module follows the Model-View-ViewModel (MVVM) pattern, separating business logic from the UI and improving state management.
- **State Management with StateFlow:** StateFlow was used to maintain a reactive data flow, dynamically updating the UI based on state changes.
- **Jetpack Compose for UI:** The entire user interface was built with Jetpack Compose, providing a declarative and intuitive approach.
- **Persistence with DataStore and Room:** Profile data was managed using DataStore, while local notifications and interactions can be integrated with Room for a more structured data management.
- **Mock Backend Simulation:** To test the app without a real server, we used Retrofit to simulate API requests, enabling the retrieval and updating of static or dynamic data.
- **Module Interaction Management**: The Feed module interacts with Post Creation to display new content in real time.
- **Comprehensive Application Testing:** Tests were divided into three categories: Repository for data management, ViewModel for business logic, and UI for verifying user interactions and interface behavior.
- **Error Handling and User Experience Optimization:** Post Creation includes error handling, providing immediate feedback to users, and allowing retries in case of failure.
- **End-to-End Android Development Approach:** This chapter covered all phases of social media app development, providing a complete and practical case study applicable to real-world projects.

Multiple Choice Questions

1. What was the main criterion for dividing the social media app into modules?
   a. Create a single module with all logic in one class.
   b. Divide the code based on UI components without considering business logic.
   c. Write all code in the main screen to reduce the number of files.
   d. Separate functionalities into independent units to improve maintainability and scalability.

2. Why was the MVVM pattern chosen for this application?
    a. To separate UI, presentation logic, and business logic.
    b. To completely avoid the use of repositories and ViewModel.
    c. To reduce the number of files in the project.
    d. To improve app performance without the need for testing.
3. What approach was used for managing notifications in the social media app?
    a. Direct implementation with Firebase Cloud Messaging.
    b. Use of a mock backend and local simulation of notifications.
    c. Notifications stored only in the local database without synchronization.
    d. No notification management planned in the app architecture.
4. What is the main purpose of the Feed module?
    a. Update the user profile.
    b. Notify the user about interactions received on their posts.
    c. Display posts published by users and allow interactions such as likes.
    d. Allow editing of user's name and bio.
5. What principle was followed to ensure the Feed updates after a new post is published?
    a. The repository call is executed again after inserting a new post.
    b. Feed data is saved statically and not updated.
    c. The ViewModel reloads the feed only after restarting the app.
    d. The feed updates only when the user presses a manual refresh button.

Answers

1. d
2. a
3. b
4. c
5. a

Questions

1. How was the architecture of the social media app organized to ensure modularity and scalability? Describe the division into modules and their roles.
2. What advantages did Jetpack Compose offer in building the user interface compared to traditional XML Layouts? Provide a practical example.
3. How was data persistence managed in the social media app? Explain the technologies used and their applications in different modules.
4. How was notification management simulated without a real backend? Describe the approach taken and the advantages of this solution.
5. What testing strategies were used to verify the correct functioning of the app? Explain the test structure and their role in ensuring application stability.

CHAPTER 14
Building a Chat App

Introduction

Messaging applications must ensure a clear data flow, real-time updates, and efficient state management. In this chapter, we will develop a chat app using Model-View-Intent (MVI), an architecture design pattern that maintains a unidirectional data flow and simplifies application state management. Unlike MVVM, where the state can be modified at multiple points, MVI uses a single state holder that represents the entire UI state. Every user interaction generates an Intent, which is processed by the Model to produce a new state, ensuring clear synchronization between the UI and business logic. **MVI fully leverages the declarative nature of Jetpack Compose.**

Figure 14.1: *Icon of the chat app*

In this chapter, we will develop a chat application following a structured approach, as we did in the previous chapters, starting from requirements analysis, moving through modular design, and concluding with implementation and testing. This will allow us to apply Android development best practices and strengthen our understanding of the MVI architecture in a practical scenario.

Structure

In this chapter, we will cover the following topics:

- Requirement Analysis
- Design
- Implementation
- Testing

Requirement Analysis

Before proceeding with the design of the chat app, it is essential to define the requirements that will guide its development. In this section, we will analyze:

- **Target Users:** Who will use the app and what their needs are.
- **Use Cases:** The main interactions users can perform within the app.
- **Key Requirements:** The functional, non-functional, and technical specifications necessary to ensure a reliable and efficient app.

This analysis will allow us to design an app that meets user needs while optimizing performance and user experience.

Target Users

A messaging app can be used in various contexts, but for this application, we will focus on two main user categories–personal users and professional users. Each category has specific needs that influence the app's design and core functionalities.

Personal Users:

- **Characteristics:** Individuals using the app for quick conversations, without the need for advanced features or complex history.
- **Key needs**
  - A simple and intuitive interface that requires no learning curve.
  - Immediate access to the conversation list and contacts.
  - Real-time messaging without additional configurations.
  - The ability to continue an existing conversation or start a new one in just a few steps.

Professional Users:

- **Characteristics:** Users who use the chat for work or organizational purposes, communicating with colleagues, clients, or partners.

- **Key Needs**
  - A clear conversation list structure, prioritizing unread messages.
  - Local persistence to ensure chat accessibility even offline.
  - Reliable synchronization of conversations across sessions.
  - Notification features to stay updated on replies.

The chat app is designed to adapt to both personal and professional use, ensuring simplicity while providing stability and organization for work-related communication.

Use Cases

To ensure an intuitive and efficient user experience, it is essential to define the key use cases of the chat app. Each use case represents an action the user can perform within the app, describing the interaction flow and objectives to be achieved. Following are the five main scenarios, which will define the core functionalities of the application.

Viewing the Conversation List

The user opens the app and sees a list of active conversations with recent contacts. Each chat displays a preview of the last received message and its read status.

Goals:

1. Load and display the conversation list in chronological order.
2. Highlight chats with unread messages.
3. Allow the user to select a chat to view its details.

Starting a New Conversation

The user accesses the contact list and selects a person to start a new chat. If the conversation already exists, it is simply reopened.

Goals:

1. Retrieve the list of available contacts.
2. Allow the user to select a contact and start a new conversation.
3. If a chat with that contact already exists, open the existing conversation directly.

Sending a Message in a Chat

The user enters a conversation, types a message, and sends it. The message appears immediately in the chat and is synchronized with the system.

Goals:

1. Allow the user to write and send a message.
2. Display the message immediately in the chat screen.
3. Simulate message synchronization with a mock backend.

Receiving a Message in Real Time

The user receives a new message while in an open chat or when the app is in the background. The system updates the UI or highlights the new message in the conversation list.

Goals:

1. Simulate the arrival of a new message in an active conversation.
   a. If the chat is open, display the message immediately.
   b. If the chat is closed, highlight the conversation in the list to indicate a new message.

Simulating Notifications for New Messages

When a user receives a message while the app is in the background, a notification alerts them to the new content and allows direct access to the chat.

Goals:

1. Simulate the arrival of a notification for a received message.
2. Display an icon or badge on the conversation list to indicate unread messages.
3. Allow the user to open the chat directly from the notification.

These use cases define the core interactions within the chat app. Their implementation will ensure a smooth, intuitive, and seamless user experience.

Main Requirements

After analyzing the main use cases of the chat app, it is essential to define the key requirements that will guide the development process. This section is divided into three categories:

- **Functional Requirements:** Define the core features of the app, such as sending and receiving messages, managing conversations, and simulating notifications.
- **Non-Functional Requirements:** Describe the quality attributes of the application, including responsiveness, scalability, and data persistence.

- **Technical Requirements**: Specify the technologies and tools used for development, such as MVI, Jetpack Compose, Room Database, and Retrofit.

These requirements will provide a solid foundation for the design and implementation of the chat app. As with the previous projects, you can find the full source code in the dedicated repository.

Functional Requirements

The functional requirements define the key features that the chat app must provide to ensure a complete and intuitive user experience. These requirements are directly derived from the previously defined use cases and represent the core actions that users can perform within the app.

- **Viewing the conversation list:** The user must be able to access a list of active conversations with a preview of the last message and read status.
    - Retrieve and display the conversation list in chronological order.
    - Highlight conversations with unread messages.
    - Update the list in real time when new messages arrive.
- **Starting a new conversation:** The user must be able to start a conversation by selecting a contact from the available list.
    - Retrieve the contact list and display it in alphabetical order.
    - Allow the selection of a contact to start a chat.
    - If a conversation already exists, open the existing chat instead of creating a new one.
- **Sending a message in a chat:** The user must be able to write and send messages within a conversation.
    - Allow text input and message sending.
    - Display the message immediately in the chat after sending.
    - Simulate message transmission to the mock backend to ensure synchronization.
- **Receiving a message in real time:** The user must be able to receive messages in an open or closed conversation.
    - If the conversation is open, display the message immediately.
    - If the conversation is closed, update the conversation list and mark it as unread.
    - Store received messages to keep them available offline.
- **Simulating notifications for new messages:** The user must receive notifications when a new message arrives in a closed chat.
    - Simulate a local notification to indicate a new received message.

  - Display an icon or badge on the conversation list to highlight unread messages.
  - Allow the user to open the conversation directly from the notification.

These functional requirements define the core actions that users can perform within the chat app. Their implementation will ensure a clear usage flow and a smooth user experience. Now, we can move on to the non-functional requirements, which describe the quality attributes of the system.

Non-Functional Requirements

In the previous chapter, we defined the key non-functional requirements necessary to ensure a stable, responsive, and scalable app. For this chat application, we will follow the same principles, ensuring performance, scalability, reliability, and accessibility.

Key aspects to consider:

- **Responsiveness**: The interface must immediately react to user input, ensuring a smooth experience.
- **Local persistence**: Conversations must be saved and accessible offline, even without an internet connection.
- **Real-time updates**: Received messages must appear automatically in the UI, without requiring a manual refresh.
- **Efficient state management**: The app's state must be clear and predictable, preventing unexpected behaviors in conversations.
- **Scalability:** The architecture must support a growing number of chats without negatively impacting performance.

By following these guidelines, we will ensure that the chat app provides an optimal user experience. Now, we can move on to the technical requirements, where we will define the tools and technologies needed to develop the application.

Technical requirements

The technical requirements define the technologies, tools, and architectures needed for developing the chat app. Following a modern and efficient approach, we will adopt an architecture based on Model-View-Intent (MVI) to ensure unidirectional state management and a clear flow between the user interface and business logic.

- **Architecture and State Management**
  - **Model-View-Intent (MVI):** Enables predictable and reactive state management, separating the UI, update logic, and user intents.
  - **StateFlow:** Keeps the UI state synchronized with data updates.

- **Repository Pattern:** Organizes data access clearly, separating business logic from persistence management.

- **Technologies Used**
  - **Jetpack Compose:** Used for declarative UI creation, optimizing state handling in chat screens.
  - **Room Database:** Ensures local message and conversation persistence, providing offline access.
  - **Retrofit:** Simulates real-time communication, handling asynchronous message reception.
  - **Dagger-Hilt:** Manages dependencies efficiently for a scalable architecture.
- **Testing Tools**
  - **JUnit and MockK:** For unit testing on Repositories and ViewModels.
  - **Espresso:** For UI tests that simulate real interactions with the app.

With these technical requirements, we ensure that the chat app is designed to be reactive, scalable, and easily testable.

We have thoroughly analyzed the users of the app, the ways in which it will be used, and the functionalities that it must offer. This has allowed us to identify key use cases and define the fundamental requirements for the project's development.

Now, we can move on to the design phase, where we will transform these requirements into a clear and efficient modular structure.

Design

In this section, we will organize the app architecture, defining the modular structure and state management. This phase is divided into two main parts:

- **General Architecture**: Defines the app structure, module organization, and component interactions.
- **Module Design**: Detailed analysis of the two main modules:
  - **Chat Module**: Manages the conversation list and chat screen.
  - **Contact Module**: Displays the list of available contacts and allows users to start new conversations.

The design will follow a modular approach, with a scalable architecture based on Model-View-Intent. This will ensure a clear and predictable data flow, improving code maintainability and state management.

General Architecture

Each module of the app is structured into three main packages—**`model`**, **`view`**, and **`intent`**.

- **Model (Data Layer & Business Logic):**
  - Contains the repository and data models.
  - Retrieves information from the database and the mock backend.
  - Implements the logic for fetching and saving messages and conversations.
- **View (UI Layer):**
  - Contains the app screens (for example, ChatScreen, ContactScreen).
  - Automatically updates based on the state provided by the Intent Layer.
- **Intent (State Management & User Actions):**
  - Defines Intents representing user actions (for example, Send Message, Open Conversation).
  - Contains the Reducer, which updates the state based on received intents.
  - Exposes StateFlow for UI state management.

Module Overview

The application is divided into three modules—Chat module, Contact module and a module that acts as a simulation of a real backend, called Mock Backend.

- **Chat Module**
  - **View**: Displays the conversation list and chat interface.
  - **Intent Layer**: Manages user input and updates the UI state.
  - **Model**: Fetches messages from the repository and updates the local database.
- **Contact Module**
  - **View**: Displays the contact list.
  - **Intent Layer**: Allows the user to select a contact to start a new conversation.
  - **Model**: Checks if a chat already exists with the selected contact or creates a new one.
- **Mock Backend**
  - Simulates sending and receiving messages.
  - Interacts with the Model to update conversation states.

Design of Individual Modules

After defining the general architecture of the chat app, we can now focus on the design of individual modules. In this section, we will analyze each module in detail, describing the main classes and their roles within the application.

Chat Module

The **Chat** module is the core of the messaging application, responsible for managing conversations and handling message sending/receiving. This module consists of two main screens:

- **Conversation List**: Displays the list of active chats with a preview of the last message.
- **Chat Screen**: Allows sending and receiving messages within a conversation.

Additionally, this module simulates notifications, which are generated when a new message arrives in a conversation not opened.

UML Diagram

Figure 14.2 shows the UML diagram of this module.

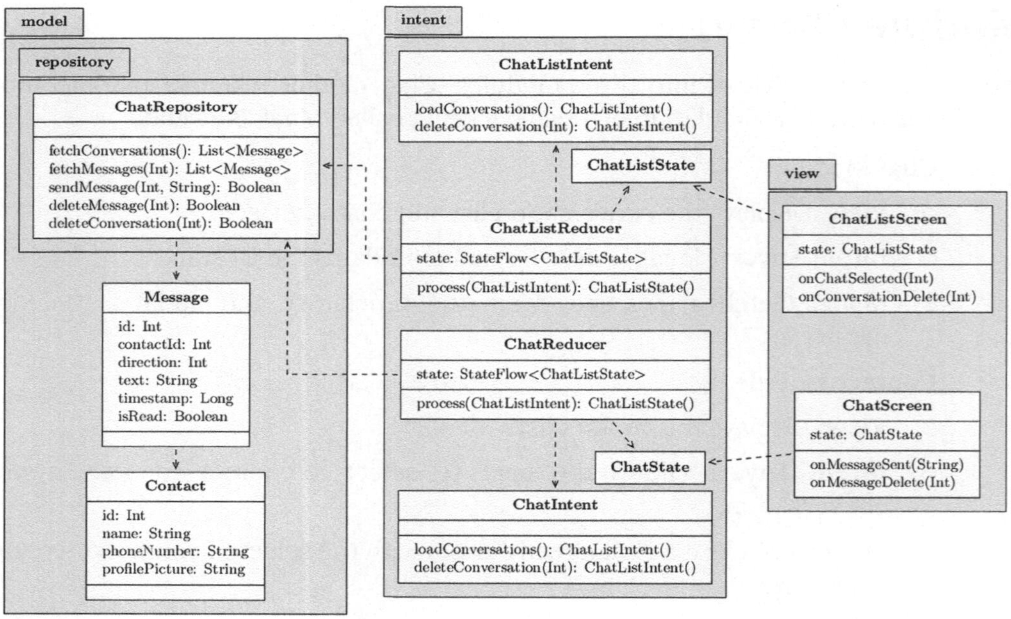

***Figure 14.2**: UML diagram of the module Chat*

Package `model`

- **Message**: Represents a message model, including content, author, and timestamp.
- **Contact**: Represent a contact (that is, a person to whom the user can send messages and from whom the user can receive messages). It has a name and a phone number.
- **ChatRepository**: Manages conversation data access, interacting with the database and simulating message reception from the mock backend.

Package `intent`

- **ChatListIntent**: Defines intents for the conversation list, such as opening a conversation or delete it.
- **ChatListReducer**: Updates chat list state based on received intents and maintains state management logic.
- **ChatListState**: Holds the current state for the list of conversations.
- **ChatIntent**: Defines user actions, such as sending a message.
- **ChatReducer**: Updates chat state based on received intents and maintains state management logic.
- **ChatState**: Holds the current chat state.

Package `view`

- **ChatListScreen**: Displays the list of active conversations with a preview of the last message.
- **ChatScreen**: Allows viewing and sending messages within a selected conversation.

Relationships

- **ChatListScreen** interacts with **ChatListState** to display the updated conversation list and with **ChatListIntent** to handle chat openings.
- **ChatScreen** interacts with **ChatState** to show real-time messages and with **ChatIntent** to send new messages.
- **ChatListReducer** and **ChatReducer** interact with **ChatRepository** to update conversation states and synchronize sent messages.

Interactions with Other Modules

- **ChatRepository** interacts with **ContactRepository** to check if a conversation already exists with a contact before creating a new one.
- **ChatReducer** interacts with the simulated notification system, updating the conversation list when new messages are received.

Contact Module

The Contact module is responsible for managing the contact list and initiating new conversations. Users can access a list of available contacts and select a person to start a chat. This module interacts with the Chat Module to check if a conversation already exists or to create a new one.

UML Diagram

Figure 14.3 shows the UML diagram of this module.

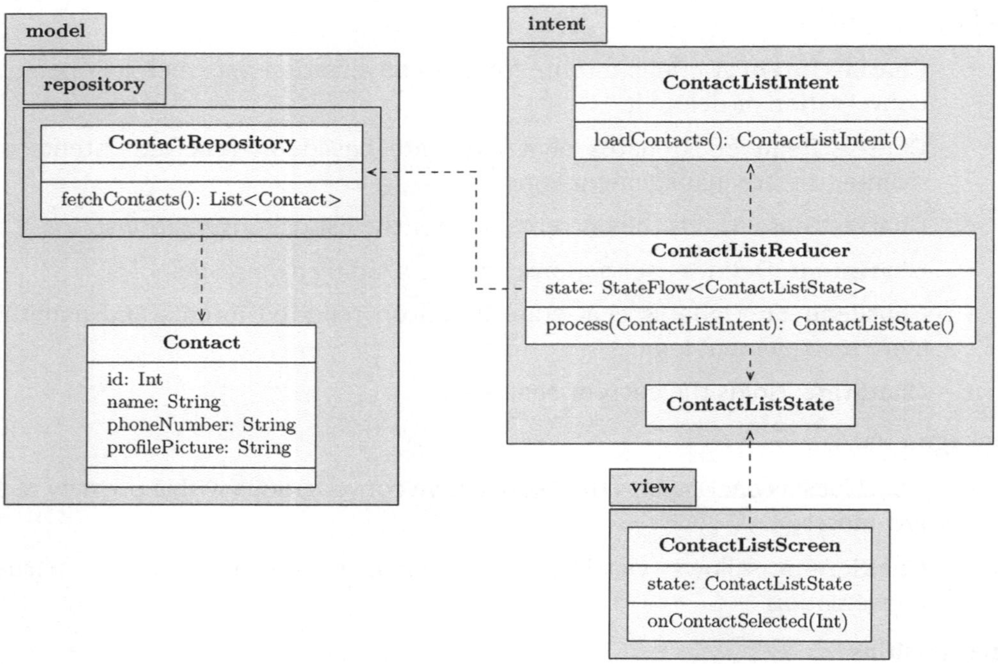

***Figure 14.3**: UML diagram of the module Contact*

Package `model`

- **Contact**: Represents a user model in the contact list.
- **ContactRepository**: Retrieves available contacts and enables starting new conversations.

Package `intent`

- **ContactListIntent**: Defines user actions, such as selecting a contact.
- **ContactListReducer**: Manages state updates for the contact list.
- **ContactListState**: Holds the current state of the contact list.

Package `view`

- **ContactListScreen**: Displays the list of contacts and allows users to start new conversations.

Relationships

- **ContactListScreen** interacts with **ContactListState** to display the contact list and with **ContactListIntent** to handle contact selection.
- **ContactListReducer** interacts with **ContactRepository** to retrieve contacts and start new conversations.

Interactions with Other Modules

This module does not interact with any other module and is completely independent.

We have completed the design phase of the chat app, defining a clear and modular structure based on the Model-View-Intent (MVI) architecture. This approach ensures predictable state management, a well-defined separation of responsibilities, and a responsive user interface.

The app has been organized into **two main modules**:

- **Chat Module**: Handles conversation management, message sending and receiving, and notification simulation.
- **Contact Module**: Displays available contacts and allows users to start new conversations.

Each module follows the MVI model, divided into three packages:

- **Model:** Manages data and access to it.
- **View:** Contains the main app screens, built with Jetpack Compose.
- **Intent:** Defines user actions, manages state, and updates the UI via the Reducer.

With this modular and scalable design, the app will be easier to maintain and test. Now, we can move on to the implementation phase, transforming these concepts into concrete code.

Implementation

After defining the design of the chat app, we can now proceed with its implementation. Following the Model-View-Intent (MVI) architecture, we will develop each module by organizing the code into **`model`**, **`intent`**, and **`view`** packages, ensuring a clear separation of responsibilities.

For simplicity, the app does not use a mock backend to simulate communication between users. Instead, all data is managed locally using Room Database, which serves both as a storage system for messages and a source for simulating real-time message reception. This approach simplifies implementation and allows testing the app without relying on external infrastructure.

As in previous chapters, for reasons of space, we will cover only the key aspects of each module's implementation, referring to the source code for further details.

Chat

The Chat module handles conversation management, message sending and receiving, and notification simulation. The implementation follows the Model-View-Intent (MVI) architecture, structuring the code into three main packages–model, intent, and view.

In this section, we will analyze the five key aspects of the implementation, with examples from the source code.

1. **Managing Conversation and Message State**
    - `ChatReducer` and `ChatListReducer` use StateFlow to keep the state updated and reactive.
    - The `process(intent: ChatIntent)` method handles user intents and updates the conversation state.

    This approach ensures a clear and unidirectional data flow.

```
class ChatReducer(
    private val repository: ChatRepository
) {
    private val _state = MutableStateFlow(ChatState())
    val state: StateFlow<ChatState> get() = _state.asStateFlow()

    private val scope = CoroutineScope(Dispatchers.IO +
SupervisorJob())

    fun process(intent: ChatIntent) {
        when (intent) {
            is ChatIntent.LoadMessages -> loadMessages(intent.
contactId)
            is ChatIntent.SendMessage -> sendMessage(intent.
contactId, intent.message)
            is ChatIntent.DeleteMessage -> deleteMessage(intent.
contactId, intent.messageId)
        }
    }
}
```

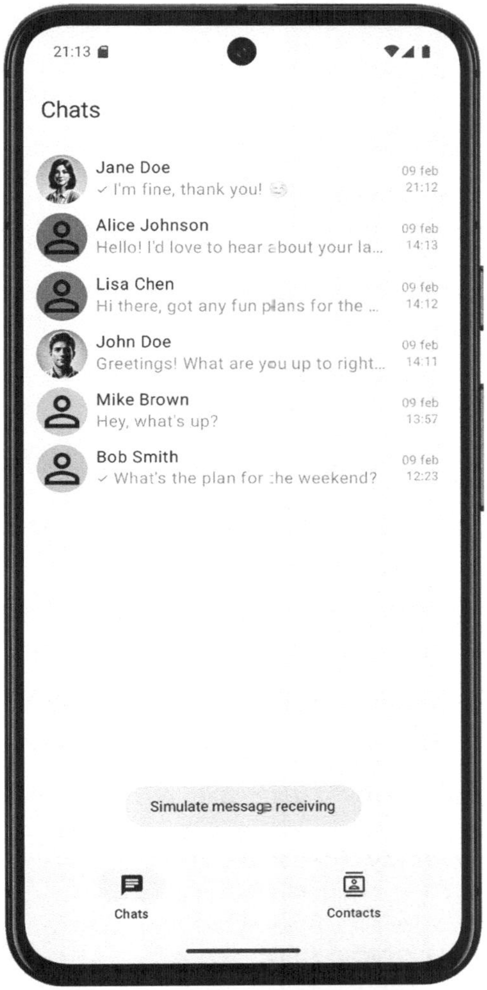

Figure 14.4: *Screen of the application showing the chat list*

2. **Message Persistence with Room Database**
    - **`ChatRepositoryImpl`** manages message persistence using Room.
    - **`MessageDao`** provides methods to retrieve and save messages.

This ensures that messages remain available even offline.

```
override suspend fun fetchMessages(contactId: Int): List<Message>
{
    return messageDao.getMessagesForContact(contactId)
        .map { it.toMessage() }
}
```

```
override suspend fun sendMessage(
    contactId: Int,
    message: Message
): Boolean {
    val messageEntity = MessageEntity(
        contactId = contactId,
        direction = MSG_SENT,
        text = message.text
    )
    messageDao.insert(messageEntity)
    return true
}
```

3. **Simulating Message Reception**

   - The **`receiveMessage()`** method generates a new message and saves it to the database.

This method allows simulating incoming messages without relying on a backend.

```
suspend fun receiveMessage(): List<Message> {
    val randomContact = contactDao.getAll().map {
        it.id
    }.random()
    val randomMessage = listOf(
        "Hello! How are you?",
        "Hey, what's up?",
        "Hi there! How's your day going so far?"
    ).random()
    val messageEntity = MessageEntity(
        contactId = randomContact,
        direction = MSG_RECEIVED,
        text = randomMessage
    )
    messageDao.insert(messageEntity)
    return listOf(messageEntity.toMessage())
}
```

Figure 14.5: *Screen of the application showing a single chat*

4. **UI with Jetpack Compose for Chat List and Conversations**
   - **`ChatListScreen`** displays the list of active conversations.

```
@Composable
fun ChatListScreen(
    state: ChatListState,
    onChatSelected: (Int) -> Unit,
    onSimulateMessageReceiving: (String, String) -> Unit
){
    Box(
        modifier = Modifier.fillMaxSize()
    ) {
        LazyColumn {
            items(state.conversations.size) { index ->
                val chat = state.conversations[index]
                ChatListItem(chat = chat, onChatSelected = on-
ChatSelected)
            }
        }
    }
}
```

- **`ChatScreen`** manages the active conversation, displaying all messages.

```
@Composable
fun ChatScreen(
    state: ChatState,
    onMessageSent: (Message) -> Unit
) {
    Column(modifier = Modifier.fillMaxSize().padding(8.dp)) {
        LazyColumn(modifier = Modifier.weight(1f)) {
            items(state.messages.size) { index ->
                val message = state.messages[index]
                MessageView(message = message)
            }
        }
    }
}
```

The Chat module was implemented using the MVI architecture, ensuring clear state management, local persistence via Room Database, and reactive updates with Jetpack Compose. By adding message and notification simulation, we created an app that feels realistic from the user's perspective, even without an external backend.

Contacts

The Contact module is a simple and independent module, responsible solely for managing the contact list. Unlike the Chat module, which interacts with multiple components to handle message state, this module focuses on retrieving and displaying available contacts without dependencies on other parts of the app.

The implementation follows the Model-View-Intent (MVI) architecture, ensuring a clear and minimal structure for efficiency and simplicity.

Now, let us analyze the three key aspects of its implementation.

1. **State Management with ContactListReducer**

   - **`ContactListReducer`** uses StateFlow to keep the state updated and reactive.
   - The **`process(intent: ContactListIntent)`** method handles user intents and updates the contact list.

This approach ensures automatic UI updates when data is loaded or an error occurs.

```
class ContactListReducer(
    private val repository: ContactRepository
) {

    private val _state = MutableStateFlow(ContactListState())
    val state: StateFlow<ContactListState> get() = _state.as-
StateFlow()
```

```
    private val scope = CoroutineScope(Dispatchers.IO + Supervi-
sorJob())

    fun process(intent: ContactListIntent) {
        when (intent) {
            is ContactListIntent.LoadContacts -> loadContacts()
        }
    }

    fun loadContacts() {
        _state.value = _state.value.copy(isLoading = true)
        scope.launch {
            try {
                val contacts = repository.fetchContacts()
                _state.value = ContactListState(contacts =
contacts, isLoading = false)
            } catch (e: Exception) {
                _state.value = ContactListState(isLoading =
false, error = e.message)
            }
        }
    }
}
```

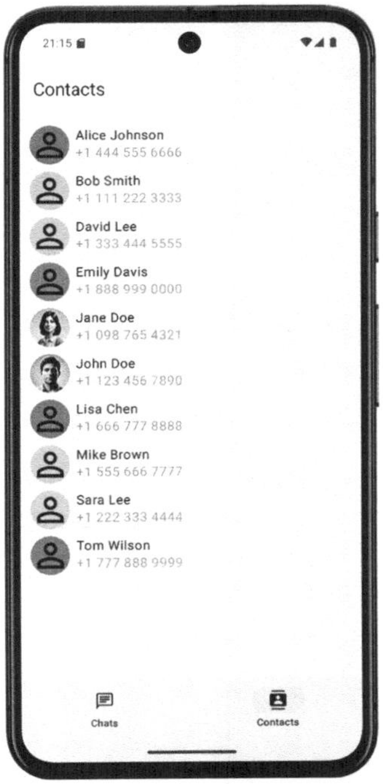

Figure 14.6: *Screen of the application showing the contact list*

2. **Contact Retrieval with Room Database**

   - **ContactRepositoryImpl** uses Room to fetch the saved contact list.
   - The **fetchContacts()** method retrieves contacts from the database and converts them into the app's required format.

```
class ContactRepositoryImpl(
    private val contactDao: ContactDao,
) : ContactRepository {

    override suspend fun fetchContacts(): List<Contact> {
        return contactDao.getAll()
            .map { it.toContact() }
    }

    fun ContactEntity.toContact(): Contact {
        return Contact(
            id = id,
            name = name,
            phoneNumber = phoneNumber,
            profilePicture = profilePicture
        )
    }
}
```

3. **UI with Jetpack Compose for Contact List**

   - **ContactListScreen** displays the list of contacts and handles user selection to start a new conversation.
   - Using **LazyColumn** ensures efficient list management, optimizing the rendering of visible elements.

```
@Composable
fun ContactListScreen(
    state: ContactListState,
    onContactSelected: (Int) -> Unit,
){
    LazyColumn {
        items(state.contacts.size) { index ->
            val contact = state.contacts[index]
            ContactListItem(
                contact = contact,
                onContactSelected = onContactSelected
            )
        }
    }
}
```

The Contact module was implemented using the MVI architecture, with state management via StateFlow, a repository leveraging Room Database for contact retrieval, and a reactive UI powered by Jetpack Compose.

We have completed the implementation of the chat app, transforming the design into concrete code while following the Model-View-Intent (MVI) architecture to ensure clear and predictable state management. The app was developed with two distinct modules:

- **Chat Module**: Handles conversation management, message sending and receiving, and notification simulation. This module required a more complex implementation to manage message state and interaction with the local database.
- **Contact Module**: A simpler and fully independent module, responsible for displaying the contact list and creating new conversations.

We adopted a reactive and modular approach, using:

- **StateFlow** for state management and UI updates.
- **Room Database** for local persistence of messages and contacts.
- **Jetpack Compose** for a fluid and declarative user interface.
- **Intents & Reducer** for a unidirectional data flow, improving code maintainability.

The absence of a mock backend simplified implementation, relying entirely on the local database for conversation management and simulating incoming messages.

Testing

After completing the implementation of the chat app, it is now time to verify the correct functionality of the code through the testing phase. In previous chapters, we developed a testing strategy divided into unit tests, integration tests, and UI tests, covering repositories, state management, and the user interface.

For this final project, we encourage the reader to develop the tests independently, applying the knowledge gained from previous projects. This approach provides an opportunity to strengthen testing skills and experiment with customized testing solutions for the chat app.

In the next section, we provide a guide for structuring tests effectively.

Testing Strategy

The recommended approach includes three levels of testing:

1. **Unit Tests:** verify the behavior of individual classes in isolation.

2. **Integration Tests:** check the interaction between multiple components of the app.
3. **UI Tests:** ensure that the graphical interface responds correctly to user inputs.

Suggested Testing Plan

To assist you in writing tests, we propose a breakdown of the most important verifications:

Unit Tests

ChatReducer and ContactListReducer

- Verify that the state updates correctly when sending or receiving a message.
- Test that the contact list loads correctly.

ChatRepository and ContactRepository

- Check that messages are saved and retrieved from the Room Database.
- Simulate receiving a new message and verify that it is added to the conversation.

Integration Tests

Communication Between Modules

- Test that selecting a contact from the list starts a new conversation in the Chat module.
- Ensure that sending a message updates both the chat state and the conversation list.

Data Persistence

- Restart the app and verify that conversation data is retained using Room Database.

UI Tests

ChatScreen and ContactListScreen

- Verify that ChatScreen correctly displays sent and received messages.
- Simulate the arrival of a new message and ensure it appears in real time.
- Check that selecting a contact from the list opens the correct conversation.

UI Interaction

- Test the behavior of the input field in ChatScreen.
- Simulate pressing a button to send a message and verify the UI updates accordingly.

Writing tests independently is an excellent exercise to strengthen the understanding of state management and best testing practices in an MVI architecture.

This phase provides an opportunity for the reader to apply the skills acquired in previous projects, developing a comprehensive testing strategy for the chat app. We have provided a guide to identify the most important tests to help the reader to design and implement a good testing strategy.

Conclusion

In this chapter, we developed a chat app using the Model-View-Intent (MVI) architecture, organizing the project in a clear and modular structure. We followed a structured process, starting from requirements analysis, moving through design and implementation, and leaving the testing phase open for the reader to develop independently.

The app was divided into two main modules: Chat Module, which handles conversation management, message sending, message receiving, notification simulation, and Contact Module, which is a simple and independent module that manages contact display and starting new conversations.

We chose to handle all data locally with Room Database, without a mock backend, simplifying implementation and allowing the app to be tested without an internet connection.

The MVI architecture ensures *predictable state management* with a unidirectional data flow, *clear separation of responsibilities* between model, intent, view, and *reactivity and smooth updates* using StateFlow and Jetpack Compose.

Finally, we encouraged the reader to develop unit, integration, and UI tests, providing a guide to structure the testing phase independently.

With this application, we demonstrated how a modern and emerging architecture like MVI can be effectively applied to a messaging app, making it scalable and maintainable.

In the next chapter, which will be the concluding one, we will try to explore the possible trends that will shape the world of Android development in the years to come.

Points to Remember

- **Model-View-Intent (MVI) Architecture**: The chat app was designed following the MVI pattern, ensuring a unidirectional data flow and predictable state management.
- **Local Data Management**: All data is stored and managed locally using Room Database, eliminating the need for a mock backend and allowing the app to work offline.

- **State Management with StateFlow**: The app utilizes StateFlow for handling chat and contact list states, ensuring reactive UI updates without manual observers.
- **Chat Module**: Manages conversations, message sending and receiving, and notification simulation to test the arrival of new messages.
- **Contact Module**: An **independent module** that manages the contact list and allows users to start new conversations, interacting with the Chat module for chat creation.
- **State Handling with Reducers**: The ChatReducer and ContactListReducer update the app's state in response to user intents, maintaining clear and predictable logic.
- **Jetpack Compose UI**: The interface was built entirely with Jetpack Compose, simplifying UI management and improving app responsiveness.
- **Message Persistence with Room**: Conversations and messages are stored in Room Database, ensuring data availability even after closing the app.
- **Scalability and Extensibility**: The app is designed to be easily extendable, allowing for the integration of new features or the addition of a real backend without significant structural modifications.
- **Real-Time Message Simulation**: Simulating incoming messages allows testing the app's behavior in real-world scenarios, improving the user experience without requiring an external server.

Multiple Choice Questions

1. Which statement correctly describes the data flow in an MVI architecture?
   a. The UI sends an intent, which is processed by the reducer to update the state, which in turn updates the UI.
   b. The UI directly updates the database, and the reducer synchronizes the data.
   c. Intents directly update the UI without passing through the state.
   d. The repository is responsible for updating the UI without needing a centralized state.
2. What is the role of the ChatReducer in the application?
   a. Retrieves data from the database and displays it in the UI.
   b. Updates the chat state based on received intents.
   c. Manages the connection with a remote backend.
   d. Stores conversation data in memory.

3. Why does the app not require a mock backend?
    a. Because all data is managed locally with Room Database.
    b. Because it uses Firebase for synchronization.
    c. Because data is temporarily stored in memory.
    d. Because it relies on external APIs to manage conversations.
4. Which test would be most useful to verify the correct functioning of the ChatReducer?
    a. Verify that the UI updates the displayed text when a message is received.
    b. Check that the database does not allow duplicate messages to be saved.
    c. Test the duration of the transition between screens when opening a conversation.
    d. Test that sending a message updates the state with the new message in the list.
5. Which scenario represents an edge case to test in the contact management module?
    a. The user selects a contact and starts a new conversation.
    b. The contact list updates automatically when the app is launched.
    c. The database is empty, and the user tries to view the contact list.
    d. The user receives a notification for a new message while writing another message.

Answers

1. a
2. b
3. a
4. d
5. c

Questions

1. How is the data flow managed in an MVI architecture, and what are the advantages compared to MVVM?
2. What are the key steps to test the behavior of the ChatReducer? Describe how you would validate the correct state management of conversations.
3. How could you optimize the handling of simulated notifications to make the app's behavior more realistic?
4. What modifications would you make to integrate a real backend instead of local management with Room Database while keeping the MVI architecture unchanged?
5. How could you extend the Contact Module to support a search functionality among contacts? Which components would need to be updated?

CHAPTER 15
The Future of Android Development

Introduction

In recent years, Android development has undergone a radical evolution, driven by the adoption of new frameworks, artificial intelligence, advanced security, and an increasingly interconnected ecosystem. Android is no longer limited to smartphones but is expanding into tablets, foldable devices, wearables, automotive, and IoT solutions, requiring developers to adapt to a constantly evolving landscape.

This chapter explores the emerging trends that will shape the future of Android development in the coming years, helping us prepare for the challenges and opportunities ahead. From the evolution of UI with Jetpack Compose to the adoption of Kotlin Multiplatform and modern design patterns, we will analyze the technologies and strategies defining the next generation of applications.

Artificial intelligence is becoming increasingly central, with tools like Gemini in Android Studio automating code writing, debugging, and documentation. At the same time, enhancements in security and privacy, performance optimization, and energy sustainability are redefining how apps are developed and distributed.

Finally, with Android's expansion into fields such as IoT and wearables, we are witnessing the emergence of a connected and intelligent ecosystem, where devices from different categories collaborate to deliver seamless and integrated experiences.

Structure

In this chapter, we will cover the following topics:

- Modern UI and UX with Jetpack Compose
- Kotlin and Multiplatform Development
- Emerging Design Patterns in Android Development
- AI and Automation

- Privacy and Security
- Sustainability and Performance
- Integration with the Connected World (IoT & Wearables)

Modern UI and UX with Jetpack Compose

In recent years, Jetpack Compose has established itself as the primary framework for building user interfaces on Android. The shift from traditional XML-based UI and View System to a declarative Kotlin-based model represents one of the most significant transformations in Android development. However, this transition is still ongoing and will continue in the coming years, leading to structural changes in how applications are designed, developed, and optimized.

The Definitive Transition from XML to Compose

Historically, Android has used XML to define the user interface, separating UI logic from application logic. However, this approach has several limitations:

- Difficulty in creating dynamic and adaptive interfaces for different screen formats.
- Increased verbosity and the need to synchronize XML code with Kotlin code.
- Performance issues related to rendering and state management.

Jetpack Compose removes these constraints by offering a fully declarative approach, allowing developers to build more fluid and modular interfaces. In the long term, Compose is set to completely replace XML, with Android Studio providing more tools to facilitate this transition.

Compose as the Standard for All UI

One of the key developments in the coming years will be the expansion of Jetpack Compose across all platforms within the Android ecosystem, including:

- **Smartphones and tablets**: More adaptive interfaces thanks to native support for different screen sizes and resolutions.
- **Foldable and flexible devices**: Dynamic layouts that adjust to foldable screens.
- **Wear OS**: Compose is already becoming the standard for smartwatch app development.
- **Android TV and automotive**: Compose will extend to more interactive interfaces with alternative input methods (voice, gestures).

This progressive unification of the framework will make it easier for developers to design a scalable UI that works seamlessly across all Android devices.

Performance Improvements and Optimizations

One of the main future goals of Jetpack Compose will be performance enhancement, focusing on:

- **Reducing memory consumption** and optimizing state management.
- **Improving UI rendering** to ensure a smooth experience even on lower-end devices.
- **More efficient compilation** to reduce application runtime.

Integration with the Kotlin 2.0 compiler enables advanced optimizations, making Compose even faster and more scalable.

Impact on User Experience (UX) Design

The shift to a declarative system also has a significant impact on user experience (UX) design. In the coming years, we will see a greater adoption of:

- **More flexible and adaptive designs**, leveraging Motion Design and smoother transitions.
- **Real-time customizable UIs**, adapting to user preferences and usage context.
- **Greater focus on accessibility**, with more intuitive and inclusive interfaces.

With these advancements, Jetpack Compose will become the foundation of Android UX, offering a more modern and dynamic approach compared to traditional UI frameworks. Jetpack Compose represents the future of Android UI, and its evolution will continue in the coming years, leading to the gradual elimination of XML and the development of more performant, adaptive, and multi-platform interfaces.

Developers adopting Compose today are already investing in the future of Android development, preparing for an environment where the UI will be declarative, scalable, and highly optimized.

Kotlin and Multiplatform Development

In recent years, Kotlin Multiplatform (KMP) has gained increasing attention as a solution for writing shared code across Android, iOS, Web, and Desktop, reducing development time and costs.

The evolution of cross-platform technologies has made the need for flexible, efficient, and native frameworks increasingly evident, and Kotlin has established itself as one of the most promising solutions in this field.

Kotlin Multiplatform: An Ongoing Revolution

Kotlin Multiplatform stands out from other cross-platform frameworks like Flutter and React Native due to its hybrid approach:

- It allows sharing business logic across multiple platforms without sacrificing performance.
- It does not require a universal UI but enables writing native interfaces for each platform.
- It is officially supported by JetBrains and Google, ensuring constant updates and compatibility with Android.

This philosophy allows companies to reduce code duplication without compromising the native user experience. In the coming years, KMP adoption is expected to grow, with increasing integration into enterprise architectures.

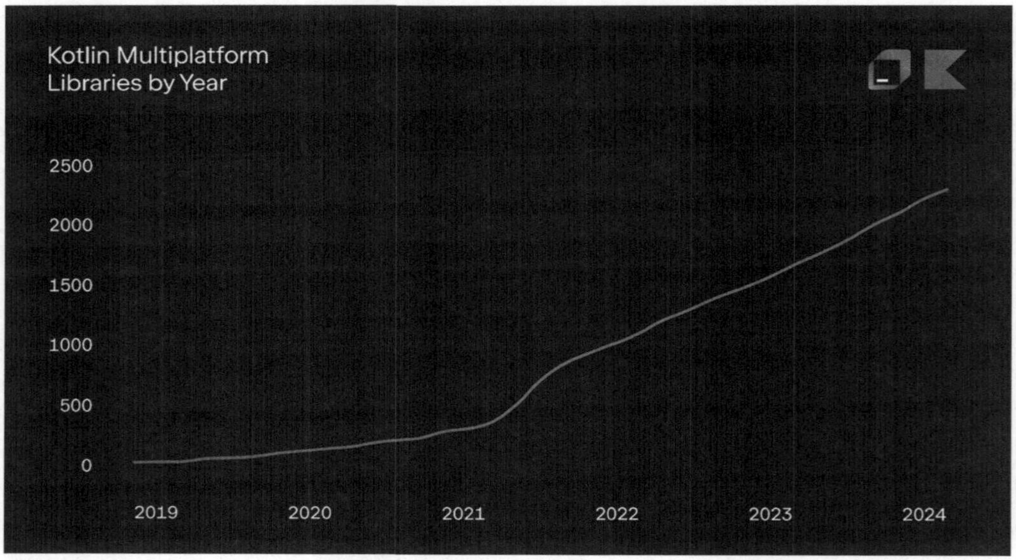

Figure 15.1: *Growth of Kotlin Multiplatform libraries over time*

Compose Multiplatform: The Future of a Unified Interface

While Kotlin Multiplatform enables logic sharing across platforms, Jetpack Compose Multiplatform aims to extend the same concept to UI development, allowing developers to build interfaces that work on:

- **Android and iOS**

- **Desktop** (*Windows, macOS, Linux*)
- Web

Compose Multiplatform is still an evolving project, but in the long run, it could become a solid alternative to Flutter, offering a single codebase for UI development without compromising native quality.

Performance and Optimization for Low-End Devices

One of the limitations of cross-platform solutions is their impact on performance. In the coming years, optimizations in KMP and Compose Multiplatform will focus on:

- **Improving memory management** to ensure optimal performance on devices with low RAM.
- **Reducing power consumption** and optimizing UI rendering.
- **Faster compilation** through improvements in the Kotlin compiler and runtime.

These enhancements will help make cross-platform apps lighter, more scalable, and more efficient, expanding their usability even on lower-end devices.

Cross-platform development is becoming an increasingly established reality, with Kotlin Multiplatform emerging as one of the most promising solutions for the future. Its flexibility, official support, and continuous optimizations make it a strategic choice for those looking to develop scalable and high-performance apps without compromising the quality of the user experience.

In the coming years, we will see the expansion of KMP and Compose Multiplatform, significantly impacting how apps will be developed for Android and beyond.

Emerging Design Patterns in Android Development

The adoption of scalable, modular, and reactive architectures has become essential in Android development. With the evolution of Jetpack Compose, Kotlin Multiplatform, and artificial intelligence, certain design patterns are emerging as standards to enhance maintainability, testability, and code reusability.

The Evolution of Android Architecture: From MVC to MVI

In recent years, Android app architecture has evolved from MVC (Model-View-

Controller) to MVVM (Model-View-ViewModel) and is now increasingly shifting toward MVI (Model-View-Intent), driven by the declarative nature of Jetpack Compose.

- **MVVM (Model-View-ViewModel):** Still one of the most widely used patterns, but with Compose, it is evolving to better manage UI state.
- **MVI (Model-View-Intent)**: Gaining popularity due to unidirectional state management, reducing bugs caused by inconsistent states.
- **Redux-like architectures**: Solutions based on StateFlow and centralized data flows are becoming more common to ensure predictable state management.

Dependency Injection and Advanced Modularization

The use of Dependency Injection (DI) continues to evolve:

- **Dagger-Hilt** remains the standard for efficiently managing component creation.
- **Koin** is emerging as a lighter alternative to Dagger-Hilt for Kotlin.
- **App modularization** with feature modules and dynamic delivery, improving code reuse and reducing build times.

Reactive Programming and State Management

The use of Flow, StateFlow, and SharedFlow is gradually replacing LiveData for more scalable state management. The new standards include:

- **State Hoisting** in Jetpack Compose, to separate UI logic from app state.
- **Repository Pattern combined with Use Case Pattern**, to keep code well-structured and testable.
- **Side Effects Management** with Coroutines and Flows, ensuring safe handling of asynchronous operations.

Clean Architecture and AI Integration

The adoption of **Clean Architecture** remains a dominant trend, but it is evolving with **integrated AI models** to optimize processes, suggest code improvements, and reduce repetitive development tasks. In the coming years, we will see:

- **LLM-assisted coding**, streamlining workflows and enhancing productivity.
- **AI-powered automatic refactoring tools**, improving code quality.

- **Hybrid architectures between MVVM and MVI**, where AI can analyze usage patterns and suggest real-time improvements.

The adoption of new design patterns in Android development is leading to more modular, reactive, and scalable architectures. with increasing integration of advanced state management, modern dependency injection, and reactive programming.

In the coming years, artificial intelligence will have a significant impact on architectural practices, enhancing efficiency, automation, and code maintainability.

AI and Automation

Artificial Intelligence (AI), as well as many other tech fields, is revolutionizing Android development by enhancing process automation, user experience personalization, and performance optimization. In the coming years, AI adoption in mobile applications will become increasingly widespread, leading to intelligent interfaces, smoother interactions, and predictive features.

Development Automation with AI

Artificial Intelligence is transforming the entire Android app development lifecycle, automating complex tasks and improving developer productivity. With the introduction of Gemini in Android Studio, AI is evolving into a true development assistant. The key AI applications in Android development include:

- **Automated Code and UI Generation**: Gemini can write Kotlin or Jetpack Compose code snippets, suggest solutions to common issues, and generate layouts based on user data and design preferences.
- **Smart Documentation**: Developers can receive detailed code explanations, automatic function documentation, and suggestions to improve readability and maintainability.
- **UX Analysis and Optimization**: AI can identify ineffective usage patterns, suggest interaction improvements, and optimize animations and transitions for a smoother experience.
- **Automated Debugging and Refactoring**: Gemini can detect bugs, propose fixes, and suggest refactoring to enhance code quality.

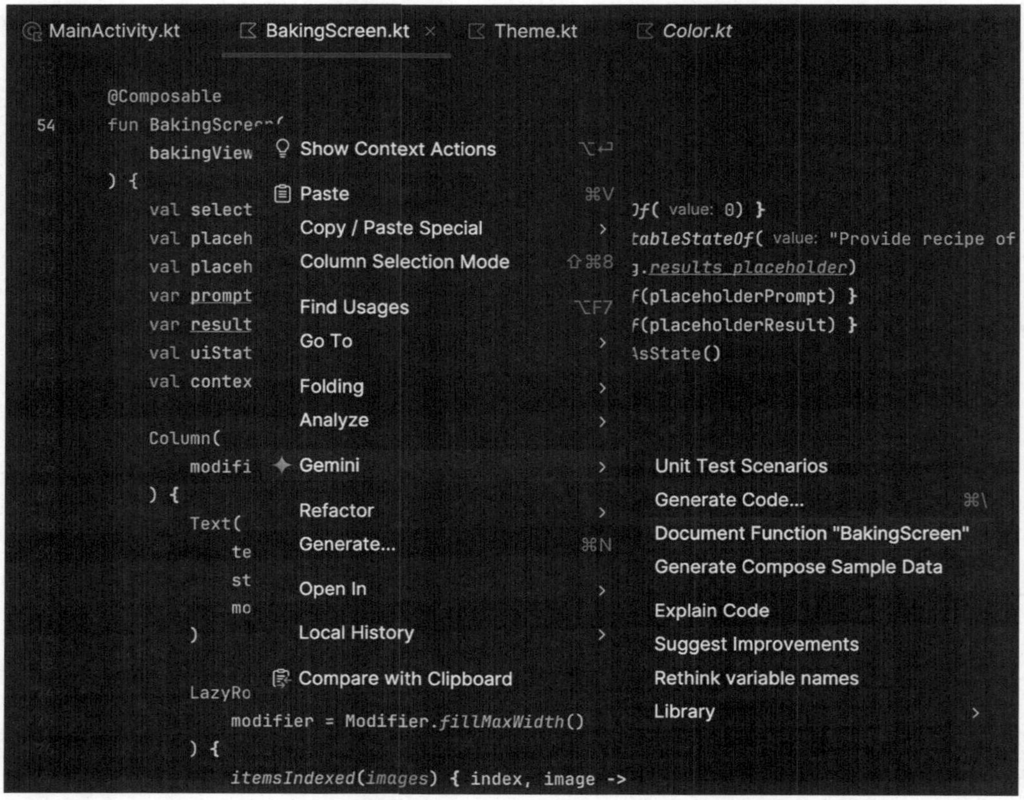

***Figure 15.2**: Code documentation with Gemini in Android Studio*

This integration marks a significant step toward more efficient and automated development, reducing the time required for repetitive tasks and allowing developers to focus on more strategic aspects of app design and architecture. In the coming years, AI will become an increasingly integral part of the workflow, transforming how Android applications are designed and developed.

Chatbot and Virtual Assistants in Android Ecosystem

In recent years, the use of chatbots and virtual assistants has grown exponentially. With the advancement of models like Google's Gemini, Android apps can now:

- Provide **personalized user assistance** based on real-time request analysis.
- Enhance **customer experience** with fast and relevant responses.
- Integrate **voice AI** more naturally, enabling smoother interactions between users and applications.

Google Assistant and Android's voice APIs continue to evolve, making voice commands and text-based interactions increasingly common in areas such as e-commerce, customer support, and digital services. With the introduction of Gemini, users can now enjoy more natural and contextual interactions, further improving the overall experience.

Predictive Analysis and Advanced Customization

Predictive analytics powered by artificial intelligence is already used in Android development, but its impact will grow significantly in the coming years. Today, many applications leverage AI to analyze user behavior and provide real-time personalized experiences. However, with improved algorithms and the increasing integration of advanced models like Gemini, this capability will become even more refined and effective.

Android applications are already implementing features such as:

- **Automated suggestions** based on user preferences and usage habits.
- **Contextual recommendations**, such as suggesting the next video to watch, an article to read, or a product to purchase.
- **Dynamic interfaces** that adapt in real time to user needs, offering personalized layouts and content.

The evolution of AI will make these functions increasingly precise, intuitive, and proactive, allowing apps to anticipate user needs even before they are expressed. This will not only enhance engagement but also significantly reduce abandonment rates, providing a smoother and more personalized experience.

In the coming years, we will see growing automation of these processes, with applications becoming capable of learning and optimizing their UX autonomously through continuous analysis of usage data. The ultimate goal is to create hyper-personalized and responsive experiences that adapt to each user naturally and seamlessly.

Artificial Intelligence and Accessibility

One of the most exciting developments is the application of AI to improve accessibility in Android apps. Emerging technologies will enable:

- **Advanced voice recognition** to facilitate app usage for people with motor disabilities.
- **Automatic transcription and text-to-speech** for users with visual impairments.

- **Adaptive UI adjustments** based on user needs (for example, automatic contrast or font size increases for visually impaired users).

Google is heavily investing in this area, and in the coming years, we will see greater use of AI to make applications more inclusive and accessible.

The integration of artificial intelligence in Android development is set to become increasingly sophisticated. UI automation, virtual assistants, advanced personalization, and improved accessibility are just some of the areas where AI will have a significant impact. In the coming years, app development will no longer be just about writing code but also about how AI can optimize user experiences and automate processes, taking Android to new levels of intelligent interaction.

Privacy and Security

In recent years, security and user privacy protection have become a central priority in Android development. Google has introduced numerous features to provide greater control over sensitive data, and in the coming years, we will see even more significant advancements in this direction.

The mobile ecosystem is becoming increasingly connected and complex, with apps handling financial, biometric, and personal data. Stricter regulations and the growing user interest in a privacy-first experience will lead to stronger security strategies throughout the app development lifecycle.

Android as a Privacy-First Ecosystem

Google has already implemented several features to ensure greater transparency and user control, such as:

- **Privacy Dashboard**: A section in Android settings that displays app access to sensitive data.
- **One-Time Permissions**: Permissions that grant access to data only for the duration of the session.
- **Automatic revocation of app permissions** for unused apps.

In the long run, Android will continue evolving as a privacy-centric operating system, with even more granular controls and greater transparency for users.

New Authentication Models and Biometric Security

Authentication is evolving toward more secure and frictionless systems, reducing reliance on traditional passwords. Future trends include:

- **Passkeys and passwordless authentication** for more secure app access management.
- **Advancements in biometrics**, with more sophisticated facial recognition and fingerprint scanning.
- **Deeper integration of Multi-Factor Authentication (MFA)** at the system level for sensitive applications.

These innovations will reduce vulnerabilities to phishing attacks and credential stuffing, making the user experience both smoother and more secure.

Blockchain and Transaction Security

The use of blockchain in mobile applications could become a key solution for enhancing security and transparency in digital transactions. The main use cases include:

- **Secure payments** through decentralized technologies.
- **Fraud prevention** in peer-to-peer transactions.
- **Improved digital identity management**, with verifiable and tamper-proof credentials.

If this technology continues to evolve, we could see greater adoption in the mobile sector, especially in financial apps and advanced authentication systems.

Advanced API and Sensitive Data Protection

Android applications rely on a vast ecosystem of APIs to interact with various services. In the coming years, we will see:

- **Enhanced API protection mechanisms** to prevent man-in-the-middle attacks.
- **More widespread end-to-end encryption** to secure user data in communications and cloud services.
- **Greater control over data shared with third parties**, with stricter regulations for developers.

The growing adoption of confidential computing will enable computations on sensitive data while keeping it encrypted, further improving application security.

Security and user privacy will become increasingly central to Android development. The future will bring stronger data protection measures, the adoption of passwordless authentication, improvements in biometric security, and greater use of advanced cryptographic technologies. Developers will be tasked with implementing solutions that balance security and usability, ensuring a safe and transparent user experience.

Sustainability and Performance

Performance optimization and energy sustainability have become key aspects of Android application development. With increasing app complexity and the proliferation of powerful yet diverse devices, developers must ensure that applications are efficient, consume less energy, and provide a smooth experience across a wide range of devices. In the coming years, the focus on these issues will grow stronger, impacting both software development and hardware design.

App Optimization to Reduce Energy Consumption

Mobile applications are one of the main sources of energy consumption on smartphones. To address this, Google is introducing tools and APIs to help developers:

- **Reduce battery consumption** by avoiding unnecessary wake-locks and background processes.
- **Optimize UI rendering** with improvements in Jetpack Compose, minimizing redundant recompositions.
- **Use Jetpack WorkManager** to schedule background tasks more efficiently.

In the future, Android could integrate even more advanced energy management systems, with algorithms that automatically limit resource usage for energy-intensive apps.

Sustainable Development to Reduce Environmental Impact

Sustainability is not just about battery consumption but also about reducing the environmental impact of software development. Key trends include:

- **Code splitting and modularization** to avoid loading entire libraries when unnecessary.
- **Support for low-end devices**, ensuring apps run efficiently even on less powerful hardware.
- **Reducing app size** by eliminating unused resources and improving memory management.

The goal is to create lighter and less resource-intensive applications, reducing the need for frequent hardware upgrades to run apps efficiently, ultimately contributing to a lower environmental footprint.

Micro-Apps and Advanced Modularization

One of the most interesting trends is the adoption of modular architectures, making apps more flexible and lightweight. In the coming years, we will see:

- **Increased use of App Bundles**, allowing users to download only the necessary parts of an app.
- **Dynamic Features**, enabling functionalities to be activated and downloaded based on usage.
- **Greater use of caching and lazy loading**, improving the user experience without overloading the CPU or memory.

This modularity will make applications more responsive, faster, and less demanding in terms of storage and performance.

Android's Push Toward Lighter and More Scalable Operating Systems

With the expansion of the Android ecosystem, Google is working on lighter and more scalable versions of the operating system, such as Android Go, to ensure a smooth user experience even on budget devices. This effort includes:

- **Optimizations in the Android runtime** to reduce memory usage.
- **Improved background process management** to limit energy consumption.
- **Support for new hardware architectures** to ensure compatibility with ARM processors and future mobile hardware advancements.

This push toward a more efficient and scalable Android will help developers create more sustainable apps without compromising functionality or performance.

Performance optimization and sustainability will become increasingly central to Android development. In the coming years, we will see improvements in energy management, lighter and more modular apps, and a more adaptable and scalable Android. Developers will be challenged to balance advanced features with efficiency, creating seamless experiences without resource waste.

Integration with the Connected World (IoT and Wearables)

The Android ecosystem is becoming increasingly interconnected with smart devices, including wearables, IoT sensors, smart home systems, automotive technology, and augmented reality. In the coming years, Android app development will no longer be limited to smartphones but will increasingly expand to devices that enhance productivity, fitness, health, and daily interactions.

Android Apps and IoT Integration

The Internet of Things (IoT) is transforming how users interact with technology. More and more devices are now connected and communicating through Android, with applications managing:

- **Smart Home** (Google Home, Nest, smart home devices) for controlling lights, thermostats, security, and automation.
- **Wearables and fitness devices**, including smartwatches, wellness trackers, and biometric sensors.
- **Automotive and Android Auto**, featuring smart interfaces for navigation and voice control.

With the expansion of 5G and low-latency networks, the integration between Android and IoT devices will become even smoother and more responsive, reducing latency and enhancing the user experience.

Wearables and Advanced Interaction Technologies

Android is becoming the leading ecosystem for wearable devices, thanks to the evolution of Wear OS and the integration of advanced features for smartwatches and wellness devices. In the coming years, we will see:

- **Greater accuracy in biometric sensors**, improving the monitoring of parameters such as heart rate, oxygen levels, and blood pressure.
- **Expansion of gesture-based and AI-driven interfaces**, allowing users to control apps without touching the screen.
- **New health and wellness applications**, with increased adoption of certified medical devices based on Android.

These advancements will lead to smarter and more independent wearables, capable of functioning autonomously without needing a smartphone.

Android and the Future of Screenless Interfaces

With the growing adoption of voice interfaces, AR, and smart devices, Android is evolving to support screenless experiences. In the coming years, we may see:

- **Deeper integration with advanced voice assistants** (Google Assistant, Gemini) for natural interactions with IoT devices.
- **Support for smart glasses and AR/VR interfaces**, expanding Android into immersive experiences.
- **Development of invisible wearables**, such as smart earbuds and biometric sensors integrated into clothing.

The goal of these innovations is to make device interactions more natural and less intrusive, enhancing productivity and quality of life.

The Convergence of Mobile, Wearables, and Ambient Computing

A key trend for the future of Android will be the convergence of mobile devices, wearables, and ambient computing. This means that devices will collaborate more seamlessly, allowing users to:

- **Start an activity on one device and continue it on another** without interruptions (for example, replying to a message on a smartwatch and continuing on a tablet).
- **Leverage environmental context to enhance the experience** (for example, a phone adjusting brightness based on ambient light or suggesting content based on location).
- **Communicate intelligently with IoT devices**, with apps adapting to usage context and optimizing energy consumption.

This seamless integration between devices will make Android not just an operating system for smartphones, but a widespread ecosystem within the connected world.

The integration of Android, IoT, and wearable devices will be a pillar of the technological future. With advancements in 5G networks, advanced sensors, screenless interfaces, and artificial intelligence, Android will increasingly become a central hub for managing a connected ecosystem, enhancing quality of life through automation, intelligent monitoring, and more natural interactions.

Conclusion

Android development is undergoing a significant transformation, driven by modern UI frameworks, artificial intelligence, advanced security, and an increasingly interconnected ecosystem.

The adoption of Jetpack Compose and Kotlin Multiplatform is redefining application development, enhancing modularity, code reusability, and cross-platform scalability.

At the same time, emerging design patterns such as MVI are optimizing state management and code organization, making applications more efficient and testable.

The integration of artificial intelligence is revolutionizing both development and user experience, with tools like Gemini in Android Studio automating code generation, debugging, and refactoring, while AI-powered applications provide advanced personalization and more natural interactions.

Security and privacy will remain a central focus, with advanced authentication, encryption, and greater transparency for users. At the same time, performance optimization and sustainability will become key aspects, emphasizing reduced energy consumption and app modularization.

Finally, Android is expanding beyond smartphones, with increasing integration into IoT, wearables, and ambient computing. In the coming years, Android development will become smarter, more efficient, and more secure, delivering high-performance and privacy-conscious applications. Developers will need to adapt to these transformations, leveraging new technologies to create more advanced and interconnected experiences.

Points to Remember

- **Jetpack Compose is the future of Android UI:** The shift from XML to a declarative system makes interfaces more flexible, scalable, and performant across all devices.
- **Kotlin Multiplatform is revolutionizing development:** With KMP, developers can share business logic across Android, iOS, Web, and Desktop, reducing duplicate code.
- **Design patterns are evolving toward reactive architectures:** The adoption of MVI, StateFlow, and Clean Architecture enhances state management and application scalability.
- **Artificial intelligence is optimizing development:** With tools like Gemini in Android Studio, code generation, documentation, and debugging are becoming faster and more efficient.
- **Security and privacy are more crucial than ever:** Passkeys, biometric authentication, and advanced encryption ensure better data protection and greater user control.
- **Apps must be lighter and more efficient:** The use of modularization, App Bundles, and advanced caching reduces energy consumption and improves performance.

- **Android is expanding beyond smartphones:** The operating system is increasingly integrated with IoT, wearables, smart home, and automotive devices, creating a connected ecosystem.
- **Screenless interfaces are becoming a reality:** The evolution of voice assistants, AR/VR, and contextual interactions is transforming the user experience.
- **Sustainability is a key objective:** Apps must optimize battery consumption and reduce environmental impact, promoting more responsible development practices.
- **The future of Android will be smarter, more secure, and highly interconnected:** The combination of AI, advanced security, and cross-platform development will lead to seamless and automated experiences.

Multiple Choice Questions

1. What is the main advantage of Jetpack Compose over the XML-based UI system?
   a. Reduces the amount of code needed to create interfaces.
   b. Allows the development of lighter apps without dependencies.
   c. Is only compatible with the latest versions of Android.
   d. Does not support responsive design.
2. What is the main advantage of Kotlin Multiplatform?
   a. Allows the creation of common graphical interfaces between Android and iOS.
   b. Enables development only for Android.
   c. Facilitates the sharing of business logic across multiple platforms.
   d. Is faster than Java for Android development.
3. Which architectural design pattern is becoming increasingly popular thanks to Jetpack Compose?
   a. MVC (Model-View-Controller)
   b. MVP (Model-View-Presenter)
   c. MVVM (Model-View-ViewModel)
   d. MVI (Model-View-Intent)

4. Which AI tool has been integrated into Android Studio to support development?
   a. OpenAI o1
   b. Google Gemini
   c. Microsoft Copilot
   d. DeepSeek R1
5. Which of these strategies helps improve the energy efficiency of Android apps?
   a. Using complex animations.
   b. Reducing the use of background processes.
   c. Increasing the UI refresh rate.
   d. Loading all app resources at startup.

Answers

1. a
2. c
3. d
4. b
5. b

Questions

1. How has Jetpack Compose revolutionized UI development in Android compared to the XML-based system?
2. What are the main advantages of Kotlin Multiplatform for cross-platform application development?
3. How does the Model-View-Intent (MVI) pattern improve state management in Android applications?
4. How is artificial intelligence automating the development process in Android Studio?
5. What strategies can be adopted to reduce energy consumption in Android applications?

References

1. **Jetpack Compose: The Future of Android Development** - https://medium.com/@themukeshsolanki/jetpack-compose-the-future-of-android-development-acf2ec318625
2. **Jetpack Compose: The Future of Android UI** - https://mentormate.com/blog/jetpack-compose-the-future-of-android-ui/
3. **Why adopt Compose - Android Developers** - https://developer.android.com/develop/ui/compose/why-adopt
4. **Jetpack Compose vs XML in Android: A Detailed Comparison** - https://medium.com/@YodgorbekKomilo/jetpack-compose-vs-xml-in-android-a-detailed-comparison-aa411f5391d9
5. **Jetpack Compose vs XML: Android UI development compared** - https://qubika.com/blog/jetpack-compose-vs-xml-android-u/
6. **Is Kotlin Multiplatform Mobile Replacing Flutter? -** https://medium.com/stackademic/is-kotlin-multiplatform-mobile-replacing-flutter-244b6b0f2645
7. **Ten reasons to adopt Kotlin Multiplatform and supercharge your projects** - https://www.jetbrains.com/help/kotlin-multiplatform-dev/multiplatform-reasons-to-try.html
8. **Introduction to Compose Multiplatform with KMP -** https://medium.com/sisaldigitalhubturkiye/introduction-to-compose-multiplatform-with-kmp-71a412578b69
9. **Meet Gemini | Android Developers** - https://developer.android.com/studio/preview/gemini
10. **AI-assisted coding | Android Studio** - https://developer.android.com/studio/preview/gemini/ai-code-completion
11. **Refactoring and documentation | Android Studio** - https://developer.android.com/studio/preview/gemini/organize
12. **AI for Compose | Android Studio** - https://developer.android.com/studio/preview/gemini/compose
13. **I/O 2024: What's new in Android security and privacy** - https://security.googleblog.com/2024/05/io-2024-whats-new-in-android-security.html
14. **New security and privacy features in Android 15** - https://www.kaspersky.com/blog/android-15-new-security-and-privacy-features/51311/

15. **Best practices for app optimization | App quality - Android Developers** - https://developer.android.com/topic/performance/appstartup/best-practices
16. **How to Design and Develop Eco-Friendly Mobile Apps - Sofy.ai** - https://sofy.ai/blog/how-to-design-and-develop-eco-friendly-mobile-apps/
17. **Sustainable App Development: Trends and Best Practices** - https://inappstory.com/blog/sustainable-app-development
18. **Android (Go edition) | Android** - https://www.android.com/versions/go-edition/
19. **Understanding IoT and Its Application in Android** - https://medium.com/@amarkumarprajapti/understanding-iot-and-its-application-in-android-e2785831ece0
20. **The Future of App Development: Wearables and IoT Integration** - https://www.invra.co/en/the-future-of-app-development-wearables-and-iot-integration/
21. **The Internet of Things (IoT) Revolution in Wearables** - https://iotbusinessnews.com/2023/11/03/97971-the-internet-of-things-iot-revolution-in-wearables/
22. **MVI Architecture Pattern in Android** - https://medium.com/@mohammedkhudair57/mvi-architecture-pattern-in-android-0046bf9b8a2e
23. **Koin - The pragmatic Kotlin Injection framework** - https://insert-koin.io/

Index

C

D

G

I

J

K

M

N

O

P

R